D1363749

KU-151-525

CANCELLED 1 9 AUG 2024

Professional Diploma in Marketing

PAPER 8:
MARKETING MANAGEMENT IN PRACTICE

For exams in December 2007 and June 2008

Study Text

In this August 2007 edition

- A **user-friendly format** for easy navigation

- Regular **fast forward** summaries emphasising the key points in each chapter

- Recent examples of marketing practice

- Fully revised

- A full **index**

BPP
LEARNING MEDIA

Fifth edition August 2007

ISBN 9780 7517 4174 2 (previous edition 0 7517 2703 2)

British Library Cataloguing-in-Publication Data
A catalogue record for this book
is available from the British Library

Published by

BPP Learning Media
BPP House, Aldine Place
London W12 8AA

www.bpp.com/learningmedia

Printed in Great Britain by
WM Print
45-47 Frederick Street
Walsall
WS2 9NE

Your learning materials, published by BPP Learning
Media Ltd, are printed on paper sourced from
sustainable, managed forests.

All our rights reserved. No part of this publication may
be reproduced, stored in a retrieval system or
transmitted, in any form or by any means, electronic,
mechanical, photocopying, recording or otherwise,
without the prior written permission of BPP Learning
Media.

We are grateful to the Chartered Institute of Marketing
for permission to reproduce in this text the syllabus,
tutor's guidance notes and past examination
questions. We are also grateful to Karen Beamish of
Stone Consulting for preparing the assignment based
assessment learning material.

©
BPP Learning Media
2007

RECEIVED 17 OCT 2007

Contents

CANCELLED 19 AUG 2024

Page

RECEIVED 17 OCT 2007

The BPP Study Text

Aims of this Study Text

To provide you with the knowledge and understanding, skills and applied techniques that you need if you are to be successful in your exams

The Study Text has been written around **Marketing Management in Practice** syllabus.

- It is **comprehensive**. It covers the syllabus content. No more. No less.

- It is targeted to the **exam**. We have taken account of the **Pilot Paper guidance** the examiner has given and the assessment methodology.

To allow you to study in the way that best suits your learning style and the time you have available, by creating and following your personal Study Plan

You may be studying at home on your own until the date of the exam, or you may be attending a full-time course. You may like to (and have time to) read every word, or you may prefer to (or only have time to) skim-read and devote the remainder of your time to question practice. Whatever approach you select, you will find the BPP Study Text meets the needs of your personal Study Plan.

To tie in with the other components of the BPP Effective Study Package to ensure you have the best possible chance of passing the exam

BPP LEARNING MEDIA

Recommended period of use	Elements of the BPP Effective Study Package
3-12 months before exam	**Study Text** Acquisition of knowledge, understanding, skills and applied techniques
1-6 months before exam	**Practice & Revision Kit** Tutorial questions and helpful checklists of the key points lead you into each area. There are then numerous Examination questions to try, graded by topic area, along with realistic suggested solutions prepared by marketing professionals in the light of the Examiner's Reports.
From three months before the exam until the last minute	**Passcards** Work through these short memorable notes which are focused on what is most likely to come up in the exam you will be sitting.

Settling down to study

By this stage in your career you may be a very experienced learner and taker of exams. But have you ever thought about *how* you learn? Let's have a quick look at the key elements required for effective learning. You can then identify your learning style and go on to design your own approach to how you are going to study this text – your personal Study Plan.

Key element of learning	Using the BPP Study Text
Motivation	You can rely on the comprehensiveness and technical quality of BPP. You've chosen the right Study Text – so you're in pole position to pass your exam!
Clear objectives and standards	Do you want to be a prizewinner or simply achieve a moderate pass? Only you can decide.
Feedback	Follow through the examples in this text and do the Action Programme and the Quick Quizzes. Evaluate your efforts critically – how are you doing?
Study Plan	You need to be honest about your progress to yourself – do not be over-confident, but don't be negative either. Make your Study Plan (see below) and try to stick to it. Focus on the short-term objectives – completing two chapters a night, say – but beware of losing sight of your study objectives.
Practice	Use the Quick Quizzes and Chapter Roundups to refresh your memory regularly after you have completed your initial study of each chapter.

These introductory pages let you see exactly what you are up against. However you study, you should

- **Read through the syllabus** – this will help you to identify areas you have already covered, perhaps at a lower level of detail, and areas that are totally new to you
- **Study the examination paper section,** where we show you the format of the exam (how many and what kind of questions and so on).

Key study steps

The following steps are, in our experience, the ideal way to study for professional exams. You can of course adapt it for your particular learning style (see below).

Tackle the chapters in the order you find them in the Study Text. Taking into account your individual learning style, follow these key study steps for each chapter.

Key study steps	Activity
Step 1 **Chapter Topic list**	Study the list. Each numbered topic denotes a **numbered section** in the chapter.
Step 2 **Setting the Scene**	Read it through. It is designed to show you **why the topics in the chapter need to be studied** – how they lead on from previous topics, and how they lead into subsequent ones.
Step 3 **Explanations**	Proceed **methodically** through the chapter, reading each section thoroughly and making sure you understand.
Step 4 **Key Concepts**	**Key concepts** can often earn you **easy marks** if you state them clearly and correctly in an appropriate exam.
Step 5 **Exam Tips**	These give you a good idea of how the examiner tends to examine certain topics – pinpointing **easy marks** and highlighting **pitfalls**.
Step 6 **Note taking**	Take **brief notes** if you wish, avoiding the temptation to copy out too much.
Step 7 **Marketing at Work**	Study each one, and try if you can to add flesh to them from your **own experience** – they are designed to show how the topics you are studying come alive (and often come unstuck) in the **real world**. You can also update yourself on these companies by going on to the World Wide Web.
Step 8 **Action Programme**	Make a very good attempt at each one in each chapter. These are designed to put your **knowledge into practice** in much the same way as you will be required to do in the exam. Check the answer at the end of the chapter in the **Action Programme review**, and make sure you understand the reasons why yours may be different.
Step 9 **Chapter Roundup**	Check through it very carefully, to make sure you have grasped the **major points** it is highlighting
Step 10 **Quick Quiz**	When you are happy that you have covered the chapter, use the **Quick Quiz** to check your recall of the topics covered. The answers are in the paragraphs in the chapter that we refer you to.
Step 11 **Illustrative question(s)**	Either at this point, or later when you are thinking about revising, make a full attempt at the **illustrative questions**. You can find these at the end of the Study Text, along with the **Answers** so you can see how you did.

Developing your personal Study Plan

Preparing a Study Plan (and sticking closely to it) is one of the key elements in learning success.

First you need to be aware of your style of learning. There are four typical learning styles. Consider yourself in the light of the following descriptions. and work out which you fit most closely. You can then plan to follow the key study steps in the sequence suggested.

Learning styles	Characteristics	Sequence of key study steps in the BPP Study Text
Theorist	Seeks to understand principles before applying them in practice	1, 2, 3, 7, 4, 5, 8, 9, 10, 11 (6 continuous)
Reflector	Seeks to observe phenomena, thinks about them and then chooses to act	
Activist	Prefers to deal with practical, active problems; does not have much patience with theory	1, 2, 8 (read through), 7, 4, 5, 9, 3, 8 (full attempt), 10, 11 (6 continuous)
Pragmatist	Prefers to study only if a direct link to practical problems can be seen; not interested in theory for its own sake	8 (read through), 2, 4, 5, 7, 9, 1, 3, 8 (full attempt), 10, 11 (6 continuous)

Next you should complete the following checklist.

Am I motivated?   (a)

Do I have an objective and a standard that I want to achieve?   (b)

Am I a theorist, a reflector, an activist or a pragmatist?   (c)

How much time do I have available per week, given: (d)

- The standard I have set myself

- The time I need to set aside later for work on the Practice and Revision Kit

- The other exam(s) I am sitting, and (of course)

- Practical matters such as work, travel, exercise, sleep and social life?

Now:

- Take the time you have available per week for this Study Text (d), and multiply it by the number of weeks available to give (e)   (e)

- Divide (e) by the number of chapters to give (f)   (f)

- Set about studying each chapter in the time represented by (f), following the key study steps in the order suggested by your particular learning style

This is your personal **Study Plan**.

Short of time?

Whatever your objectives, standards or style, you may find you simply do not have the time available to follow all the key study steps for each chapter, however you adapt them for your particular learning style. If this is the case, follow the Skim Study technique below (the icons in the Study Text will help you to do this).

Skim study technique

Study the chapters in the order you find them in the Study Text. For each chapter, follow the key study steps 1–2, and then skim-read through step 3. Jump to step 9, and then go back to steps 4–5. Follow through step 7, and prepare outline Answers to the Action Programme (step 8). Try the Quick Quiz (step 10), following up any items you can't answer. You should probably still follow step 6 (note-taking).

Moving on...

However you study, when you are ready to embark on the practice and revision phase of the BPP Effective Study Package, you should still refer back to this Study Text:

- As a source of **reference** (you should find the list of key concepts and the index particularly helpful for this)
- As a **refresher** (the Chapter Roundups and Quick Quizzes help you here)

A note on pronouns

On occasions in this Study Text, 'he' is used for 'he or she', 'him' for 'him or her' and so forth. Whilst we try to avoid this practice it is sometimes necessary for reasons of style. No prejudice or stereotyping according to sex is intended or assumed.

BPP
LEARNING MEDIA

Syllabus

Aims and objectives

The *Marketing Management in Practice* module practises participants in developing and implementing marketing plans at an operational level in organisations. A key part of this module is working within a team to develop the plan and managing teams implementing the plan by undertaking marketing activities and projects. Its aim is to assist participants in integrating and applying knowledge from all the modules at Stage 2, particularly as part of a team. This module also forms the summative assessment for Stage 2.

Learning outcomes

Participants will be able to:

- Explain the roles and structure of the marketing function and the nature of relationships with other functions within various types of organisation.

- Plan and undertake or commission marketing research for an operational marketing plan or business decision.

- Interpret qualitative and quantitative data and present appropriate and coherent recommendations that lead to effective marketing and business decisions.

- Develop marketing objectives and plans at an operational level appropriate to the organisation's internal and external environments.

- Develop an effective plan for a campaign supporting customers and members of a marketing channel.

- Use appropriate management techniques to plan and control marketing activities and projects.

- Use appropriate techniques to develop, manage and motivate a team so that it performs effectively and delivers required results.

- Define measures for, and evaluate the performance of, marketing plans, activities and projects and make recommendations for improvements.

Knowledge and skill requirements

Element 1: Managing people and teams (30%)		Covered in chapter(s)
1.1	Describe the functions, roles of marketing managers and typical marketing jobs and the nature of relationships with other functions in organisations operating in a range of different industries and contexts.	1, 2
1.2	Develop and maintain effective relationships with people in other functions and disciplines within the organisation.	1
1.3	Identify and explain the key challenges of managing marketing teams in a multi-national or multi-cultural context.	6
1.4	Explain how you would use the techniques available for selecting, building, developing and motivating marketing teams to improve performance.	2, 3
1.5	Allocate and lead the work of marketing teams, agreeing objectives and work plans with teams and individuals.	1, 2
1.6	Respond to poor performance within a marketing team by minimising conflict, supporting team members, overcoming problems and maintaining discipline.	4
1.7	Explain the sources and nature of change affecting organisations and the techniques available for managing change.	5
1.8	Evaluate individual and team performance against objectives or targets and provide constructive feedback on their performance.	4

Element 2: Managing market projects (10%)		
2.1	Describe the main stages of a project and the roles of people involved at each stage.	7
2.2	Describe the main characteristics of successful and less successful projects and identify the main reasons for success or failure.	7
2.3	Explain the importance of, and techniques for, establishing the project's scope, definition and goals.	8
2.4	Use the main techniques available for planning, scheduling, resourcing and controlling activities on a project.	8
2.5	Explain the importance of preparing budgets and techniques for controlling progress throughout a project to ensure it is completed on time and within budget.	8
2.6	Explain the main techniques for evaluating the effectiveness of a project on its completion.	8

BPP LEARNING MEDIA

Element 3: Managing knowledge and delivering marketing research projects (20%)		Covered in chapter(s)
3.1	Explain the concept, and give examples, of the application of information and knowledge management, highlighting the role of marketing and employees within the organisation.	10
3.2	Design a research project aimed at providing information as part of a marketing audit or for marketing and business decisions.	10
3.3	Manage a marketing research project by gathering relevant information on time and within the agreed budget.	10
3.4	Make arrangements to record, store and, if appropriate, update information in the MkIS, a database created for the purpose or another system.	10
3.5	Analyse and interpret information and present, as a written report or oral presentation, appropriate conclusions or recommendations that inform the marketing and business decisions for which the research was undertaken.	10
3.6	Review and evaluate the effectiveness of the activities and the role of the individual and team in this process.	10

Element 4: Developing and implementing marketing plans (20%)		
4.1	Develop an operational marketing plan, selecting an appropriate marketing mix for an organisation operating in any context such as FMCG, business-to-business (supply chain), large or capital project-based, services, voluntary and not-for-profit, or sales support (eg SMEs).	11
4.2	Use the main techniques available for planning, scheduling and resourcing activities within the plan.	11
4.3	Identify appropriate measures for evaluating and controlling the marketing plan.	11
4.4	Review and evaluate the effectiveness of planning activities and the role of the individual and team in this process.	11

Element 5: Delivering communications and customer service programmes (20%)		
5.1	Plan the design, development, execution and evaluation of communications campaigns by a team of marketers, including external agencies and suppliers.	12
5.2	Use appropriate marketing communications to develop relationships or communicate with a range of stakeholders.	12
5.3	Manage and monitor the provision of effective customer service.	12
5.4	Use marketing communications to provide support for members of a marketing channel.	12
5.5	Use marketing communications techniques for an internal marketing plan to support management of change within an organisation.	12
5.6	Review and evaluate the effectiveness of communications activities and the role of the individual and team in this process.	12

Related key skills for marketers

There is only so much that a syllabus can include. The syllabus itself is designed to cover the knowledge and skills highlighted by research as core to professional marketers in organisations. However, marketing is performed in an organisational context so there are other broader business and organisational skills that marketing professionals should also posses. The 'key skills for marketers' are therefore an essential part of armoury of the 'complete marketer' in today's organisations. They have been identified from research carried out in organisations where marketers are working.

'Key skills for marketers' are areas of knowledge and competency common to business professionals. They fall outside the CIM's syllabus, providing underpinning knowledge and skills. As such they will be treated as systemic to all marketing activities, rather than subjects treated independently in their turn. While it is not intended that the key skills are formally taught as part of programmes, it is expected that tutors will encourage participants to demonstrate the application of relevant key skills through activities, assignments and discussions during learning.

Using ICT and the Internet

Planning and using different sources to search for and select information; explore, develop and exchange information and derive new information; and present information including text, numbers and images.

Using financial information and metrics

Planning and interpreting information from different sources; carrying out calculations; and presenting and justifying findings.

Presenting information

Contributing to discussions; making a presentation; reading and synthesising information and writing different types of document.

Improving own learning and performance

Agreeing targets and planning how these will be met; using plans to meet targets; and reviewing progress.

Working with others

Planning work and agreeing objectives, responsibilities and working arrangements; seeking to establish and maintain cooperative working relationships; and reviewing work and agreeing ways of future collaborative work.

Problem solving

Exploring problems, comparing different ways of solving them and selecting options; planning and implementing options; and applying agreed methods for checking problems have been solved.

Applying business law

Identifying, applying and checking compliance with relevant law when undertaking marketing activities.

BPP
LEARNING MEDIA

Assessment

CIM will normally offer two forms of assessment for this module from which centres or participants may choose: written examination and continuous assessment. CIM may also recognise, or make joint awards for, modules at an equivalent level undertaken with other professional marketing bodies and educational institutions.

Marketing journals

In addition to reading core and supplementary textbooks participants will be expected to acquire a knowledge and understanding of developments in contemporary marketing theory, practice and issues. The most appropriate sources of information for this include specialist magazines, e.g. Marketing, Marketing Week, Campaign and Revolution; dedicated CIM publications, e.g. Marketing Business and Marketing Success; and business magazines and newspapers, e.g. The Economist, Management Today, Business Week, The Financial Times, and the business pages and supplements of the quality press. A flavour of developments in academic marketing can be derived from the key marketing journals including:

- Admap
- European Journal of Marketing
- Journal of the Academy of Marketing Science
- Journal of Consumer Behaviour: An International Research Review
- Journal of Consumer Research
- Marketing Intelligence and Planning
- Journal of Marketing
- Journal of Marketing Management

Websites

The Chartered Institute of Marketing

www.cim.co.uk	CIM website with information and access to learning support for participants.
www.cim.co.uk/learningzone	Direct access to information and support materials for all levels of CIM qualification
www.cim.co.uk/tutors	Access for Tutors
www.shapethagenda.com	Quarterly agenda paper from CIM

Publications online

www.ft.com	Extensive research resources across all industry sectors, with links to more specialist reports. (Charges may apply)
www.thetimes.co.uk	One of the best online versions of a quality newspaper.
www.economist.com	Useful links, and easily-searched archives of articles from back issues of the magazine.
www.mad.co.uk	Marketing Week magazine online.
www.brandrepublic.com	Marketing magazine online.
www.westburn.co.uk	Journal of Marketing Management online, the official Journal of the Academy of Marketing and Marketing Review.
http://smr.mit.edu/smr/	Free abstracts from Sloan Management Review articles
www.hbsp.harvard.edu	Free abstracts from Harvard Business Review articles
www.ecommercetimes.com	Daily enews on the latest ebusiness developments
www.cim.co.uk/knowledgehub	3000 full text journals titles are available to members via the Knowledge Hub – includes the range of titles above - embargoes may apply.
www.cim.co.uk/cuttingedge	Weekly round up of marketing news (available to CIM members) plus list of awards and forthcoming marketing events.

Sources of useful information

www.1to1.com	The Peppers and Rogers One-to-One Marketing site which contains useful information about the tools and techniques of relationship marketing
www.balancetime.com	The Productivity Institute provides free articles, a time management email newsletter, and other resources to improve personal productivity
www.bbc.co.uk	The Learning Zone at BBC Education contains extensive educational resources, including the video, CD Rom, ability to watch TV programmes such as the News online, at your convenience, after they have been screened
www.busreslab.com	Useful specimen online questionnaires to measure customer satisfaction levels and tips on effective Internet marketing research
www.lifelonglearning.co.uk	Encourages and promotes Lifelong Learning through press releases, free articles, useful links and progress reports on the development of the University for Industry (UFI)
www.marketresearch.org.uk	The Market Research Society. Contains useful material on the nature of research, choosing an agency, ethical standards and codes of conduct for research practice
www.nielsen-netratings.com	Details the current levels of banner advertising activity, including the creative content of the ten most popular banners each week (within Top Rankings area)
www.open.ac.uk	Some good Open University videos available for a broad range of subjects

www.direct.gov.uk	Gateway to a wide range of UK government information
www.srg.co.uk	The Self Renewal Group – provides useful tips on managing your time, leading others, managing human resources, motivating others etc
www.statistics.gov.uk	Detailed information on a variety of consumer demographics from the Government Statistics Office
www.durlacher.com	The latest research on business use of the Internet, often with extensive free reports
www.cyberatlas.com	Regular updates on the latest Internet developments from a business perspective
http://ecommerce.vanderbilt.edu	eLab is a corporate sponsored research centre at the Owen Graduate School of Management, Vanderbilt University
www.kpmg.co.uk	The major consultancy company websites contain useful research
www.ey.com/uk	reports, often free of charge
www.pwcglobal.com	PriceWaterhouseCooper
http://web.mit.edu	Massachusetts Institute of Technology site has extensive research resources
www.adassoc.org.uk	Advertising Association
www.dma.org.uk	The Direct Marketing Association
www.theidm.co.uk	Institute of Direct Marketing
www.export.org.uk	Institute of Export
www.bl.uk	The British Library, with one of the most extensive book collections in the world
www.managers.org.uk	Chartered Management Institute
www.cipd.co.uk	Chartered Institute of Personnel and Development
www.emerald-library.com	Article abstracts on a range of business topics (fees apply)
www.w3.org	An organisation responsible for defining worldwide standards for the Internet

Case studies

Case studies

www.1800flowers.com	Flower and gift delivery service that allows customers to specify key dates when they request the firm to send them a reminder, together with an invitation to send a gift
www.amazon.co.uk	Classic example of how Internet technology can be harnessed to provide innovative customer service
www.broadvision.com	Broadvision specialises in customer 'personalisation' software. The site contains many useful case studies showing how communicating through the Internet allow you to find out more about your customers
www.doubleclick.net	DoubleClick offers advertisers the ability to target their advertisements on the web through sourcing of specific interest groups, ad display only at certain times of the day, or at particular geographic locations, or on certain types of hardware
www.facetime.com	Good example of a site that overcomes the impersonal nature of the Internet by allowing the establishment of real time links with a customer service representative
www.hotcoupons.com	Site visitors can key in their postcode to receive local promotions, and advertisers can post their offers on the site using a specially designed software package
www.superbrands.org	Access to case studies on international brands

The Exam Paper

Format of the paper

		Number of marks
Part A:	A compulsory multi-part question, relating to a case study or scenario (Answers generally required in report form)	50
Part B:	Two questions from a choice of four (25 marks each)	50
		100

Analysis of past papers

December 2006

Part A (compulsory question worth 50 marks)

A successful hair salon is looking to expand its chain in a new area.

1   (a)   Outline marketing communications plan for the new salon
     (b)   Change management issues in moving from local to national

Part B (two questions, 25 marks each)

2   Information needed to select new locations, and means of obtaining it
3   Branding issues; communications activities to build brand value
4   Use of management/marketing theory in recruitment, induction and training
5   Project management approaches for salon opening; actions to project manage launch marketing

What the examiner said

Common causes of poor exam performance include:

- Generic answers, with little application of selected theory to the specific context of (a) the case study and (b) the question.

- Unstructured lists of action points, without citing relevant underpinning theory. ('lack of knowledge and understanding of relevant theory results in superficial answers that will not achieve a pass grade at this level'.)

- Failure to answer the specific focus and instructions of each question.

- Failure to structure answers and/or leaving gaps in the treatment of the issues. ('It is vital to plan answers'.)

- Wasting time on overly-detailed report format (title pages, lengthy introductions, contents listings etc): not required. ('Conversely, focused tables and context-developed diagrams are welcomed'.)

Future themes will include: consumer, B2B, product, service and international themes.

June 2006

Part A (compulsory question worth 50 marks)

Trade association representing the fragrance industry is organising its first international conference.

1   (a)   Marketing plan for the conference
      (b)   Monitoring staff performance and development

Part B (two questions, 25 marks each)

2   Development of conference programme – information requirements
3   Use of the internet in co-ordinated communications
4   Development of successful multidisciplinary/ multicultural teams
5   Project management issues

December 2005

Part A (compulsory question worth 50 marks)

Successful motorbike business has outgrown its current facilities and is constructing a new 'complex'.

1   (a)   Segmentation for profitable opportunities
      (b)   Marketing plan
      (c)   Marketing initiatives to attract female enthusiasts

Part B (two questions, 25 marks each)

2   Marketing communications for additional revenue and profit
3   Actions to develop a marketing orientation
4   Website development and launch; project management
5   Customer satisfaction and service quality

June 2005

Part A (compulsory question worth 50 marks)

Company manufacturing plastic wrap is looking to extend its application to new markets.

1   (a)   Outline marketing plan
      (b)   Selection of brand manager to develop the export market

Part B (two questions, 25 marks each)

2   Information for market development
3   Integrated marketing communications activities for launch
4   Change management issues
5   Project management tools for product launch

December 2004

Part A (compulsory question worth 50 marks)

The case study scenario is based on a film developing and printing business.

1   (a)   Prepare a marketing plan to develop a profitable regional business. Partnership arrangements with local organisations

       (b)   Selection, appointment and induction of a webmaster

Part B (two questions, 25 marks each)

2   (a)   Information requirements for developing an online digital business
       (b)   Methods of gathering the necessary information

3   Integrated marketing communications activities to promote an online digital image processing service

4   Identification of change management issues and effective actions required

5   Exhibition launch and project management tools

June 2004

Part A (compulsory question worth 50 marks)

North American based perfume company looking for international expansion via construction of a new facility.

1   (a)   Marketing communications plan for new site
       (b)   Collecting information on the macro environment
       (c)   Selection and training of new marketing assistant

Part B (two questions, 25 marks each)

2   (a)   Information on profitable customers
       (b)   Key client information

3   (a)   Planning the opening event – stakeholders, objectives, schedule
       (b)   Project management

4   MkIS framework to track market developments

5   'Customer care' workshop for front line staff

December 2003

The case study relates to the future development of a golf course resort and its facilities that has recently been purchased by a global operator.

Part A (compulsory question worth 50 marks)

1   (a)   Selection, training and team-building
       (b)   Marketing plan for developing midweek business

Part B (two questions, 25 marks each)

2   Marketing research and marketing information system
3   Marketing communications activities
4   Building and retaining membership and customer relationships; customer care
5   Project management for a shop opening

Pilot Paper

The case study setting relates to an international hotel firm that has just opened a new hotel and appointed a new marketing manager

Part A (compulsory question worth 50 marks)

1 (a) Selection, training and motivation of a suitable marketing team
   (b) Marketing plan for developing weekend business

Part B (two questions, 25 marks each)

2 Marketing research and marketing information system
3 Marketing communications activities
4 Internal marketing and monitoring quality
5 Arrangements for a sales launch conference

The Pilot Paper and BPP's suggested answer plans are reproduced at the back of the Study Text.

Guide to the assignment route

- Aims and objectives of this guide
- Introduction
- Assignment route, structure and process
- Preparing for assignments: general guide
- Presentation
- Time management
- Tips for writing assignments
- Writing reports
- Resources to support Assignment Based Assessment

Aims and objectives of this guide to the assignment route

- To understand the scope and structure of the route process
- To consider the benefits of learning through the assignment route
- To assist students in preparation of their assignments
- To consider the range of communication options available to students
- To look at the range of potential assignment areas that assignments may challenge
- To examine the purpose and benefits of reflective practice
- To assist with time-management within the assignment process

Introduction

At time of writing, there are over 80 CIM Approved Study Centres that offer the assignment route option as an alternative to examinations. This change in direction and flexibility in assessment was externally driven by industry, students and tutors alike, all of whom wanted a test of practical skills as well as a knowledge-based approach to learning.

At Stage 1, all modules are available via this assignment route. The assignment route is however optional, and examinations are still available. This will of course depend upon the nature of delivery within your chosen Study Centre.

Clearly, all of the Stage 1 subject areas lend themselves to assignment-based learning, due to their practical nature. The assignments that you will undertake provide you with an opportunity to be **creative in approach and in presentation.** They enable you to give a true demonstration of your marketing ability in a way that perhaps might be inhibited in a traditional examination situation.

The assignment route offers you considerable scope to produce work that provides existing and future **employers** with **evidence** of your **ability.** It offers you a **portfolio** of evidence which demonstrates your abilities and your willingness to develop continually your knowledge and skills. It will also, ultimately, help you frame your continuing professional development in the future.

It does not matter what type of organisation you are from, large or small, as you will find substantial benefit in this approach to learning. In some cases, students have made their own organisation central to their assessment and produced work to support their organisation's activities, resulting in subsequent recognition and promotion: a success story for this approach.

So, using your own organisation can be beneficial (especially if your employer sponsors you). However, it is equally valid to use a different organisation, as long as you are familiar enough with it to base your assignments on it. This is particularly useful if you are between jobs, taking time out, returning to employment or studying at university or college.

BPP
LEARNING MEDIA

To take the assignment route option, you are required to register with a CIM Accredited Study Centre (ie a college, university, or distance learning provider). **Currently you would be unable to take the assignment route option as an independent learner**. If in doubt you should contact the CIM Education Division, the awarding body, who will provide you with a list of local Accredited Centres offering the Assignment Route.

Structure and process

The **assignments** that you will undertake during your studies are normally set **by CIM centrally** and not usually by the study centre. All assignments are validated to ensure a structured, consistent, approach. This standardised approach to assessment enables external organisations to interpret the results on a consistent basis.

Each module at Stage 1 has one assignment, with four separate elements within it. This is broken down as follows.

- The **Core Section** is compulsory and worth 40% of your total mark.

- The **Elective Section** has four options, from which you must complete **two**. Each of these options is worth 25% of your total mark. Please note here that it is likely that in some Study Centres the option may be chosen for you. This is common practice and is done in order to maximise resources and support provided to students.

- The **Reflective Statement** is also compulsory. It is worth 10%. It should reflect what you feel about your learning experience during the module and how that learning has helped you in your career both now and in the future.

The purpose of each assignment is to enable you to demonstrate your ability to research, analyse and problem-solve in a range of different situations. You will be expected to approach your assignment work from a professional marketer's perspective, addressing the assignment brief directly, and undertaking the tasks required. Each assignment will relate directly to the syllabus module and will be applied against the content of the syllabus.

All of the Assignments clearly indicate the links with the syllabus and the assignment weighting (ie the contribution each assignment makes to your overall marks).

Once your Assignments have been completed, they will be marked by your accredited centre, and then **moderated** by a CIM External Moderator. When all the assignments have been marked, they are sent to CIM for further moderation. After this, all marks are forwarded to you by CIM (not your centre) in the form of an examination result. Your **centre** will be able to you provide you with some written feedback on overall performance, but **will not** provide you with any detailed mark breakdown.

Preparing for assignments: general guide

The whole purpose of this guide is to assist you in presenting your assessment professionally, both in terms of presentation skills and overall content. In many of the assignments, marks are awarded for presentation and coherence. It might therefore be helpful to consider how best to present your assignment. Here you should consider issues of detail, protocol and the range of communications that could be called upon within the assignment.

Presentation of the assignment

You should always ensure that you prepare two copies of your Assignment, keeping a soft copy on disc. On occasions assignments go missing, or second copies are required by CIM.

- Each Assignment should be clearly marked up with your name, your study centre, your CIM Student registration number and ultimately at the end of the assignment a word count. The assignment should also be word-processed.

- The assignment presentation format should directly meet the requirements of the assignment brief, (ie reports and presentations are the most called for communication formats). You **must** ensure that you assignment does not appear to be an extended essay. If it does, you will lose marks.

- The word limit will be included in the assignment brief. These are specified by CIM and must be adhered to.

- Appendices should clearly link to the assignment and can be attached as supporting documentation at the end of the report. However failure to reference them by number (eg Appendix 1) within the report and also marked up on the Appendix itself will lose you marks. Only use an Appendix if it is essential and clearly adds value to the overall Assignment. The Appendix is not a waste bin for all the materials you have come across in your research, or a way of making your assignment seem somewhat heavier and more impressive than it is.

Time management for assignments

One of the biggest challenges we all seem to face day-to-day is that of managing time. When studying, that challenge seems to grow increasingly difficult, requiring a balance between work, home, family, social life and study life. It is therefore of pivotal importance to your own success for you to plan wisely the limited amount of time you have available.

Step 1   Find out how much time you have

Ensure that you are fully aware of how long your module lasts, and the final deadline. If you are studying a module from September to December, it is likely that you will have only 10-12 weeks in which to complete your assignments. This means that you will be preparing assignment work continuously throughout the course.

Step 2   Plan your time

Essentially you need to **work backwards** from the final deadline, submission date, and schedule your work around the possible time lines. Clearly if you have only 10-12 weeks available to complete three assignments, you will need to allocate a block of hours in the final stages of the module to ensure that all of your assignments are in on time. This will be critical as all assignments will be sent to CIM by a set day. Late submissions will not be accepted and no extensions will be awarded. Students who do not submit will be treated as a 'no show' and will have to resubmit for the next period and undertake an alternative assignment.

Step 3   Set priorities

You should set priorities on a daily and weekly basis (not just for study, but for your life). There is no doubt that this mode of study needs commitment (and some sacrifices in the short term). When your achievements are recognised by colleagues, peers, friends and family, it will all feel worthwhile.

BPP
LEARNING MEDIA

Step 4   Analyse activities and allocate time to them

Consider the **range** of activities that you will need to undertake in order to complete the assignment and the **time** each might take. Remember, too, there will be a delay in asking for information and receiving it.

- Preparing terms of reference for the assignment, to include the following.

  1. A short title

  2. A brief outline of the assignment purpose and outcome

  3. Methodology – what methods you intend to use to carry out the required tasks

  4. Indication of any difficulties that have arisen in the duration of the assignment

  5. Time schedule

  6. Confidentiality – if the assignment includes confidential information ensure that this is clearly marked up and indicated on the assignment

  7. Literature and desk research undertaken

This should be achieved in one side of A4 paper.

- A literature search in order to undertake the necessary background reading and underpinning information that might support your assignment

- Writing letters and memos asking for information either internally or externally

- Designing questionnaires

- Undertaking surveys

- Analysis of data from questionnaires

- Secondary data search

- Preparation of first draft report

Always build in time to spare, to deal with the unexpected. This may reduce the pressure that you are faced with in meeting significant deadlines.

Warning!

The same principles apply to a student with 30 weeks to do the work. However, a word of warning is needed. Do not fall into the trap of leaving all of your work to the last minute. If you miss out important information or fail to reflect upon your work adequately or successfully you will be penalised for both. Therefore, time management is important whatever the duration of the course.

Tips for writing assignments

Everybody has a personal style, flair and tone when it comes to writing. However, no matter what your approach, you must ensure your assignment meets the **requirements of the brief** and so is comprehensible, coherent and cohesive in approach.

Think of preparing an assignment as preparing for an examination. Ultimately, the work you are undertaking results in an examination grade. Successful achievement of all four modules in a level results in a qualification.

There are a number of positive steps that you can undertake in order to ensure that you make the best of your assignment presentation in order to maximise the marks available.

Step 1 Work to the brief

Ensure that you identify exactly what the assignment asks you to do.

- If it asks you to be a marketing manager, then immediately assume that role.

- If it asks you to prepare a report, then present a report, not an essay or a letter.

- Furthermore, if it asks for 2,500 words, then do not present 1,000 or 4,000 unless it is clearly justified, agreed with your tutor and a valid piece of work.

Identify whether the report should be **formal or informal**; who it should be **addressed to**; its **overall purpose** and its **potential use** and outcome. Understanding this will ensure that your assignment meets fully the requirements of the brief and addresses the key issues included within it.

Step 2 Addressing the tasks

It is of pivotal importance that you address **each** of the tasks within the assignment. **Many students fail to do this** and often overlook one of the tasks or indeed part of the tasks.

Many of the assignments will have two or three tasks, some will have even more. You should establish quite early on, which of the tasks:

- Require you to collect information
- Provides you with the framework of the assignment, i.e. the communication method.

Possible tasks will include the following.

- *Compare and contrast.* Take two different organisations and compare them side by side and consider the differences ie the **contrasts** between the two.

- *Carry out primary or secondary research.* Collect information to support your assignment and your subsequent decisions

- *Prepare a plan.* Some assignments will ask you to prepare a plan for an event or for a marketing activity – if so provide a step-by-step approach, a rationale, a time-line, make sure it is measurable and achievable. Make sure your actions are very specific and clearly explained. (Make sure your plan is SMART.)

- *Analyse a situation.* This will require you to collect information, consider its content and present an overall understanding of the situation as it exists. This might include looking at internal and external factors and how the current situation evolved.

- *Make recommendations.* The more advanced your get in your studies, the more likely it is that you will be required to make recommendations. Firstly **considering and evaluating your options** and then making justifiable **recommendations**, based on them.

- *Justify decisions.* You may be required to justify your decision or recommendations. This will require you to explain fully how you have arrived at as a result and to show why, supported by relevant information. In other words, you should not make decisions in a vacuum; as a marketer your decisions should always be informed by context.

BPP LEARNING MEDIA

- *Prepare a presentation*. This speaks for itself. If you are required to prepare a presentation, ensure that you do so, preparing clearly defined PowerPoint or overhead slides that are not too crowded and that clearly express the points you are required to make.

- *Evaluate performance*. It is very likely that you will be asked to evaluate a campaign, a plan or even an event. You will therefore need to consider its strengths and weaknesses, why it succeeded or failed, the issues that have affected it, what can you learn from it and, importantly, how can you improve performance or sustain it in the future.

All of these points are likely requests included within a task. Ensure that you identify them clearly and address them as required.

Step 3 — Information search

Many students fail to realise the importance of collecting information to **support** and **underpin** their assignment work. However, it is vital that you demonstrate to your centre and to the CIM your ability to **establish information needs**, obtain **relevant information** and **utilise it sensibly** in order to arrive at appropriate decisions.

You should establish the nature of the information required, follow up possible sources, time involved in obtaining the information, gaps in information and the need for information.

Consider these factors very carefully. CIM are very keen that students are **seen** to collect information, **expand** their mind and consider the **breadth** and **depth** of the situation. In your *Personal Development Portfolio*, you have the opportunity to complete a **Resource Log**, to illustrate how you have expanded your knowledge to aid your personal development. You can record your additional reading and research in that log, and show how it has helped you with your portfolio and assignment work.

Step 4 — Develop an assignment plan

Your **assignment** needs to be structured and coherent, addressing the brief and presenting the facts as required by the tasks. The only way you can successfully achieve this is by **planning the structure** of your Assignment in advance.

Earlier on in this unit, we looked at identifying your tasks and, working backwards from the release date, in order to manage time successfully. The structure and coherence of your assignment needs to be planned with similar signs.

In planning out the Assignment, you should plan to include **all the relevant information as requested** and also you should plan for the use of models, diagrams and appendices where necessary.

Your plan should cover your:

- Introduction
- Content
- Main body of the assignment
- Summary
- Conclusions and recommendations where appropriate

Step 5   **Prepare draft assignment**

It is good practice to always produce a **first draft** of a report. You should use it to ensure that you have met the aims and objectives, assignment brief and tasks related to the actual assignment. A draft document provides you with scope for improvements, and enables you to check for accuracy, spelling, punctuation and use of English.

Step 6   **Prepare final document**

In the section headed 'Presentation of the Assignment' in this unit, there are a number of components that should always be in place at the beginning of the assignment documentation, including **labelling** of the assignment, **word counts**, **appendices** numbering and presentation method. Ensure that you **adhere to the guidelines presented**, or alternatively those suggested by your Study Centre.

Writing reports

Students often ask 'what do they mean by a report?' or 'what should the report format include?'.

There are a number of approaches to reports, formal or informal: some report formats are company specific and designed for internal use, rather than external reporting.

For Continuous Assessment process, you should stay with traditional formats.

Below is a suggested layout of a Management Report Document that might assist you when presenting your assignments.

- A *Title Page* includes the title of the report, the author of the report and the receiver of the report

- *Acknowledgements* – this should highlight any help, support, or external information received and any extraordinary co-operation of individuals or organisations

- *Contents page* provides a clearly structured pathway of the contents of the report – page by page.

- *Executive summary* – a brief insight into purpose, nature and outcome of the report, in order that the outcome of the report can be quickly established

- *Main body of the report divided into sections, which are clearly labelled.* Suggested labelling would be on a numbered basis eg:

    - 1.0   Introduction
    - 1.1   Situation Analysis
    - 1.1.1 External Analysis
    - 1.1.2 Internal Analysis

- *Conclusions* – draw the report to a conclusion, highlighting key points of importance, that will impact upon any recommendations that might be made

- *Recommendations* – clearly outline potential options and then recommendations. Where appropriate justify recommendations in order to substantiate your decision

- *Appendices* – ensure that you only use appendices that add value to the report. Ensure that they are numbered and referenced on a numbered basis within the text. If you are not going to reference it within the text, then it should not be there

BPP
LEARNING MEDIA

- *Bibliography* – whilst in a business environment a bibliography might not be necessary, for an **assignment-based report it is vital**. It provides an indication of the level of research, reading and collecting of relevant information that has taken place in order to fulfil the requirements of the assignment task. Where possible, and where relevant, you could provide academic references within the text, which should of course then provide the basis of your bibliography. References should realistically be listed alphabetically and in the following sequence

  - Author's name and edition of the text
  - Date of publication
  - Title and sub-title (where relevant)
  - Edition 1st, 2nd etc
  - Place of publication
  - Publisher
  - Series and individual volume number where appropriate.

Resources to support assignment based assessment

The aim of this guidance is to present you with a range of questions and issues that you should consider, based upon the assignment themes. The detail to support the questions can be found within your BPP Study Text and the 'Core Reading' recommended by CIM.

Additionally you will find useful support information within the CIM Student website www.cim.co.uk -: www.cimvirtualinstitute.com, where you can access a wide range of marketing information and case studies. You can also build your own workspace within the website so that you can quickly and easily access information specific to your professional study requirements. Other websites you might find useful for some of your assignment work include www.wnim.com - (What's New in Marketing) and also www.connectedinmarketing.com - another CIM website.

Other websites include:

www.mad.com	– Marketing Week
www.ft.com	– Financial Times
www.thetimes.com	– The Times newspaper
www.theeconomist.com	– The Economist magazine
www.marketing.haynet.com	– Marketing magazine
www.ecommercetimes.com	– Daily news on e-business developments
www.open.gov.uk	– Gateway to a wide range of UK government information
www.adassoc.org.uk	– The Advertising Association
www.marketresearch.org.uk	– The Marketing Research Society
www.amazon.com	– Online Book Shop
www.1800flowers.com	– Flower and delivery gift service
www.childreninneed.com	– Charitable organisation
www.comicrelief.com	– Charitable organisation
www.samaritans.org.uk	– Charitable organisation

Part A
Managing people and teams

What is management?

Syllabus content – knowledge and skill requirements

- The functions and role of marketing managers and typical marketing jobs and the nature of relationships with other functions in organisations operating in a range of different industries and contexts (1.1)
- Maintenance of effective relationships with people in other functions and disciplines within the organisation (1.2)
- Allocating and leading the work of marketing teams, agreeing objectives and work plans with teams and individuals (1.3)

Introduction

This chapter introduces you to some of the main ideas of management theory, to give you an overview of its context within the organisation, and to put the personal skills and development discussed in the later chapters in a suitable context.

A manager works in an **organisation,** which is a group of people who are directed to achieving goals. The best way of getting people to achieve organisational goals has been much disputed. Traditional theories of management are described in Section 1 and are contrasted with more recent theories of what managers' roles should be: a manager should be able to plan and control the activities of the organisation – but a manager's own job can appear completely chaotic, with interruptions and many demands.

In Section 2, we discuss **organisational culture**. As a marketing manager you will find it necessary to be sensitive to the cultural imperatives of your organisation so that you can effectively promote marketing priorities.

In Sections 3 and 4 we offer you an overview of how the management role has changed and relate these changes to the marketing orientation, with which you must by now be familiar. The sort of stresses managers and workers are under as firms react to new technology and global competition are discussed. We then look at how the role of the manager may develop in the future.

Finally we discuss the **specific role of the marketing manager**, who is the customer's champion within the organisation, as well as the organisation's main communicator with customers.

1 The management task

1.1 The manager and the organisation

FAST FORWARD

Managers play a critical role in the organisation. They act as **catalysts**, responsible for the transformation of resource inputs into desired and valued outputs.

Any business is an example of an organisation, that is, a social system created and maintained in order to achieve predetermined objectives.

Organisations exist to attain results which individuals cannot achieve alone, because of limitations imposed on them by the environment and their own physical, or biological limitations.

Management is needed in organisation so that individuals work effectively towards the common goal. Whatever the function or department, management involves the same activity.

- Vision and a sense of direction to pursue the goals and objectives
- A plan to achieve the objectives
- Organisation of the productive resources
- Co-ordination of activities
- Control, to ensure that scarce resources are used efficiently and that the organisation is on track to achieve the set objectives
- Personal skills to lead and motivate the organisation's human resources

Marketing managers do these things just as much as managers in other activities.

There have been a number of different approaches to a theory of management over the years.

(a) The **classical school**, exemplified by a 19th-century French industrialist, Henri Fayol, tried to lay down universal principles for the structure and organisation of a business.

(b) **Scientific management** was based on the work of FW Taylor, an American engineer and manager working at the end of the 19th century. Taylor suggested that organisations would be more efficient if their knowledge, experience and practices were analysed, and the best methods established by management.

(c) The **human relations** school shifted attention towards the **people** in organisations, and how they could be motivated to make the organisation more efficient. The early writers like Mayo thought that the most important factor for people at work was their relationships with other people. Later writers, such as Herzberg, considered that people have many different reasons for working, and suggested that management would have to pay attention to their **needs for challenge, interest, recognition and self development.**

(d) The **systems approach** is based on the idea that a work organisation is a system; it takes in inputs from its environment (eg people, money and materials), processes them and sends outputs back to the environment (eg goods and information).

(e) The **contingency approach**, one of the more modern management approaches, says widely accepted today, says that organisations have to adapt to different influences and demands; there is no single best way to design or run an organisation.

(f) The **empowered teams approach**. This modern approach is geared to be more responsive to market and customer needs while at the same time being more efficient. Such structures tend to work best where the organisation has a strong mission statement, core values and reporting system which serve as guiding principles for flexible and responsive teamwork.

(g) The **organic organisation approach**. Here again, the organisation is highly responsive and flexible. There are divisions of responsibility but these are broadly based and not standardised. Employees tend to be well trained, skilled and empowered. Such an approach emphasises examining the business case for doing things rather than being governed by rules and policies.

 Marketing at Work

Sun Life Assurance of Canada

A bane of customers' lives when phoning a financial institution for help is being transferred from one department to another.

Sun Life has addressed this issue by organising its customer services function into eight person teams. Team members receive proper training so that customers are not bounced around from one department to another. A small multi-disciplinary team is able to deal with all of a client's needs.

1.2 Functions of management

FAST FORWARD

Managers are responsible for the **scarce resources** entrusted to them, which must be used efficiently if value is to be added to the organisation, and if its objectives are to be achieved.

The functions of the manager define the nature of the manager's job. Even the roles of professionals, such as lawyers and accountants, involve not only the dispensing of knowledge, but the provision of a service to a consumer and the application of a high level of service standards.

Many writers have sought to analyse the manager's operational functions The weighting of the various responsibilities will change according to the seniority of the manager, his/her specialist function, and the structure and culture of the organisation.

1.3 Henri Fayol: the classical school

Going back to the 19th century, *Henri Fayol* undertook one of the first systematic approaches to analysing and defining the manager's job. Although management has progressed significantly since then, it is worth reviewing Fayol's ideas.

    (a)   **Planning**. Selecting the objectives and methods for achieving them, either for the organisation as a whole or for a part of it.

    (b)   **Organising**. Establishing the structure of tasks to be performed to achieve the goals of the organisation; grouping these tasks into jobs for an individual; creating groups of jobs within departments; delegating authority to carry out the jobs, providing systems of information and communication and co-ordinating activities within the organisation.

    (c)   **Commanding**. Giving instructions to subordinates to carry out tasks over which the manager has authority for decisions and responsibility for performance.

    (d)   **Co-ordinating**. Harmonising the activities of individuals and groups within the organisation. Management must reconcile differences in approach, effort, interest and timing.

    (e)   **Controlling**. Measuring and correcting activities to ensure that performance is in accordance with **plans**. Plans will not be achieved unless activities are monitored, and deviations identified and corrected as soon as they become apparent.

Several writers followed Fayol with broadly similar analyses of management functions. Other functions which might be identified are **staffing** (filling positions in the organisation with people), **leading** (unlike commanding, 'leading' is concerned with the interpersonal nature of management) and acting as the **organisation's representative** in dealing with other organisations.

Obviously, society has advanced a long way since the 19th century and in the 21st century, words such as commanding and subordinates, do not chime well with a modern view of the state of human relations. Modern analyses add functions such as *communication*, *inspiration*, *culture creation* and human resource *development*.

1.4 Jack Welch: the boundaryless organisation

Jack Welch a former CEO of General Electric, transformed this vast departmentalised multi-national corporation into a dynamic and high performing business. He achieved this by turning the business into what he termed a boundaryless organisation and was able to:

- Articulate a vision
- Set stretch goals
- Elevate change into a competitive weapon
- Focus on ideas generation
- Motivate employees

Welch worked to eliminate vertical and horizontal boundaries within the business and also break down the barriers between the group and its suppliers and customers. Departments were replaced with empowered teams.

The removal of horizontal (status) barriers allows the business to benefit from shorter chains of command and a more participative approach to decision making.

BPP LEARNING MEDIA

The removal of horizontal (functional) barriers facilitates the use of cross-functional team working. Activities are organised around work process rather than being governed by traditional departmental remits.

The boundaryless organisation has many benefits but tends to be used by more contemporary minded managers who have the confidence to operate without the security of traditional bureaucracy.

The approach avoids focusing on specific growth strategies, but rather on the cultural and behavioural forces underpinning the strategies. Welch emphasises the importance of employees taking pride in the company and its products and the creation of a learning environment.

In spite of GE being a mega corporation, Welch maintained an open management style, and preferred to have frontline employees, rather than bureaucrats, provide him with business advice.

1.5 Managerial roles: Mintzberg

Another way of looking at the manager's job is to observe what managers **actually do**, and from this to draw conclusions about what **roles** they play. *Henry Mintzberg* (1989) identified **ten managerial roles**, which managers take on as appropriate to their personalities and the nature of the task in hand.

1.5.1 Interpersonal roles

•	Figurehead	Performing ceremonial and social duties as the organisation's representative, for instance at conferences
•	Leader	Uniting and inspiring the team to achieve objectives
•	Liaison	Communication with people outside the manager's work group or the organisation

1.5.2 Informational roles

•	Monitor	Receiving information about the organisation's performance and comparing it with objectives
•	Disseminator	Passing on information, mainly to the workforce
•	Spokesman	Transmitting information outside the unit or organisation, on behalf of the unit or organisation

1.5.3 Decisional roles

•	Entrepreneur	Mobilising resources to get things done and to seize opportunities
•	Disturbance handler	Rectifying mistakes and getting operations, and relationships, back on course
•	Resource allocator	Distributing resources in the way that will most efficiently achieve defined objectives
•	Negotiator	Bargaining for required resources and influence

Most managers will discharge the majority of these roles. Different 'hats' will be worn more frequently according to the seniority and situation of the manager. **Brand managers** are likely to be very involved in liaison, monitoring and disturbance handling, whilst the **marketing director** has an important role as a leader, perhaps figurehead, negotiator and entrepreneur.

An equally important aspect of roles is skills. Being a good manager has similar requirements as being a good footballer. Knowing how to dribble a ball in theory is one thing but to be effective the player requires skills. Similarly, managers need good personal skills if they are to be successful in leading, motivating, communicating, negotiating or being entrepreneurial.

Action Programme 1

Consider your own role as a manager, or that of a manager you know.

1   What functions and roles are performed routinely?

2   What weightings would you allocate in terms of Mintzberg's role analysis?

3   If possible, compare your analysis with the job description for the post. How accurate do you think the description is? How would you recommend changing it if there was the need to appoint someone new to the post?

4   Now consider the role and functions of a more senior manager in the organisation. How do they differ? Can you identify the kind of new skills a manager might need to develop in order to be prepared for promotion within the organisation?

Probably you identified a further dimension to the work of the manager when completing this exercise: the operational or specialist **functional responsibilities** of being a sales manager, say, or a financial or production specialist.

1.6 The value of management

Management is essential for converting the inputs of the operation into valued outputs and for satisfying stakeholders' needs. Managers are the element which economists call **enterprise**, without which the other factors (land, labour and capital) cannot function. They are the custodians of the organisation's resources and are responsible for making the best use of them.

2 Organisational culture

FAST FORWARD

Culture is important both in organisations and in the wider world. It is the knowledge, beliefs, customs and attitudes which people adhere to.

Organisations often have their own distinctive **culture**. In wider society, culture is defined by such things as shared history, attitudes and opinions, aesthetic activities and accepted patterns of behaviour. An organisation's distinctive culture is established in the same way. However, unlike a society, an organisation is defined largely by its purpose, and this is a further influence on its culture.

Key concept

The word, **culture** is used by sociologists and anthropologists to encompass 'the sum total of the beliefs, knowledge, attitudes of mind and customs to which people are exposed in their social conditioning.'

Knowledge of the culture of a society is clearly of value to businesses in a number of ways.

(a)   **Marketers** can adapt their products accordingly, and be fairly sure of a sizeable market. This is particularly important in export markets.

(b)   **Human resource managers** may need to tackle cultural differences in recruitment. For example, some ethnic minorities have a different body language from the majority, which may be hard for some interviewers to interpret.

Key concept

> **Organisation culture** is the sum total of the beliefs, knowledge, attitudes of mind and customs to which people are exposed during their interaction with the organisation.

Culture is both internal to an organisation and external to it. The culture of an organisation is embedded in the culture of the wider society.

All organisations will generate their own cultures, whether spontaneously or under the guidance of positive managerial strategy. *Trompenaars* (1997) suggested that in fact there are different levels at which culture can be understood: Figure 1.1

Figure 1.1: The cultural iceberg

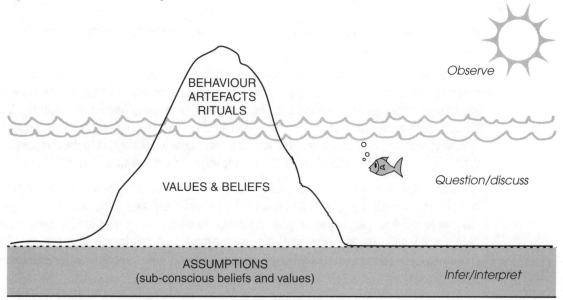

(a) The **observable** or explicit elements of culture include the following:

- **Behaviour**: norms of personal and interpersonal behaviour, including forms of address, communication styles, expression of emotion and use of body language

- **Artefacts**: concrete expressions such as art and literature, architecture and interior design, dress codes, symbols and heroes or role models

- **Rituals**: patterns of collective behaviour which have customary or symbolic value, such as greeting behaviours, business formalities and social courtesies

(b) Beneath these observable phenomena are the **values** and **beliefs** which invest the behaviour, artefacts and rituals with meaning. For example, the design of office space may imply status and honour, or reflect the importance of privacy, or reflect spiritual beliefs (as in feng shui) within a culture: their significance goes beyond the observable features. Values and beliefs cannot be directly observed but may be discovered by **questioning.**

(c) Beneath this level again is the realm of **assumptions**: the foundational beliefs and values that are no longer consciously recognised or questioned by the culture, but which programme cultural meanings and expressions and form the culture's perceptual world. Because these are sub-conscious, they can only be analysed by **inference** and **interpretation**.

Action Programme 2

Return to the ten managerial roles and analyse your own experience and expertise in each area. Turn this into a personal strengths and weaknesses analysis.

[Key Skill for Marketers: Improving own learning and performance]

Marketing at Work

Business Week (Asian edition, May 6 2002) featured the following comments by John A Byrne on the collapse of US corporate giant Enron.

'While Enron's culture emphasized risk-taking and entrepreneurial thinking, it also valued personal ambition over teamwork, youth over wisdom, and earnings growth at any cost. What's more, the very ideas Enron embraced were corrupted in their execution. Risk-taking without oversight resulted in failures. Youth without supervision resulted in chaos. And an almost unrelenting emphasis on earnings, without a system of checks and balances, resulted in ethical lapses that ultimately led to the company's downfall. While Enron is the extreme case, many other companies show the same symptoms.

'If the challenge for executives in the 1990s was to transform corporate behemoths into nimble competitors, the challenge in coming years will be to create corporate cultures that encourage and reward integrity as much as creativity and entrepreneurship. To do that, executives need to start at the top, becoming not only exemplary managers but also the moral compass for the company.'

Action Programme 3

What are the key terminal and instrumental values of your work organisation? How far do these 'fit' your own key values?

3 The activities of the manager

FAST FORWARD

The **role of the manager** has changed over time, influenced by changes in the **environment** and the prevalent business **culture**. Pressures on the role of management include the speed of change, customer power and global competition.

The manager has many functions and must take responsibility for a range of business activities. In this section, we provide you with an overview of these activities to give a context for the development of the management skills covered in detail in this course.

3.1 Planning

Planning enables the organisation to cope with the uncertainty of the future in a way that will allow its objectives to be achieved. There are three important steps to planning.

- **Objective-setting**. Deciding what the organisation, and units within it, should achieve

- **Forecasting**. Anticipating, as far as possible, what opportunities and threats are likely to be offered by the future

- **Detailed planning**. Making decisions about what to do, how and when to do it and who should be responsible for it

Even the best plans may go wrong, but plans give direction and predictability to the work of the organisation, and enable it to adapt to environmental changes without crisis.

Planning affects all levels of management from the determination of overall direction, down to the detail of day-to-day operational tasks. There is a **hierarchical structure** of plans in which broad, long-term strategies lead to medium-term policies which are supported by short-term operational decisions.

3.1.1 An approach to planning

A systematic approach to planning, based on results and objectives involves:

Step 1. **Aims**; which dictate

Step 2. **Key result areas**; for which there should be

Step 3. **Standards**; and

Step 4. **Detailed targets**; so that

Step 5. **Action plans**; can be formulated and implemented, subject to

Step 6. **Monitoring**; and

Step 7. **Control action** where required.

Exam tip

> Through your studies at Advanced Certificate and Diploma Level and your work as a practising marketer you will be called upon to produce specific and often detailed plans. The framework above can be used as a basis for section headings within a report or plan.

Key concept

> **Control** is the process of monitoring the performance of individuals and units, and taking whatever actions may be necessary to bring performance into line with plans, by adjusting performance or, possibly, the plans themselves.

3.2 Control

Control is required because unpredictable events occur and actual performance deviates from what was expected and planned. For example, a powerful new competitor may enter the market, or there may be an unexpected rise in labour costs. Control systems allow managers to identify deviations from plan and to do something about them before they have adverse consequences.

Planning and control are intimately linked.

(a) It is necessary to verify whether or not the plan has worked or is working, and whether the objectives of the plan have been/are being achieved. This is where control becomes part of the planning process.

(b) Actual results and performance are therefore compared to the plan. If there are deviations, weaknesses or errors, **control measures** will be taken – which involves adjusting or setting further plans for ongoing action. Thus planning becomes part of the control process: Figure 1.2.

Figure 1.2: Basic control cycle

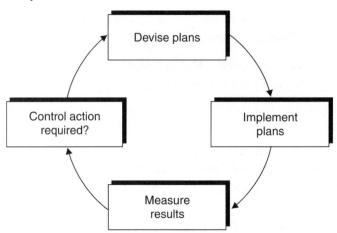

3.3 Budgets

An important aspect of both planning and control activity is the **budget** and you may be asked to make budget recommendations in the examination. Do not worry about the actual costs of various activities; the examiners are more interested in the fact you have been through the process of **identifying the key cost areas**.

Key concepts

A **budget**, since it has different purposes, might mean different things to different people.

- As a **forecast** of the expected performance of the organisation, it helps managers to look into the future. Given conditions of rapid change and uncertainty, however, this function will only be helpful over short periods of time. Budgets will often be updated or superseded.

- As a **means of allocating resources**, it can be used to decide what resources are needed and how much should be given to each area of the organisation's activities. Resource allocation is particularly important when some resources (usually finance and qualified staff) are in short supply. Budgets often set ceilings on spending by administrative and service departments – or project teams.

- As a **yardstick** against which to compare **actual performance**, the budget provides a means of indicating where and when **control action** may be necessary (and possibly where some managers or employees are open to censure for achieving poor results).

- As a **target** for achievement, a budget might be a means of **motivating the workforce** to greater personal accomplishment.

 Action Programme 4

So what do things cost? Over the next few weeks do some comparative shopping, ask questions or do some research to find out some basic costs. These will be useful when you need to select financial budgets.

BPP
LEARNING MEDIA

Cost   £

- 1 day's management consultancy
- 1 day's training (in house)
- 1 week's training course
- ½ page of advertising in a newspaper:
    local paper
    national paper
- 1 direct mail shot per 1,000
- Recruiting 1 new salesperson

3.4 Decision making and problem solving

In a business, a **decision** is usually the result of choosing between available or anticipated options and is often taken on the grounds of future projections. **The decision-making process thus involves value judgements and risk taking.** Traditionally, decision-making is a key difference between management and workers.

How systematic should decision-making be? The amount of time devoted to decision making depends on the nature of the problem, its complexity and the business risk of a poor outcome. However small the problem, it should be approached with conscientious professionalism. It is usually risky behaviour to trivialise any business problem.

The impact of a decision on peoples' reactions must be given due consideration. Initially, the organisation will depend on its personnel to successfully implement the decision. On the other hand, the outcome of the decision will inevitably affect other personnel or external customers. The good manager need to ensure these parties are brought on board and fully committed to the solution.

There are various approaches, which are applicable to different types of decision.

(a) **Scientific decision making** depends on the quantitative techniques of management, which measure and express all viable alternatives. It assumes that full and complete information will lead to the ideal solution. For example, the use of marginal costing and break-even models to set sales targets.

(b) **Creative decision making.** This requires managers to think not only systematically but also perhaps laterally or creatively. This is also sometimes referred to *thinking outside the box*. For example, creative thinking is usually beneficial in developing new products or introducing innovative services.

(c) **Reaction decision** theory assumes that once policies and corporate plans are established, decisions that are required follow as a natural result of those plans. In this way, decision making is regarded as an extension of the process of implementing corporate plans. Decisions are therefore partly predetermined by the detail of the plans.

(d) **Firefighting**. This entails making decision under pressure as and when events occur. Usually this type of decision making is used in businesses that do not adopt a proactive approach; they allow crises to brew and then everybody moves into action. A typical excuse for this mode of operation is lack of time. However, such organisations usually lack time to do things properly the first time around but seem to have time to have time to do things a second time, sorting out the original mess.

3.4.1 A problem solving process

There are as many suggested problem solving processes as there are textbooks. Here is a comprehensive process which has been drawn from a variety of sources.

We have a problem	Identify and define the problem
	Analyse the issues involved
	Define objectives of solution
	Define how success will be measured
What solution can we find?	Gather sufficient valid information
	Appraise available resources
	Consult relevant stakeholders
	List and evaluate alternative solutions
	Select the optimum solution
Now implement the solution	Draw up action plan to implement solution
	Communicate plan to stakeholders
	Carry out plan
	Gather feedback on progress and effectiveness of solution

You cannot find an answer unless you are asking the right question. Careful **definition of the problem** and examination of its causes frequently produce a definition of the solution. For example, a manager concerned with declining sales volume might concentrate on improving sales staff performance because there appears to be a direct link, while ignoring more subtle effects like product obsolescence and changes in fashion.

It is important to gather as much good quality information about the situation as it is possible to obtain with reasonable effort and at reasonable cost. The criteria for how much information should be collected is that it should be sufficient and what is obtained is verified to be valid.

There is rarely only one solution to a problem and much of a manager's skill will be exercised in framing, comparing and finally choosing between alternative solutions. Especially where creativity or innovation is required, it is advisable to generate as many options as possible. **Brainstorming** is a technique usually involving a group, where ideas are generated without immediate evaluation or comment so that creativity is not stifled.

In practice, many plans fail because of lack of consultation and plans are sprung on a surprised workforce who acquiesce in carrying out the plan. Sophisticated and sensible managers usually provide their personnel with enough participation in developing the solution to ensure they have some ownership of the plan. If a manager has to resort to selling a decision to staff, it probably means that they have not been consulted properly in the evaluation of alternatives. We will discuss consensus in decision making, and gaining acceptance of decisions later.

When an action plan had been developed, it must be properly and skilfully communicated to the people who are expected to implement it. Those tasked with delivery of the plan should be fully briefed and given the opportunity to raise questions. The dumping of a plan on staff may well reduce the likelihood of a quality outcome. It is usually better to over-communicate rather then to under-communicate.

Action Programme 5

You have been given the opportunity from your employer to attend a two-week marketing manager's course at the CIM's training centre at Moor Hall, or to work on secondment for six weeks helping in the launch of a national charity appeal.

Summarise the process which you would go through to evaluate these options and make a decision between them.

[Key Skill for Marketers: Problem solving]

Managers get decisions wrong, perhaps up to half the time. It helps if these are not decisions critical to the success of the business, but what is more important is that managers recognise and review their poor decisions, both to take corrective action and to learn from the decision and improve their decision making generally.

Action Programme 6

Make a list of five significant decisions which you have made over the last month or so, either at home or work. Can you remember the steps you went through to come to the decision?

To be effective as decision makers, managers need a framework that can be used as a reference point throughout their work: Figure 1.3.

Figure 1.3: The decision sequence

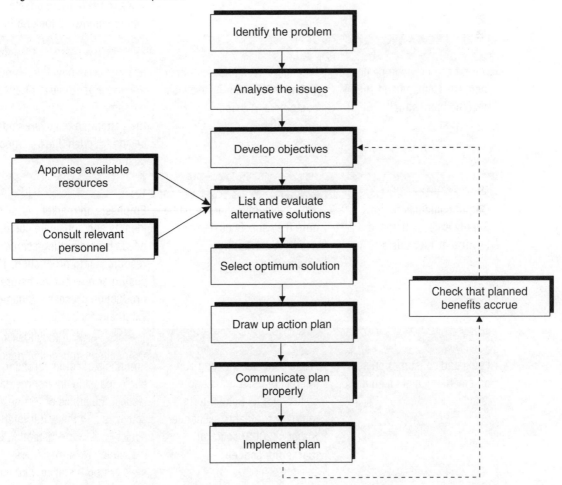

4 A forward look at the role of marketing managers

FAST FORWARD   Today's view is more **competencies** rather than task based – emphasising skills rather than the science of management.

4.1 The changing environment

The external environment contains both challenges and opportunities for the marketing manager. New technology and operational methods have increased output whilst free trade has increased competition. Economic fluctuations, government policy and legal changes have all influenced the business environment over time. An obvious change is the change in the balance of power between manufacturer and customer, forcing managers to change their views or **philosophy of business**. A developing business may well pass through the following, classic stages of business orientation.

Stage 1	Philosophy	Emphasis
Demand exceeds supply: a seller's market	Managers are centred on needs of operation: **production oriented**.	The organisation could grow be more successful by producing more, so managers concentrate on processes, operations, seeking ways to make more effective use of inputs: an inward looking focus.
Stage 2		
Output and new competitors increase. Demand and supply become more equal.	Managers seek to ensure their output is taken up by available customers. A **sales orientation**.	Production is now fine – but there are no longer queues of unsatisfied customers. Managers now turn their attention to advertising and selling to 'push' finished goods at customers
Stage 3		
Output continues to grow. Supply exceeds demand – a buyer's market exists	To survive, managers must be sure they satisfy customer needs. A **marketing orientation**.	Emphasis on market research to identify and anticipate customer needs before putting scarce resources into production. The customer now comes before the production process. Managers are externally focused.
Stage 4		
Legal and consumer pressures on environmental and quality issues	Firms consider the long-run interest of customers and society not just short-term mutually profitable exchange. *Kotler's* (2002) **societal marketing concept**.	Emphasis becomes broader, encompassing environmental issues, the ethics of business activities and the wider interests of society not just satisfaction of the individual. Now managers have needs of both society *and* the customer to satisfy.

BPP LEARNING MEDIA

Action Programme 7

How would you go about identifying the management philosophy of a particular organisation? Produce yourself a checklist and use it to evaluate the development stage of managers in the organisations below.

- Your organisation
- Your local doctor's surgery
- Your bank
- Your sports club/leisure centre
- The suppliers/intermediaries of your company

Managers have been driven to change their approaches and attitudes, as the external environment has changed. The modern bushiness environment demands a high level of management skills to ensure that essential changes are implemented smoothly, efficiently and effectively. The criteria of success is in deliveries of added value and increases in corporate wealth.

Responding to changes, or staying adaptable enough to be able to respond to changes, is often awkward for organisations. Their formal organisation structures and detailed job definitions may not be flexible enough to respond to unexpected events or quick changes of direction. They make long-term plans which cannot quickly be altered. Staff job descriptions tend to be set and require formal approval for any changes to be made.

Perhaps the trickiest problem with managing organisational change is the fact that people dislike it. They frequently resist changes to their jobs.

(a) Any change makes people feel insecure and uncertain

(b) They fear a threat to their competence or success in their jobs

(c) Change disrupts the social structure and relationships they are used to, for example, if there is relocation or redundancies.

The implementation of change is often not easy. Changes in crisis situations may sometimes be resisted less than routine changes, because people understand that there is an urgent **need** for change and that change is in their own interests. The traditional advice is that managers should address and try to overcome resistance rather than simply pushing change on people eg by developing a sound and fair business case supporting the change initiative.

An alternative approach is to build a flexible change-oriented organisation. Examples discussed earlier in this chapter include the organic organisation or the boundaryless organisation. Change is likely to be easier to swallow if it is delivered continuously in smaller chunks.

4.2 Pressures for change

Traditionally structured organisations tend to have certain characteristics in common.

(a) Belief in **universal laws** like the **span of control** principle (a small number of subordinates for each manager)

(b) Very **tall structures** (ie lots of different management levels) with **close supervision** at every level

(c) **Hierarchical control** through a rigid chain of command (as in an army)

(d) **Problem-solving** of a fragmented, directive, mechanistic kind, solely devoted to putting things right once they had gone wrong (instead of making sure they did not go wrong in the first place)

(e)   **Single function specialisms** like 'production' and 'sales', with departmental barriers and careers concentrated in one activity

(f)   **Individualism** reflected in incentive systems and the encouragement of competitive behaviour

(g)   **Focus on tasks and responsibilities** in job descriptions rather than the concept of adding value and using initiative for the organisation as a whole and for its customers

(h)   **Systems** which were reactive and procedure-bound with opportunity being seen as a very positive employee asset

In the past, also, managers have been able to impose change on other people. Nowadays, **change has a dramatic impact on managers themselves**. The impetus for these changes has come from a number of external forces, most importantly the following.

(a)   **New technology**. Improved information systems have meant that many middle managers previously involved in passing information have effectively been made redundant. Senior managers no longer need them to access or transmit information. New technologies have also increased the proportion of **knowledge workers** in the organisation. These people need less supervision as they plan and control their own work.

(b)   **Recession**. The economic downturn, experienced across the world in the late 1980s and early 1990s effectively reduced demand, forcing many mature organisations into buyers' markets. In an attempt to get closer to customers and cut costs, senior management has **delayered** the organisational structure. Organisations are **flatter**, with senior management closer to the market. There are thousands fewer managers employed today in giant organisations such as IBM and British Telecom.

(c)   The problems associated with the management of large bureaucratic organisations have been recognised. Many, such as the former ICI, have given up on the strategy of decades based on building competitive advantage through scale and cost economies and instead are looking for flexibility and responsiveness from smaller autonomous and de-centralised units. ICI demerged into two new companies, the 'new ICI' and the pharmaceuticals firm, Zeneca.

(d)   Similarly the flexible manager encourages communication across the organisation with **cross-functional teams**. These are **task-centred**, replacing the vertical communication of functionally orientated tall structures.

Action Programme 8

What have been the recent changes in your organisation, or one with which you are familiar? Take time to talk to the managers involved – find out how those changes have affected them and their roles.

4.3 Organisation structure

FAST FORWARD

Recent changes in ideas as to what makes the best **organisation structure** have led to a flattening and inversion of the old tall pyramid. There are resulting changes for the manager of today who needs to be more flexible and take on more responsibilities. There is a shift to breaking down boundaries and barriers within organisations and more sharing of information.

BPP
LEARNING MEDIA

Key concept

> **Organisation structure** is a formal framework intended to link individuals in an established network of relationships; group and allocate tasks; allocate and define authority and accountability for task performance; and co-ordinate information and work flows.

A classic **hierarchical structure** (organised by function and specialism) is illustrated in the organisation chart below: Figure 1.4.

Figure 1.4: Hierarchical (functionally-based) structure

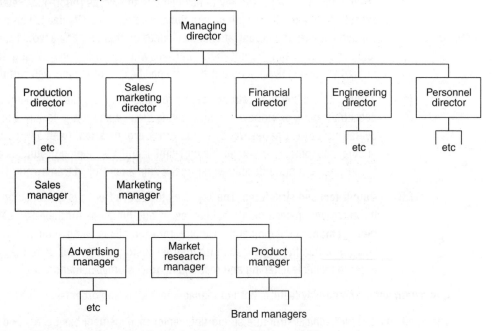

This type of structure gives clear lines of authority and responsibility.

A **matrix structure** may be used when lines of authority and responsibility are more complex: Figure 1.5.

Figure 1.5: Matrix structure

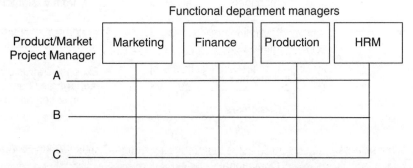

(a)   Horizontal lines of authority and responsibility are superimposed on the normal vertical departmental lines. Thus allows manager A, B, and C to improve efficiency by providing tight coordination across departments. Some employees report to two managers. This idea can also be used temporarily when a multi-department project is to be managed.

(b)   Whilst flexible and easing cross-company communication, this suggests that managers need even more effective communication and team building skills than hitherto.

4.3.1 The new organisation

Some recent trends (identified by writers such as Tom Peters) have emerged from the focus on **flexibility** as a key organisational value.

(a)   **Flat structures.** The flattening of hierarchies does away with levels of organisation which lengthened lines of communication and decision-making and encouraged ever-increasing specialisation. Flat structures are more responsive, because there is a more direct relationship between the organisation's strategic centre and the operational units serving the customer.

(b)   **'Horizontal structures'.** What Peters *(Liberation Management)* calls 'going horizontal' is a recognition that functional versatility (through multi-functional project teams and multi-skilling, for example) is the key to flexibility. In the words (quoted by Peters) of a Motorola executive: 'The traditional job descriptions were barriers. We needed an organisation soft enough between the organisational disciplines so that … people would run freely across functional barriers or organisational barriers with the common goal of getting the job done, rather than just making certain that their specific part of the job was completed.'

(c)   **'Chunked' and 'unglued' structures**. So far, this has meant teamworking and decentralisation, or empowerment, creating smaller and more flexible units within the overall structure. Charles Handy's **'shamrock organisation'** (with a three-leafed structured of core, subcontractor and flexible part-time labour) is gaining ground as a workable model for a leaner and more flexible workforce, within a controlled framework.

(d)   **Output-focused structures**. The key to all the above trends is the focus on results, and on the customer, instead of internal processes and functions for their own sake. A **project management** orientation and structure, for example, is being applied to the supply of services within the organisation (to internal customers) as well as to the external market, in order to facilitate listening and responding to customer demands.

Empowerment is another key feature, both of management style *and* organisation structure.

The traditional **tall** hierarchical structure supporting senior management has been stood on its head.

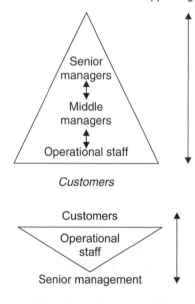

- Managers were a long way from customers

- Only the lowest grade of staff had customer contact!!

- Expensive structure of middle managers to support the organisation and its systems

- The organisation is flatter

- Senior management now perceive their role as facilitating and supporting the operational staff in direct customer contact

4.3.2 The implications for managers

There have been changes in roles and in attitudes. The manager of the future must possess certain vital qualities.

- Flexibility
- The ability to promote change and cope with it
- Obsession with quality and customer care

BPP
LEARNING MEDIA

- Effective communication skills
- Leadership
- Teambuilding skills
- The ability to look at the organisation as a whole ('helicopter vision')

He or she will be a member of a smaller team, will be expected to take on more responsibility and will be more accountable than previously. Finally, the reduction in management layers means that there will be fewer managers.

4.3.3 Grounds for optimism about management

(a) **Managerial roles are now more generalist**, with increased responsibilities and more tasks.

(b) **Managers are managing larger teams** or groups of people, with a wider mix of staff.

(c) **The new manager is more accountable:** this greater focus on performance means attempts to measure added-value more carefully and, hence, redesigned performance review (appraisal) systems.

(d) Because of the explosion in IT, **managers have better information** on which to base their decisions.

(e) Moreover, because IT has taken much of the drudgery out of the manager's administrative activities, **the manager has more time** for the people aspects, for strategic thinking, for 'customer' service, and for dealing with routine tasks more efficiently.

(f) **Managers are learning new skills**, concerned with managing change, financial know-how, marketing, strategic planning and the motivation of multi-function teams.

In some research studies, the majority of participating managers are positive about the changes and how these changes are influencing their roles. Indeed, many argue that previous frustrations have been removed.

(a) **Flatter hierarchies** mean that most managers are closer to top management in the strategic and policy-making areas. Further, most managers have clear domains of responsibility, plus more control over the resources needed to achieve results.

(b) **'Empowerment'** is generating the opportunity to take on new challenges, to broaden expertise, to innovate and to take risks.

(c) Managerial careers may be more problematic, but it is a mistake to assume that all managers are continually striving for advancement.

Management career planning nowadays tends to focus on the development and acquisition of **generic transferable skills** such as communication, making effective presentations, teamworking, people development, business diagnostics, performance management, relationship management, active listening, business development, project management, negotiation and leadership, coaching.

 Marketing at Work

If you follow the fortunes of top company chairman and chief executive officers, you will recognise how these people rely on their generic transferable skills.

For example Adam Crozier went from running the Football Association to running the Royal Mail. Sir Peter Davis moved from the Prudential to the top of Sainsbury.

Delayering has recently been very fashionable, as it promises to save money. It tends to be justified by increased use of information technology and the growth of self-managed teams. However, some authorities argue that middle managers are essential for implementation: they also hold the company's 'corporate memory', in other words, practical lessons learnt about past successes and failures.

On the other hand, there are others who argue for more open and virtually boundaryless structures. Here information is shared freely and not discarded or blocked by individual managers. Within this approach, **information belongs to the business and not individual managers**. This accords more with modern corporate governance and stewardship requirements and minimises the business risk of the organisation in being held to ransom by managers who hold its information and knowledge base in their heads.

4.3.4 The Internet

Information and Communications Technology have had a significant impact on management and communications. Networks generate an increase in information flow, which empowers front-line employees (facilitating delayering and virtual team working) while at the same time giving better quality control and decision-support information for managers.

5 The responsibilities of the marketing manager

Marketing at Work

Here is a CIM job description for a marketing manager (www.cim.co.uk)

Description

Responsible for the strategic direction of all marketing activity on specific products/services.

Personal specification

- 3 years experience in marketing or product management
- Able to think strategically and direct delivery
- Works well in multi-disciplined teams
- Forms close knit relationships with outside agencies

Suggested Professional Qualifications (CIM)

- CIM Postgraduate Diploma in Marketing (DipM)
- Chartered Marketer

Responsibilities

- Reports to Marketing Director
- Ensures product/service matches brand positioning
- Identifies target markets and works with data manager to provide external agencies with relevant data
- Plans communication strategy and liaises with all members of the campaign team to ensure effective and efficient delivery
- Analyses results of all marketing activity and presents findings and recommendations to management
- Builds close knit teams, own and cross departmental
- Liaises with external agencies to ensure clear understanding of the marketing strategy.

BPP LEARNING MEDIA

5.1 General management and specialist managers

So far we have been considering the general role of management but now we need to turn our attention specifically to **the role of marketing management.**

All managers wear two hats.

- They are leaders and organisers of the marketing team
- They deploy specialist skills

However, the marketing manager also acts as the bridge between the company and its external audiences, particularly customers: Figure 1.6.

(a) . The marketing manager represents the **customer's** needs and interests within the organisation. The marketing manager is the customer's champion, often dealing with customer complaints.

(b) Marketing managers often have the ambassadorial or figurehead role in the organisation; many of their **teams** also share this responsibility. Moreover, the marketing department generally creates relationships with customers, and controls the firm's **communications** with them.

Figure 1.6: The marketing manager as interface

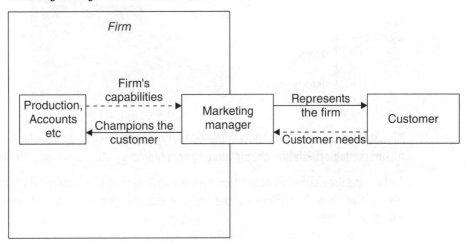

5.2 Embedding the market oriented culture

Marketing is often perceived as being the same as advertising, selling or promotion and have often there are no **strategic** expectations of the marketing expert. An important role of marketing management is the liaison with senior management to further the chosen marketing strategy.

In many sectors, marketers have reinforced the product focus of the business with their system of brand management in which managers are given responsibility for individual brands, **rather than the needs of customers**. A number of FMCG manufacturers are re-assessing the value of the traditional brand manager, replacing them with more **market-oriented managers** who can liaise with other functions to improve customer service.

Much of the marketing philosophy has been picked up with the concepts of **internal customers**, **relationship marketing** and quantification of **value added** at each stage of the process. Whether these developments are called marketing or something else is relatively unimportant, as long as the philosophy of **customer satisfaction** is effected within the business. An important role will remain for the managers responsible for external liaison, and for identifying and anticipating the changing needs of their customer base.

5.3 Influencing the mix

The degree of freedom the marketing department has to determine the mix elements varies, because of required financial targets, existing production equipment and distribution systems: Figure 1.7. The marketing department probably has most control over promotion.

(a)   The **product** element will be affected by the degree to which the marketing department has an influence over production and R&D.

(b)   The **place** element will be affected by the degree to which the marketing department can influence distribution.

(c)   The type of **price** demanded for a product will reflect the cost to a degree, and the finance department will have an inevitable influence. This also includes credit offered and payment terms each of which has an impact.

(d)   The **promotion** element is under the direct control of the marketing department, even though many activities will be subcontracted.

Figure 1.7: Marketing department influences

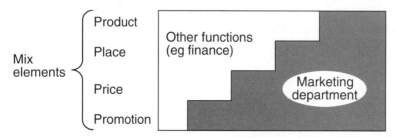

Degree of influence

Arguably although the personnel in the **marketing department** may have limited influence in some cases, the **marketing orientation should have been adopted by all** in the organisation.

Embedding the marketing orientation means convincing other departments that for long-term success they should place the customer at the focus of their decision-making, and use their specialist expertise with this in mind.

Exam tip

You are unlikely to come across purely theoretical questions in this exam: all questions will relate directly to a specific practical scenario.

However, you cannot rely solely on common sense and experience: the Senior Examiner has explicitly called for candidates to underpin their action points with relevant theory. A good approach is to put yourself in the shoes of the marketing manager in the scenario – but to assume that the people you are writing the reports for are the types who want sound theoretical justification or explanations (ie examiners!).

BPP
LEARNING MEDIA

5.4 Becoming an effective marketing manager

Going over the points that have been made in this section, we can summarise as follows.

Activity	Example management skills needed
1 Heading and organising	
	Communication
• Controlling the marketing team	Project management
• 'Representing' the customer	Team working
• Liaising with senior management on strategy	Negotiation
• Liasing with other organisational functions	Conflict resolution
	Appraisal/coaching
	Performance management
2 Specialist	
	Conflict resolution
• Handling complaints	Communication
• Building relationships	Listening skills
• Technical marketing knowledge	Project management
• Controlling communications	Negotiation
• Internal marketing	Technical training

Remember often management may develop an excellent strategy and formulate logical and detailed plans on paper. However, to actually make it work effectively **in practice** requires the highest level of management and personal skills.

Chapter Roundup

- **Managers** play a critical role in the organisation. They act as **catalysts**, responsible for the transformation of resource inputs into desired and valued outputs.

- Managers are responsible for the **scarce resources** entrusted to them, which must be used efficiently if value is to be added to the organisation, and if its objectives are to be achieved.

- **Culture** is important both in organisations and in the wider world. It is the knowledge, beliefs, customs and attitudes which people adhere to.

- The **role of the manager** has changed over time, influenced by changes in the **environment** and the prevalent business **culture**. Pressures on the role of management include the speed of change, customer power and global competition.

- Recent changes in ideas as to what makes the best **organisation structure** have led to a flattening and inversion of the old tall pyramid. There are resulting changes for the manager of today who needs to be more flexible and take on more responsibilities. There is a shift to breaking down boundaries and barriers within organisations and more sharing of information.

- Today's view is more **competencies** rather than task based – emphasising skills rather than the science of management.

Quick Quiz

1   What were the five management functions identified by Fayol?

2   Mintzberg identified ten roles of managers and sub-divided these into three broad categories: what are they?

3   What are the explicit elements of culture?

4   What steps are involved in a systematic approach to planning?

5   What is control?

6   Distinguish between scientific and reaction decision-making.

7   What characterises product orientated management philosophies, sales orientated management philosophies, and customer orientated management philosophies?

8   Suggest a possible change in the senior management role as a result of flatter organisations.

9   What is the role of the marketing manager?

10   What is the significance of a new focus upon internal customers and relationship marketing?

Answers to Quick Quiz

1   Planning, organising; commanding; co-ordinating; controlling

2   Interpersonal: figurehead, leader, liaison
Information: monitor, disseminator, spokesman
Decisional: entrepreneur, disturbance handler, resource allocator, negotiator

3   Behaviour, artefacts, rituals

4   Aims – key results – standards – detailed targets – action plans – monitoring – control action

5   The process of monitoring performance and taking any action required to maintain it at the desired standard

6   Scientific decision making assumes consideration of complete information will lead, via quantitative analysis to a rational solution. Reaction decision making is an extension of the process of implementing corporate plans.

7   Production orientation assumes unlimited demand and concentrates on increasing output and production efficiency. Sales orientation concentrates on persuading people to buy current production.

8   More emphasis on supporting and facilitating

9   To be the champion of the customer

10   They both reflect the philosophy of the importance of ensuring customer satisfaction

BPP
LEARNING MEDIA

Action programme review

1 The differences between levels of management will normally reflect breadth of scope and responsibility. Authority over spending is usually carefully controlled. Did you find any anomalies, especially with regard to job descriptions and what is actually done? It is not uncommon for job descriptions to lag behind what is actually done.

2 Whilst doing this, try to identify opportunities for developing areas of weaknesses. Here are some examples.

- Internal training programmes
- Job shadowing with colleagues
- Observation, secondments or work with community or social groups

3 Your answer to this will depend upon your own experiences, but think about what differences the compatibility or incompatibility of values make to your experience of working in the organisation.

4 Your findings will vary, depending on your own definitions of the items to be costed!

5 **Problem definition** is crucial to this decision. Before you can assess the options you must establish **decision criteria**. What do you want to get out of the activity you choose? Something prestigious for your CV? Specific career relevant experience? General personal development? Wider benefits such as social interaction and knowledge of the wider world? The two, theoretically distinct, stages of problem definition and appraisal of potential solutions may interact, since you may not be aware of all the possible benefits you could derive without considering what the solutions offer.

6 This will depend upon your own experiences, but you could ask yourself some further questions:

- How would you assess those decisions?
- Were they the right ones?
- What actions could you take to put bad decisions right?

7 You might consider the points below.

- Stated aims of values
- Status of sales and marketing people
- Any listing of customer complaints or other feedback
- Behaviour of management in relation to products and markets
- Perceived quality of products and service

8 You might consider not only the nature of the changes, but the timescales over which may they have happened, the key drivers behind the change, internal and external to the organisation and the cultural adjustments required. If involving other people in your discussions be sensitive to their time and make sure your questions are focused and within their authority to answer.

Now try Question 1 at the end of the Study Text

BPP LEARNING MEDIA

Managing the team

2

Syllabus content – knowledge and skill requirements

- Functions and roles of marketing managers and typical marketing jobs and the nature of relationships with other functions in organisations operating in a range of different industries and contexts (1.1)
- Techniques available for selecting, building, developing and motivating marketing teams to improve performance (1.4)
- Allocating and leading the work of marketing teams, agreeing objectives and work plans with teams and individuals (1.5)

Introduction

In this chapter, we discuss some of the issues in managing a team. In Section 1 we discuss teams and groups in general, why they are needed, what they do, some examples in a marketing context, and some key management issues.

In Section 2, we discuss the problems of forming new teams, and the type of developmental stages a team goes through before it can get down to work. Team formation in difficult or unusual circumstances has been stressed as important for this paper. In Section 3, we offer some rules of thumb for you to assess whether a team is effective or not, with the proviso that a team which is too cohesive can be blind to new or different ideas – group think.

Sections 4 and 5 deal with two modern types of team: the virtual team and the cross-functional team. Cross-functional teams are likely to be used more and more in modern, flexible organisations and have a particular contribution to make in the field of marketing. Virtual teams exploit the potential of IT to make possible new structures and approaches to work. In Section 6 we focus on your role, as a possible team leader. Teams often need some sort of direction, but the approach to leadership you adopt (leadership style) can vary, depending on the task and the followers.

In this chapter we offer some detailed examples for you to try out your diagnostic skills.

1 Teams and groups

FAST FORWARD

An **effective group** is one which achieves its allotted task *and* satisfies its members. **Teams** are becoming more important as a means of carrying out work in a contemporary business environment.

Key concept

Handy defines a **group** as **'any collection of people who perceive themselves to be a group'**. The point of this definition is the distinction it implies between a random collection of individuals and a group of individuals who share a **common sense of identity and belonging.**

Group dynamics is the name given to the system of relationships and behaviour which exists in any group of people. Membership of a group tends to modify or develop personal characteristics to the extent that the group appears to have a personality of its own.

A group has certain attributes that a random 'crowd' does not possess.

- **The members have a sense of identity**: there are acknowledged boundaries to the group which define it.

- **Members are loyal to the group**, and conform to the norms of behaviour and attitude that bind the group together.

- **Purpose and leadership**. Most groups have a **purpose or set of objectives** and will, spontaneously or formally, choose individuals or sub-groups to lead them towards those goals.

1.1 Formal and informal groups in organisations

Some groupings will be part of the **formal organisation**: for example, specialists may be in a committee investigating a particular problem; a department split into small work teams to facilitate supervision. Other groups are **informal**.

BPP LEARNING MEDIA

(a) **Formal groups** will have a formal structure; they will be consciously organised for a function allotted to them by the organisation, and for which they are held responsible – they are task oriented, and become **teams.** Leaders may be chosen within the group, but are typically given authority by the organisation. Permanent formal groups include work sections and management teams such as the board of directors. **Temporary** formal groups include *ad hoc* committees and project teams.

(b) **Informal groups** will invariably be present in any organisation. Informal groups include workplace cliques and networks who socialise outside work. They have a constantly fluctuating membership and structure, and leaders usually emerge because of their personal qualities. The purposes of informal groups are usually related to group and individual member satisfaction, rather than to a task.

Key concept

> A **team** is a small number of people with complementary skills who are committed to a common purpose, performance goals and approach, for which they hold themselves mutually accountable.
>
> *(Katzenbach & Smith)*

1.2 The strengths of team working

FAST FORWARD

Groups function through **interaction** between individual members and the **blend** of their skills and abilities.

From the organisation's standpoint groups and teams are particularly valuable for several key functions:

- Performing **tasks** which require the collective skills of more than one person
- Yielding of **efficiencies** by smoothing out peaks and troughs in individual workloads
- Testing and ratifying **decisions** made outside the group
- Consulting or negotiating, especially to resolve **disputes** within the organisation
- Creating **ideas** from the interaction of group members
- Collecting and transmitting **information** and ideas
- Co-ordinating the **work** of different individuals or other groups
- **Motivating** individuals to devote more energy and effort into achieving the organisation's goals

 Marketing at Work

Teamworking at Royal Mail

Traditionally each postal delivery person had a designated area or route. Thus A might be responsible for delivery post to area X and B was responsible for servicing area Y. If there were few letters on a specific day for area X, A would not be very busy. If on that day area Y had a big mail load, B would have to work harder and might even have to work overtime.

The introduction of teamwork helped to eliminate the job demarcations that were hindering efficiency savings. Hence, in the above case, A being less busy would help out B or share the workload.

1.3 Limitations of team working

FAST FORWARD Problems with teams include **conflict** on the one hand, and **groupthink** (excessive cohesion) on the other.

1.4 Examples of teams in marketing

Team working may be used for a variety of purposes in a marketing context.

(a)   **Quality circles** discussing and improving quality of service

(b)   **Project groups**

- **A new product development team**

- A **key account team** responsible for all aspects of a marketing for a key client or customer segment

- A **specialist marketing function team** responsible for research or the creative dimensions of marketing

(c)   **Brainstorming groups,** brought together to generate new ideas and suggestions, for problem-solving or planning

(d)   **Cross-functional teams** to perform a variety of tasks such as new product development, setting up operational systems, identifying service standards and bringing the product or service to market.

(e)   **Training or study groups**

Action Programme 1

What (a) formal and (b) informal groups are you involved with? What are their functions? Why can these functions be performed better by a group than by an individual?

Pick a group of which you are a member. How do you define who is 'in' the group and who isn't? Does the leader of the group make a positive effort to keep the group close-knit and to make it **feel** like a team? Would you say your department or section was a team?

Do you personally **like** working in a group, or do you prefer to be and function better alone? Do you think you could succeed by being either a team player or a loner? Or does your work and the marketing culture require you to be both, at appropriate times?

[Key Skill for Marketers: Working with others]

Marketing at Work

Team focus at General Electric

In the transformation of General Electric, Jack Welch, the CEO introduced the idea of team focus. He expected managers to be team players.

Welch puts forward the example of a multi-functional business consisting of marketing, engineering and components manufacturing. This business has a brilliant manufacturing manager who is highly numerate and delivers high quality output and meets his deadlines.

BPP LEARNING MEDIA

However, Welch explains that "this person won't talk with people in engineering and manufacturing. He won't share ideas with them, and won't behave in a boundaryless way with them.

Now we're replacing that person with someone who may not be quite perfect but who is a good team player and lifts the team's performance.

Maybe the predecessor was working at 100% or 120%, but that person didn't talk with team members, didn't swap ideas. As a result, the whole team was operating at 65%. But the new manager is getting 90% or 100% from the whole total. That was a discovery."

Welch advocates taking steps against those managers who are not willing to be team players.

2 Team formation and development

If you are faced with starting a team from scratch, you can begin by identifying what the **task** is and what **skills** and **characteristics** are needed to achieve it. Then group members can be identified from within or outside the organisation.

In the flatter organisation of today the formation of teams for relatively short periods is becoming more common. These may be **project teams** which bring together individuals from different disciplines, backgrounds and even different companies. In these situations the manager has two key roles.

- Selecting the right mix of individuals
- Actively working to turn individuals into effective teams in as short a time as possible

 Marketing at Work

Nicky Wnek described the 'innovation squad' in *Marketing Business*

'**Mr Blue Skies** is the broad thinker who keeps the long-term vision but needs to be kept-in-touch with reality. His colleague, **Mr Margin** gets margins up and thus delivers the all-important profit. However, he cannot see that innovation relies on intangibles such as faith and judgement.

Ms Misery takes her name from her tendency to focus on the negative. But innovation needs her rigorous approach.

Ms Me-Too could bring about a first-to-market situation by keeping a valuable eye on the competition – for instance an innovation abroad. Every innovation needs someone to champion the cause but **Mr Hobby-Horse** can be in danger of backing the wrong horse. **Mr Cavalier** is the classic self-confident entrepreneur with high energy levels and a healthy disregard for the established way of doing things; he genuinely cares about a result and is faster at effecting change.

Ms Brands is the player who contributes the strong understanding of the consumer, but unfortunately not everyone shares her passion for her particular brand. **Mr Out-of-Depth** is unlikely to have that big idea, but he is keen, hard-working and sufficiently junior to do the essential donkey work.'

2.1 Who should belong in the team?

Team members should be selected for their potential to contribute to getting things done (**task performance**) and establishing good working relationships (**group maintenance**). This may include:

(a) **Specialist skills**. A team might exist to combine expertise from different departments.

(b)   **Power** in the wider organisation. Team members may have influence.

(c)   **Access to resources**

(d)   The **personalities and goals** of the individual members of the team. These will determine how the group functions.

The blend of the individual skills and abilities of its members will (ideally) **balance** the team.

2.2 Belbin: team roles

FAST FORWARD

Ideally team members should perform a balanced mix of **roles**. **Belbin** suggests: co-ordinator, shaper, plant, monitor-evaluator, resource-investigator, implementer, team-worker, completer-finisher and specialist.

R Meredith **Belbin** (1981) researched business game teams at the Henley Management College and drew up a widely-used framework for understanding roles within work groups.

Belbin insisted that a distinction needs to be made between:

(a)   **Team (process) role** ('a tendency to behave, contribute and interrelate with others at work in certain distinctive ways'), and

(b)   **Functional role** ('the job demands that a person has been engaged to meet by supplying the requisite technical skills and operational knowledge')

His model of nine roles addresses the mix of team/process roles required for a fully functioning team.

2.2.1 Nine team roles

Belbin identifies nine team roles.

Role and description	Team-role contribution	Allowable weaknesses
Plant Creative, imaginative, unorthodox	Solves difficult problems	Ignores details, too preoccupied to communicate effectively
Resource investigator Extrovert, enthusiastic, communicative	Explores opportunities, develops contacts	Over-optimistic, loses interest once initial enthusiasm has passed
Co-ordinator (chairman) Mature, confident, a good chairperson	Clarifies goals, promotes decision-making, delegates well	Can be seen as manipulative, delegates personal work
Shaper Challenging, dynamic, thrives on pressure	Has the drive and courage to overcome obstacles	Can provoke others, hurts people's feelings
Monitor evaluator Sober, strategic and discerning	Sees all options, judges accurately	Lacks drive and ability to inspire others, overly critical
Team worker Co-operative, mild, perceptive and diplomatic	Listens, builds, averts friction, calms the waters	Indecisive in crunch situations, can be easily influenced

Role and description	Team-role contribution	Allowable weaknesses
Implementer (company worker) Disciplined, reliable, conservative and efficient	Turns ideas into practical actions	Somewhat inflexible, slow to respond to new possibilities
Completer – Finisher Painstaking, conscientious, anxious	Searches out errors and omissions, delivers on time	Inclined to worry unduly, reluctant to delegate, can be a nitpicker
Specialist Single-minded, self-starting, dedicated	Provides knowledge and skills in rare supply	Contributes only on a narrow front, dwells on technicalities, overlooks the 'big picture'

2.2.2 A balanced team

These team roles are not fixed within any given individual. Team members can occupy more than one role, or switch to 'backup' roles if required: hence, there is no requirement for every team to have nine members. However, since role preferences are based on personality, it should be recognised that:

- Individuals will be naturally inclined towards some roles more than others
- Individuals will tend to adopt one or two team roles more or less consistently
- Individuals are likely to be more successful in some roles than in others

The nine roles are complementary, and Belbin suggested that an 'ideal' team should represent a mix or balance of all of them. If managers know employees' team role preferences, they can strategically select, 'cast' and develop team members to fulfil the required roles.

Question

The following phrases and slogans project certain team roles: identify which. (Examples are drawn from Belbin, 1993.)

(a) The small print is always worth reading.
(b) Let's get down to the task in hand.
(c) In this job you never stop learning.
(d) Without continuous innovation, there is no survival.
(e) Surely we can exploit that?
(f) When the going gets tough, the tough get going.
(g) I was very interested in your point of view.
(h) Has anyone else got anything to add to this?
(i) Decisions should not be based purely on enthusiasm.

Answer

(a) Completer – finisher
(b) Implementer/company worker
(c) Specialist
(d) Plant
(e) Resource investigator
(f) Shaper
(g) Teamworker

(h) Co-ordinator/Chairman

(i) Monitor evaluator

Action Programme 2

Over the next month make a note of the sort of roles you play in meetings and group situations. Are any of the roles absent from the group? Did this make the task harder than necessary in hindsight?

If there is the opportunity, perhaps in syndicate work at college, make a conscious effort to take on a different role.

[Key Skills for Marketers: Working with others]

2.3 Team development

You probably have had experience of being put into a group of people you do not know. Many teams are set up this way and it takes some time for the team to become effective.

> **FAST FORWARD**
>
> A team develops in **stages**: forming, storming, norming, performing (**Tuckman**) and dorming or mourning/adjourning.

Four stages in group development were identified by *Tuckman* (1965).

Step 1 **Forming**

The team is just coming together. Each member wishes to impress his or her personality on the group. The individuals will be trying to find out about each other, and about the aims and norms of the team. There will at this stage probably be a wariness about introducing new ideas. The objectives being pursued may as yet be unclear and a leader may not yet have emerged.

Step 2 **Storming**

This frequently involves more or less open conflict between team members. There may be changes agreed in the original objectives, procedures and norms established for the group. If the team is developing successfully this may be a fruitful phase, as more realistic targets are set and trust between the group members increases.

Step 3 **Norming**

A period of settling down: there will be agreements about work sharing, individual requirements and expectations of output. Norms and procedures may evolve which enable methodical working to be introduced and maintained.

Step 4 **Performing**

The team sets to work to execute its task. The difficulties of growth and development no longer hinder the group's objectives.

Later writers added two stages to Tuckman's model.

(a) **Dorming**. Once a group has been performing well for some time, it may get complacent, and fall back into self-maintenance functions, at the expense of the task.

BPP LEARNING MEDIA

(b) **Mourning/adjourning**. The group sees itself as having fulfilled its purpose – or, if it is a temporary group, is due to physically disband. This is a stage of confusion, sadness and anxiety as the group breaks up. There is evaluation of its achievements, and gradual withdrawal of group members. If the group is to continue, going on to a new task, there will be a re-negotiation of aims and roles: a return to the forming stage.

Question

Read the following descriptions of team behaviour and decide to which category they belong (forming, storming, norming, performing, dorming).

(a) Two of the group arguing as to whose idea is best
(b) Progress becomes static
(c) Desired outputs being achieved
(d) Shy member of group not participating
(e) Activities being allocated

Answer

Categorising the behaviour of group members in the situations described results in the following: (a) storming, (b) dorming, (c) performing, (d) forming, (e) norming.

Exam tip

A past question has asked about team building in an organisation culture focused on individuals. The examiner complained about answers that consisted of little more than a Tuckman 'theory dump'. This is a very important point. Theory is very important but you must *apply* it to the setting given in the question. The particular issues faced at each stage of development will be different if the team is brand new (as in the December 2006 exam) adding to the 'forming' needs; temporary (and therefore likely to get to the adjourning stage); or multi-disciplinary and multicultural (as in the June 2006 exam), to the 'storming' and 'norming' needs.

Apart from anything else, don't waste time talking about 'forming' if your team in a scenario has been together for years – and don't neglect 'forming' issues if your team is brand new!

Action Programme 3

Read the following descriptions of team behaviour and decide to which category they belong (forming, storming, norming, performing, dorming).

(a) Two of the group arguing as to whose idea is best
(b) Progress becomes static
(c) Desired outputs being achieved
(d) Shy member of group not participating
(e) Activities being allocated

2.4 Building a team

In paragraph 2.3 we suggested that teams have a natural evolutionary life cycle, and that four stages can be identified. Not all teams develop into mature teams and might be stuck, stagnating, in any one of the stages.

So, it often falls to the supervisor or manager to build the team. There are three main issues involved in team building.

Issues	Comments
Team identity	Get people to see themselves as part of this group
Team solidarity	Encourage loyalty so that members put in extra effort for the sake of the team
Shared objectives	Encourage the team to commit itself to shared work objectives and to co-operate willingly and effectively in achieving them.

FAST FORWARD ⟫

Team development can be facilitated by active **team building** measures to support team identity, solidarity and commitment to shared objectives.

2.4.1 A contingency approach to team effectiveness

A useful way of looking at the problem of how a supervisor or manager can create an effective team is to take a **contingency approach**. *C B Handy* (1992) suggested that group effectiveness (**outcomes**) depends on the **givens** and **intervening factors**: Figure 2.1.

Figure 2.1: Handy's model of team effectiveness

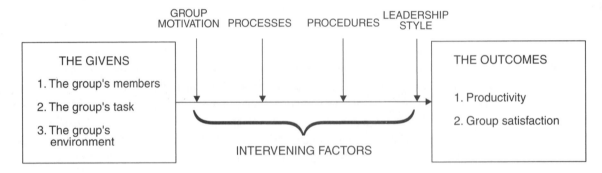

2.4.2 The givens

The personalities of the members of the team, and their personal goals, will help to determine the group's personality and goals. Individuals are likely to be influenced more strongly by a small group than by a large group in which they may be unable to participate effectively in team decisions.

The nature of the task must have some bearing on how a group should be managed.

- If a job must be done urgently, it is often necessary to apply close hand-on supervision of how things should be done, rather than to encourage a participatory style of working.

- Jobs that are routine and undemanding are unlikely to motivate either individuals or the group as a whole. In consequence, the manager may have to inspire the staff so as to get things going.

The group's environment relates to the physical surroundings at work and to inter-group relations. An open-plan office, in which the members of the group are closely situated, is usually conducive to group cohesion. A group's attitudes will also be affected by its relationship with other groups, which may be friendly, neutral or hostile. Where groups are in competition with other groups, an element of group bonding and motivation might arise. Managers of sports teams try hard to develop team bonding to motivate players to win.

BPP
LEARNING MEDIA

2.4.3 Intervening factors

Of the intervening factors, we will be discussing **motivation** in more detail later and we will go on to talk about **leadership** and leadership style at the end of this chapter. With regard to processes and procedures, groups are much the same as individuals: research indicates that a team which tackles its work systematically will be more effective than one which muddles through. Note that it is the intervening factors that a manager is likely to be able to control.

2.4.4 The outcomes

Ideally, the group and its work will be managed so that efforts towards high productivity will also lead to the satisfaction of personal and group needs such as job satisfaction, respect and cohesion. A **participative style of management** may contribute to this.

Opponents of teamwork usually like to give the erroneous impression that teams somehow act spontaneously and hence may be ineffective. In practice, even self-managed teams exercise some form of target setting and performance appraisal. Hence, teams might be ineffective not simply because it is a team, but because it is badly managed.

3 Effective and ineffective teams

FAST FORWARD

The management problem is how to create an **efficient work group**.

3.1 Characteristics of an effectively functioning team

(a) The team has a **clear mission**, **values** and **objectives** which are understood and **shared** by all members.

(b) Members are **aware** of each others **differences**, respect them and realise the **synergistic effect** of individual contributions.

(c) The actual **mix of personalities and skills** is sufficiently diverse and complimentary.

(d) Each individual gets the **support of the team and a sense of identity and belonging** which encourages loyalty and hard work on the group's behalf.

(e) **Skills, information and ideas are shared**, so that the team's capabilities are greater than those of the individuals.

(f) **New ideas** are welcomed and built upon. **Persuasion skills** are brought into play in **group discussion for decision making and problem solving.**

(g) Each member is encouraged to have a **voice and participate**, and becomes personally **involved in and committed to the team's activities.**

(h) There is **trust and openness** so that individuals and task problems can be addressed effectively.

(i) There are effective forums for maintaining **communication**. These include regular **formal meetings** as well as **informal get-togethers**, for example around the coffee machine or drinks/food after work.

(j) The team **bonds well** together and acquires a good *esprit de corps*.

Teamworking may suffer problems if not properly managed.

(a) **Rigid leadership** and procedures may **strangle initiative and creativity** in individuals.

(b) **Over enforcement of group norms** may **restrict individual personality** and flair.

(c) **Too much discord.** Conflicting **roles and relationships** can cause difficulties in communicating effectively.

(d) **Personality problems** will harm performance if one member dislikes or distrusts another; is too dominant or so timid that the value of his ideas is lost; or is so negative that constructive communication is rendered impossible.

(e) **Rivalry** and political conflicts of interest may surface.

(f) **Too much harmony.** Teams work best when there is room for disagreement. The cosy consensus of the group may prevent consideration of alternatives, constructive criticism or conflict. This is called **group think**. Similarly, efforts to paper over differences lead to bland recommendations.

(g) **Corporate culture and reward systems.** Teams may fail if the company promotes and rewards the individual at the expense of the group.

(h) **Lack of focus.** There is often a mistaken belief that things will happen simply because a team has been formed.

(i) **Powerlessness.** People will not bother to work in a team or on a task force if its recommendations are ignored.

Teamworking is an invaluable working practice in a contemporary business environment. Sensible managers will acknowledge the benefits of teamworking and recognise that many of the arguments against team working are in effect the consequences of poor management.

There is no divine reason why individual working should *per se* be better than team working. If an individual is badly managed, his or her performance could well be ineffective or poor.

3.2 Appraising group effectiveness

Supervisors who wish to improve the effectiveness of their work groups must be able to identify the different characteristics of an effective and an ineffective group. No one factor on its own will be significant, but taken collectively the factors may indicate how well or badly the group is doing.

The effectiveness of the group should be assessed initially in terms of the group itself, the group's task and the group's working environment.

(a) The **personalities, characteristics, skills and experience** of each individual group member should be assessed. Inter-personal hostility between particular individuals should be identified. Habitual absentees should be identified.

(b) The **tasks** of the group should be assessed. Are the tasks of the group too difficult for the group members? Is the workload too heavy for a group of ten?

(c) The **environment** of the group should be examined. Do the individuals who have to co-operate closely with each other actually sit close together? Is the equipment used by the group adequate for their job?

 Action Programme 4

How would you determine whether a team was effective or ineffective? Think about both quantitative and qualitative factors which may characterise the two extremes. Remember that individual attitudes will affect many things, as well as the dynamics of the group.

BPP
LEARNING MEDIA

Action Programme 5

Consider your group at work. How effective is it in terms of (a) doing what the organisation wants it to do in the way of tasks and (b) offering satisfaction to its members?

What can you (or your manager) do to improve the effectiveness of the group? Think about your contribution, if you are a member, and your ability to adjust the 'intervening factors' in the group situation, if you are its leader. What is there in the group membership, the task and the environment (ie the 'givens') that hold the group back from being as effective as it might be?

3.2.1 Example case study

You have recently been appointed to manage a group of 10 people and you have found evidence that all is not well. The output of the section is not high. Although overtime is regularly worked, there are substantial backlogs and targets are missed. Absenteeism is high with the same people absent regularly. They produce poor excuses or none at all. People fall out over trivial issues and the lack of co-operation impairs efficiency. You feel a general air of lethargy, if not hostility. What do you propose to do about it? How will you know when you are succeeding?

Solution

Generally it seems as if there is a casual, hands off management style being applied. That so many things have gone wrong, seems to suggest the manager has taken his/her eye off the ball. The failure to achieve targets might be due to inadequate planning, failure of the manager to communicate targets effectively. Poor selection may mean that individual group members might be unsuited to their jobs and this might help to explain poor efficiency. Inadequate working conditions and poor organisation of the group's work routines might also be at fault. The workload of the group might be excessive so that group members no longer try to achieve targets. However, an improvement in efficiency would increase output and the group is clearly not performing well enough.

The problem of absenteeism might be caused by low morale, but the absence of disciplinary action against persistent offenders can only create a sense of unfairness amongst the others. This could help to explain the hostility and conflicts over trivial matters between group members. Absenteeism is often caused by some form of dissatisfaction. Good managers should try to identify and address the underlying cause.

The lack of co-operation might be caused by poor planning and supervision, or by poor motivation of staff and inter-personal dislikes. Staff have clearly been reluctant to refer matters to their manager, since conflicts have arisen over trivial matters. Good managers should be sensitive to minor disagreements and prevent these from escalating into conflict in the first place.

3.3 Managing performance problems

After the initial assessment, the leader should call a **group meeting** to discuss the issues. The group members should be encouraged to state **their own views**, after which the leader should state his or her **intention** to do something about the problem. An outline of the proposed steps should be given.

(a) The group as a whole must know what its **planning targets** are, and each individual member of the group should be given standards or targets to work towards.

(b) If there is a need for **overtime**, the quantity of overtime that ought to be required should be built into the plan. You should ask individuals whether they are unable or unwilling to work these amounts of overtime. If there is a need for more staff, you could pursue the matter through your superior, and let the staff know what is happening about it.

(c)   There should be regular **feedback** to individual group members on their performance, against target. If performance is below standard, you should discuss what control action or remedies might be necessary.

(d)   **Persistent absenteeism** must be **stopped**. It should be made clear to all group members that disciplinary measures will be taken against offenders. You should than apply discipline consistently and keep to your word.

(e)   The need for **co-operation** between group members should be made clear and can be improved by good planning. You should set a timescale for improvements and use regular group meetings to review progress, identify problems and work out difficulties.

(f)   You should give **time and attention to individual members** of the group. **Training needs** should be identified, and group members given appropriate training where required. You should get to know each individual, identifying their needs and interests, and trying to encourage them. If some individuals continue to show personal animosity, or to perform badly, you should express concern, and indicate that their next formal appraisal will not be favourable.

(g)   The **techniques and equipment** used by the group should be improved where necessary (and if resources are available). You should make whatever alterations to the office layout and environment seem beneficial and practicable.

3.4 How to gauge success

Two things should happen when matters are improving.

- The productivity of the group should improve and targets will be achieved.
- There should be an apparent improvement in the **attitudes** of group members.

More specific improvements will occur. Several of these can be quantified and monitored.

- **Absenteeism** should be much lower.

- There should be **higher output**.

- **Individual targets** as well as group targets should be achieved.

- Individuals should display a **greater commitment** to their work and the achievement of targets.

- **Communication** between group members should be more free and open.

- **Conflicts** over minor matters should no longer occur.

- Group members should show signs of trying to help each other by offering **constructive suggestions and ideas**.

- Group members will show signs of wanting to develop their abilities further.

It is the manager's responsibility to monitor the effectiveness of the group and be constantly seeking ways of improving it. The manager should bring in new ideas and set new challenges and targets.

3.5 Proactive approach

FAST FORWARD

Opponents of teamwork compare the performance of a poor team management approach with diligently managed **individual working**. To be effective, teams (like individuals) need to be appropriately managed.

In practice, within a well managed business, the need to perform assessments of a groups success or effectiveness should be mere formality. Issues regarding selection of the wrong members, excessive

BPP
LEARNING MEDIA

workloads and inappropriate equipment should not arise if the manager has performed his/her **planning** with **due skill and conscientiousness**.

The desired approach for a good marketing manager should be to **exercise proper management skills** to ensure that whatever is being managed, whether it be individual work, project work or team work is **carried out smoothly and efficiently** and produces **high quality outcomes**.

Planning is a key part of effective management. If planning is too casual, there is likely to be an increased risk of objectives and targets being missed.

Briefing and communication are also critical management activities, These should be comprehensive and not too cryptic. If staff are left to work things out for themselves, there is a chance that they may get the wrong end of the stick and be going down the wrong path until it is too late. A well structured and clear briefing is vital to the success of any activity.

Monitoring. This should be on a formal and informal basis.

- **Informal**. This might comprise of regular chats and brief "how are you doing?" questions. This might be done when an opportunity arises, say at the coffee machine or perhaps at an after work drink or snack. The opportunity to uncover real problems over a drink or snack is probably an underestimated management practice!

- **Formal meetings**. Meetings are subject to a lot of 'knee jerk' criticism but are nevertheless an extremely valuable management tool. The fact that staff are required to physically report progress on a regular basis and be subject to searching questions keeps them on their toes and avoids work slippages from occurring.

Action Programme 6

Draft a short report to the manager of a team you are involved with. In it you should make three specific recommendations for improving team performance and the ways in which you suggest the effect of these changes is monitored.

[Key Skills for Marketers: Presenting information]

4 Managing team diversity

FAST FORWARD

Cross-functional teams are a key feature of contemporary working practice.

There are two basic approaches to the organisation of cross-functional team working, in other words teams which carry out a number of business activities: **multi-disciplinary** teams and **multi-skilled** teams.

4.1 Multi-disciplinary teams

Multi-disciplinary teams bring together individuals from different functional specialisms, so that their competencies can be **pooled or exchanged**.

Multi-disciplinary teams have three important capabilities.

(a) They increase team members' awareness of the wider context of their tasks and decisions.

(b) They help to generate solutions to problems and suggestions for improvements by integrating disparate ideas

(c)   They aid co-ordination across functional boundaries by increasing the flow of communication, informal relationships and co-operation.

On the other hand, the members of such teams have different reporting lines and responsibilities within their line departments, which creates the ambiguity of dual responsibility. They may have a range of different backgrounds, work cultures, specialist skills and terminology. This creates a particular challenge for the team leader: to build a sense of team identity, role clarity and co-operative working.

4.2 Multi-skilled teams

Multi-skilled teams bring together a number of functionally versatile individuals, each of whom can perform *any* of the group's tasks: work can thus be **allocated flexibly**, according to who is best placed to do a given job when required.

(a)   Performing a whole meaningful job is more **satisfying** to people than performing only one or two of its component operations.

(b)   Allowing team members to see the big picture enables and encourages them to **contribute information and ideas** for improvements.

(c)   Empowering team members to take initiatives enhances **organisational responsiveness** to customer demands and environmental changes (particularly in front-line customer service units).

(d)   A focus on overall task objectives reduces the need for tight **managerial control** and supervision.

(e)   **Labour resources** can be allocated more flexibly and efficiently, without potentially disruptive demarcation disputes.

 Marketing at Work

The Hewlett-Packard way

The Hewlett-Packard way is an approach to management that places great importance on its core values and treats them as a management tool. They actively serve as guidelines for day to day business development and decision making.

Part of the Hewlett-Packard way entails the *integration and reinforcement of critical opposites*. Within the HP culture, teamwork and individualism are not mutually exclusive concepts. Instead both approaches are recognised as HP working practices. HP personnel are trained to work in cross-functional teams but are also appraised on individual performance.

Most other businesses recruit people along functional criteria and offer bottom-up vertical career paths. HP recruits people with diverse skills and personalities and provides them with career paths that include vertical as well as horizontal routes. In consequence, the HP employees on average moves through six functional areas during their careers with the company.

This approach produces *cross-functional individuals* with a broad range of skills and a comprehensive understanding of the company's business, its people and its products/services. The approach is flexible and conducive to either individual performance or cross-functional teamworking depending on circumstances.

BPP)))
LEARNING MEDIA

4.3 Project teams

Project teams may be set up to handle specific **strategic developments** (such as the introduction of a Just in Time approach), tasks relating to particular **processes** (such as the computerisation of the payroll system), tasks relating to particular **cases** or **accounts** (such as co-ordination of work for a client or client group) or special **audits** or **investigations** of procedures or improvement opportunities (such as a review of recruitment and selection methods).

The key management challenge of project teams arises from the fact that:

(a) They have a limited life span: managers have to accelerate the process of team development, in order to achieve the performing stage quickly (as required by the project plan);

(b) They frequently involve members from different functions, different sites/branches and/or different organisations (eg the organising committee for a trade exhibition). This creates logistical challenges (getting people together for meetings etc) as well as team building challenges (potentially wide differences in goals, cultures, specialisms etc).

4.4 Multi-cultural and diverse teams

We will discus international management challenges in Chapter 6, but it is worth noting here that teams are increasingly diverse in terms of the cultures, interests, specialisms, stakeholders and personalities represented.

As our discussion of Belbin suggests, successful teamworking depends on a mix and balance of different viewpoints and contributions. Diverse (and even divergent) styles and backgrounds are a positive asset to teamworking as they:

(a) Widen the range of information and ideas taken into account in problem-solving and decision-making;

(b) Demonstrate willingness to take into account the views and concerns of different stakeholders in decisions;

(c) Challenge and test dominant and habitual viewpoints, helping to control the risk of 'groupthink' (blinkered and complacent thinking in ultra-cohesive, homogeneous groups); and

(d) Create a climate of mutual respect and learning within which all team members are able to contribute fully.

However, team diversity also poses challenges, because of the potential for misunderstanding, conflict, disintegration and costly efforts to maintain communication and co-ordination. These should be seen clearly as management challenges – *not* arguments against having diverse teams!

Exam tip

The issues of a multi-disciplinary (ie from different functional specialisms), multi-cultural (ie from different cultural backgrounds) and multi-organisation (ie with different stakeholder interests and goals) project team were the focus of a June 2006 exam question. The Senior Examiner has emphasised that international contexts are a potential future theme – so think these diversity issues through.

5 Virtual teams

Computer systems have enabled communication and collaboration among people at diverse and far-flung locations, via teleconferencing and video-conferencing, networked PCs and email. This has created the concept of the **virtual team**: an interconnected group of people who may never be present in the same office but who share information and tasks, make joint decisions and fulfil the collaborative functions of a team.

Virtual teams have existed for some time in the form of **teleworking**: the process of working from home, or from a satellite office close to home, with the aid of computers, facsimile machines, modems or other forms of telecommunication equipment. The main benefits cited for such work include savings on office overheads and the elimination of the costs and stresses of commuting for employees.

More recently, however, the globalisation of business, the need for fast responses to marketplace demands and the increasing sophistication of available technologies has brought about an explosion in **global virtual teamworking**. More and more organisations are attempting to conduct business 24 hours a day, seven days a week, with people on different continents and in different time zones. Electronic collaboration allows organisations to do the following things.

(a)   Recruit and collaborate with the best available people without the constraints of location or relocation. A team can co-opt a specialist when required, from a global pool of skills.

(b)   Offer more scheduling flexibility for people who prefer non-traditional working hours (including the handicapped and working parents, for example).

(c)   Maintain close contact with customers throughout the world.

(d)   Operate 24-hour working days (for example, for global customer support) – without having to have staff on night shifts.

6 Team leadership

FAST FORWARD

> **Leadership is** the process of influencing others to work willingly towards the achievement of organisational goals. **Theories of leadership** have taken several different approaches.

6.1 Leadership

Key concept

> **Leadership** is the process of influencing others to work **willingly** towards a goal, and to the best of their capabilities.

Leadership comes about in a number of different ways.

- A manager is **appointed** to a position of authority within the organisation. Leadership of staff is a function of the position.

- Some leaders are **elected**.

- Other leaders **emerge** by popular choice or through their personal drive.

The personal, physical or expert power of leaders is more important than position power alone. Within teams and groups of equal colleagues leadership can and does change.

If a manager has indifferent or poor leadership qualities then the team might still do the job, but probably not efficiently. A good leader can ensure more than simply a compliance with orders. **Leadership and management are different**. **Managing** is concerned with logic, structure, analysis and control. If done well, it produces predictable results on time. **Leadership** requires a different mind set and the leader has different tasks.

- **Creating a sense of direction**
- **Communicating the vision**
- **Energising, inspiring and motivating**

All of these activities involve dealing with people rather than things. A manager needs leadership skills to be effective. A person's **leadership style** is determined by the amount of autonomy his or her followers enjoy.

 Marketing at Work

An article in *Band T* magazine (June 2007) explored how **strong internal brand culture** gives companies such as Virgin Airlines, Google and Australian bank ANZ a competitive edge.

- Richard Branson is cited as one of the best-known practitioners of internal branding through the global Virgin brands. He is an embodiment of the brand and leads the company with a clear vision of how the brand should be communicated throughout the organisation. The 'irreverent style' of Virgin Airlines expresses the brand values and helps staff to deliver service in a distinctive way. The brand is prominent throughout recruitment, induction and training of team members.

- The 'Breakout' programme was launched by ANZ to shape the internal culture and how the brand is expressed in everything from branch-fit-out to above-the-line advertising. Based on the value of 'humanity', ANZ staff engage in customer service training and community development programmes, to emphasise that 'it is people that make a difference' – overcoming the faceless image of many large financial institutions.

- One of the ways in which Google maintains its key innovation culture is to allow staff to work on their own projects – on the company's time! 'We encourage our employees to create, discuss, experiment and innovate. To this end, we have many on-line innovation blogs, and discussion points.

Recruitment, training, involvement and communication are key tools of internal branding.

6.2 Issues in leading groups

John Adair's (1983) work on leadership identified three overlapping sets of **needs** which need to be satisfied when teams are managed, and the **roles the team leader needs to play** to satisfy these needs: Figure 2.2.

Figure 2.2: Adair's action-centred leadership model

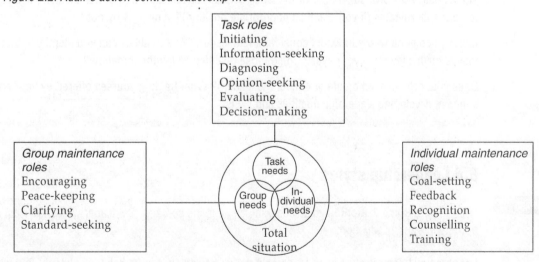

For effective performance all three sets of needs must be identified and satisfied. Without an overlap of these three circles, the group will be unsuccessful.

The total situation dictates the relative priority that must be given to each of the three sets of needs. Effective leadership involves identifying and acting on those priorities to create a balance between the needs. Meeting the various needs implies specific management roles.

Around this framework, Adair developed a scheme of leadership training based on precept and practice in each of **eight leadership activities** as applied to task, team and individual.

- Defining the task
- Planning
- Briefing
- Controlling
- Evaluating
- Motivating
- Organising
- Setting an example

Adair argued that the common perception of leadership as 'decision-making' was inadequate to describe the range of action required by the complex situations in which managers find themselves. This model is therefore more practical. It clearly identifies the responsibilities of the manager or leader in ensuring that the required task is achieved, but also that team and individual needs are satisfied as part of the process.

Exam tip

> Since team working is such an important part of this syllabus, you wil often be placed (in exam scenarios) in the position of *team leader* – whether or not this is explicitly stated. It is worth considering a department, section, task force or committee a 'team' for the purposes of questions!.

6.3 Leadership traits

Early writers believed that leadership was an inherent characteristic: you either had it, or you didn't: leaders were born, not made. Studies on leadership concentrated on the personal traits of existing and past leadership figures.

It is now felt that leadership appropriate to a given work situation can be learned.

Action Programme 7

Think about your own supervisor or manager. Would you consider him or her a leader? Are you a leader to your subordinates (if you are in an appropriate position)? Why, or why not?

Identify someone who you would consider a real leader. What qualities can you identify in that person that makes them a leader in your eyes? Could those qualities be taught somehow?

Does your organisation create or encourage leaders? What training courses offered by your employer are aimed at developing leadership qualities and skills?

6.4 Leadership styles

FAST FORWARD

> According to **Blake & Mouton** ideal leadership style is the so-called 9:9 leader who shows concern for both people and production.

Leadership styles are clusters of leadership behaviour which leaders habitually adopt – but which are, ideally, adapted or selected according to the situation. While there are many different classifications of style, they mainly relate to the extent to which the leader is focused primarily on task/performance (directive behaviour) or relationships/people (facilitative/supportive behaviour).

6.4.1 A continuum of styles

Tannenbaum and Schmidt proposed a continuum of behaviours (and associated styles) which reflected the balance of control exercised in a situation by the leader and the team.

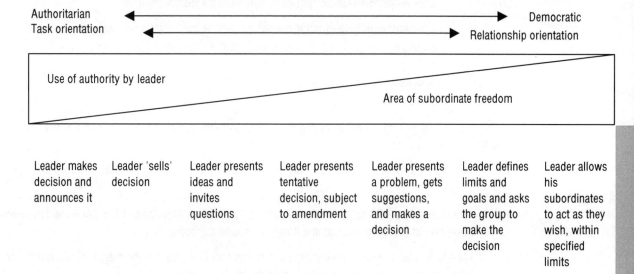

| Leader makes decision and announces it | Leader 'sells' decision | Leader presents ideas and invites questions | Leader presents tentative decision, subject to amendment | Leader presents a problem, gets suggestions, and makes a decision | Leader defines limits and goals and asks the group to make the decision | Leader allows his subordinates to act as they wish, within specified limits |

6.4.2 Blake and Mouton's managerial grid

R R Blake and J S Mouton focused on two basic dimensions of leadership: concern for production/task and concern for people. Along each of these dimensions, a manager could be located at any point from very low (1) to very high (9). Blake and Mouton argued that the two concerns do not correlate: a high concern in one dimension does not imply a high or low concern in the other. Managers can, therefore, reflect various permutations, depicted on a grid: Figure 2.3.

Blake and Mouton (1994) tried to address there two-dimensional view with their **managerial grid** (Figure 2.3).

Figure 2.3: Blake & Mouton's managerial grid

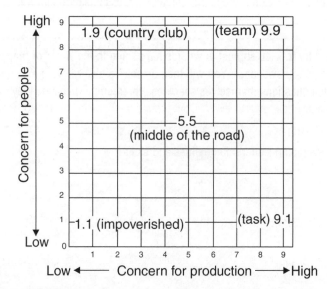

Extreme cases shown on the grid are:

(a)   1.1 **impoverished**: manager is lazy, showing little effort or concern for staff or work targets.

(b)   1.9 **country club**: manager is attentive to staff needs and has developed satisfying relationships. However, little attention is paid to achieving results.

(c)   9.1 **task management**: almost total concentration on achieving results. People's needs are virtually ignored and conditions of work are so arranged that people cannot interfere to any significant extent.

(d)   5.5 **middle of the road**: adequate performance through balancing the necessity to get out work while maintaining morale of people at a satisfactory level.

(e)   9.9 **team**: high performance manager who achieves high work accomplishment through leading committed people who identify with the organisational aims.

 Action Programme 8

Here are some statements about a manager's approach to meetings. Which position on Blake's Grid do you think each might represent?

(a)   I attend because it is expected. I either go along with the majority position or avoid expressing my views.

(b)   I try to come up with good ideas and push for a decision as soon as I can get a majority behind me. I don't mind stepping on people if it helps a sound decision.

(c)   I like to be able to support what my boss wants and to recognise the merits of individual effort. When conflict rises, I do a good job of restoring harmony.

Note that Blake and Moulton assume that 9.9 is the ideal model for effective leadership. Later **contingency or 'situational' models** have argued that this is not necessarily the case: rather, 'it all depends' (the essence of contingency theory). A 9.1 (task) style may be most appropriate where only compliance is required (eg where the task is highly programmed or automated); or where team members are unwilling, unable or otherwise 'unready' to carry out the task without a strong degree of direction; or in a crisis situation, where swift, decisive action is required.

Exam tip

> Always take a contingency approach in exams! What is the most appropriate leadership style? It depends on the context, the leader, the team, the task, the organisation culture – and so on.

Exam tip

> You should try to keep abreast of what is happening in the world of management by reading the business pages of a good newspaper. You will then be able to give relevant examples in your answers. You will also find that the questions themselves seem less threatening, because they are often based on contemporary developments.

BPP
LEARNING MEDIA

Chapter Roundup

- An **effective group** is one which achieves its allotted task *and* satisfies its members. **Teams** are becoming more important as a means of carrying out work in a contemporary business environment.

- Groups function through **interaction** between individual members and the **blend** of their skills and abilities.

- **Tuckman's** model suggests that **team development** involves four stages. Good management entails building a culture which does not entail the negative effects that Tuckman envisages.

- In practice, **teambuilding** is a pragmatic approach entailing good management, judgement and skills.

- **Belbin** developed a model of the eight **roles** required – evenly spread – in an effective team.

- The management problem is how to create an **efficient work group**.

- Opponents of teamwork compare the performance of a poor team management approach with diligently managed **individual working**. To be effective, teams, like individuals, need to be appropriately managed.

- **Cross-functional teams** are a key feature of contemporary working practice.

- **Leadership is** the process of influencing others to work willingly towards the achievement of organisational goals. Theories of leadership have taken several different approaches.

- According to **Blake and Mouton** the ideal leadership style is the so-called 9:9 leader who shows concern for both people and production.

Quick Quiz

1   What attributes distinguish a group or team from a random collection of individuals?

2   What are the functions of groups from the point of view of the organisation?

3   What are the main issues to be taken into account when managing a group?

4   What stages does a team go through as it matures?

5   What happens during the norming stage?

6   What does Handy mean by the term 'outcomes' in his contingency approach?

7   List four of the characteristics you would expect in an ideally functioning group.

8   How will you know when your measures to improve the performance of a team are being successful?

9   How does leadership come about?

10   Are all managers leaders?

Answers to Quick Quiz

1   Sense of identity; loyalty to the group; purpose and leadership

2   Performing tasks; testing decisions; consulting over disputes; creating ideas; collecting and transmitting information; co-ordinating work; motivating individuals

3   Task roles; individual needs; group needs

4   Forming, storming, norming, performing

5   Roles are established, cohesiveness increases, acceptable norms of behaviour emerge

6   Productivity and group satisfaction

7   • A sense of identity, belonging and support
        • Sharing of skills information and ideas
        • participative problem solving
        • Individual commitment
        • Good communication

8   Low absenteeism; high output; achievement of group and individual targets; individual commitment; open communication; reduced conflict; constructive suggestions; emergence of individual's need for self-development.

9   Leaders may be appointed or elected or they may emerge as a result of personal qualities.

10   Management and leadership are different but connected ideas. Management is about planning and controlling the use of resources; leadership is about getting the best out of people.

Action Programme Review

1, 2   There are no set answers to these Action Programmes as they are wholly dependant on your individual circumstances. Thinking through your own experience, should help you to understand the theory and how it applies in practice.

3   (a), storming, (b) dorming, (c) performing, (d) forming, (e) norming

4

Effective teams	Ineffective teams
Quantifiable factors	
Low rate of labour turnover	High rate of labour turnover
Low absenteeism	High absenteeism
High output and productivity	Low output and productivity
Good quality of output	Poor quality of output
There are few stoppages and interruptions to work	Much time is wasted owing to disruption of work flow

Qualitative factors	
There is a high commitment to the achievement of targets and organisational goals	There is a low commitment to targets
There is a clear understanding of the group's work	There is no understanding of organisational goals or the role of the group (or there are no clear organisational goals)
There is a clear understanding of the role of each person within the group	There is confusion about the role of each person and uncertainty
There is free and open communication between members of the group and trust between members	There is mistrust between group members and suspicion of group's leader
There is idea sharing	There is little idea sharing
The group is good at generating new ideas	The group does not generate any good new ideas

BPP)))
LEARNING MEDIA

Qualitative factors	
Group members try to help each other out	Group members make negative and hostile criticisms about each other's work
There is group problem solving which gets to the root causes of the work problem	Work problems are dealt with superficially, with attention paid to the symptoms but not the cause.
Group members seek a united consensus of opinion	Group members hold strongly opposed views
The group is sufficiently motivated to be able to carry on working in the absence of its leader	The group needs its leader there to get work done

5   Thinking through Action Programme 4 should assist you with this exercise.

6   If you are stuck, review paragraph 3.3 for some ideas. Consider the factors which create a successful team and brainstorm how you might create a climate for these conditions to thrive. Ensure your report is in an appropriate format.

7   Your own reflection.

8   (a) 1.1, (b) 9.1, (c) 1.9.

Now try Question 2 at the end of the Study Text

3

Recruitment and selection

Syllabus content – knowledge and skill requirements

- Techniques available for selecting, building, developing and motivating marketing teams to improve performance (1.4)

Introduction

Chapter 2 discussed how teams might be formed and managed, but often the membership of a team or department changes. As people leave, or the department grows, new people are needed.

In Section 1, we start with the circumstances in which the need for new recruits is identified, and we show how the overall human resources needs of a firm can be broken down into the need for individuals to fill specific jobs.

In Section 2, we discuss the labour market in which the firm is perhaps a seller. The firm needs to identify the people it is advertising to, draw up an appropriate job description, and develop the right job advertisements in the right media: after all, the firm is 'selling' the job to a potential 'customer', the successful recruit.

We then discuss in Section 3 what happens to those applicants who apply, and here we show the use of application forms, selection interviews and testing.

In Chapter 4, we go on to see how employees' performance can be appraised and improved. New recruits – and existing workers – need training and appraisal.

1 Expanding the team: the importance of search and selection

FAST FORWARD

All teams will need to **recruit new members** at some time and the marketing manager will be very involved in that process, possibly supported by Human Resource specialists.

Exam tip

Remember to address the context of each question. For example, the human resources strategy for an organisation with a growth strategy in place will be quite different from one that is facing decline. (Don't talk about recruitment, or raising salaries, if the company is facing redundancies, for example! More subtly, think about the benefits of external recruitment, as opposed to internal promotion, say, if the company is suffering from a dysfunctional culture).

It will often be necessary to bring new people into the team.

- To fill an identified skills gap
- To replace staff who have been promoted or who have left
- Because the work of the team has expanded

The process of recruitment is very important. Getting the wrong person can cause problems within the existing group, and the person will require either extensive training and development, or will require replacing, with all the attendant disruption this involves.

The overall aim of the recruitment and selection process is to obtain the employees required with maximum efficiency. This process can be broken down into three main stages: a **definition of requirements** (including the preparation of job descriptions and specifications), **recruitment** and **selection**.

Key concepts

Recruitment. The identification and attraction of potential applicants, inside and outside the organisation.

Selection. Selection is the part of the employee resourcing process which involves choosing between applicants for jobs: it is largely a 'negative' process, eliminating unsuitable applicants.

A marketing manager may have the help and support of **human resources (HR) specialists** during the process but in smaller organisations, he or she will be responsible for all aspects of the search and selection process. Many firms outsource the early stages of the process to consultants or agencies.

1.1 A systematic approach to recruitment and selection

FAST FORWARD

The process of **search and selection** needs to be thoroughly planned and professionally managed if the right candidate for the post is to be identified.

If not approached systematically, the process of recruitment and selection can become costly and time-consuming. A methodical approach will probably involve the following stages:

(a) Detailed **human resource planning,** defining the people and skills the organisation needs to meet its objectives and how they are to be provided. At marketing team level, this activity would require an analysis of the future marketing skills needed. This requirement will flow from the overall marketing plan which, in turn, is one of the outputs from the wider **corporate planning** process. The recruitment of an individual member of marketing staff is thus set in the context of the overall strategic control of the organisation.

(b) **Job analysis**, so that for any given job there are two things.

- **A job description** describing the nature and responsibilities of the job
- **A person specification** describing the ideal candidate for the job

(c) An identification of **vacancies**, from the requirements of the human resources plan or by a **job requisition** from the section needing a new post holder.

(d) Evaluation of the **sources of labour**, which should be in the HR plan. Internal and external sources, and media for reaching both, will be considered.

(e) **Advertising** has three functions.

- To attract the attention and interest of potentially suitable candidates
- To give a favourable (but accurate) impression of the job and the organisation
- To tell candidates how to apply

(f) **Processing applications** and assessing and selecting candidates

(g) **Notifying applicants** of the results of the selection process

Figure 3.1: The recruitment process

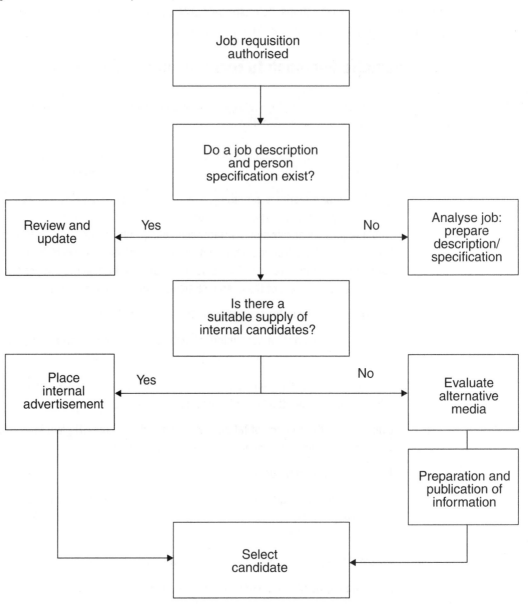

 Action Programme 1

Find out what the recruitment and selection procedures are in your organisation and who is responsible for each stage. A procedures manual might set this out, or you may need to ask someone – perhaps in the Personnel or Human Resources department. In your own experience, what part does the manager play in these procedures? Get hold of some of the documentation your company uses. We show specimens in this chapter, but practice and terminology varies, so your own experience will be invaluable. Try to find three things.

- The job description for your job
- The personnel specification (if any) for your job
- If your firm is currently recruiting, a full set of the paperwork including the job ad

None of the stages in the recruitment process can be ignored or taken lightly if the best candidate for the post is to be found. Practical advice for running an interview is included in section 4 of this chapter.

Before the search process can begin managers have a great deal to do. When the need for a new member of the team is recognised, a careful review should be undertaken to ensure that an extra full time post is **justified by the contribution the person is expected to make**. Particular care is needed when the vacancy is due to a team member leaving. Simple replacement is not always appropriate. During the job holder's time in the job, the task itself may have changed, or the individual may have shaped the role differently from how it was advertised originally.

1.1.1 Recent trends

Recent trends towards **flexibility** and **multi-skilling** have encouraged an approach which is oriented towards fitting the job to the person rather than fitting the person to the job.

(a) In a highly innovative market or technological environment rigid job descriptions would not be suitable. Organisations should look at the skills and attributes of the people they employ and gifted outsiders, and ask: 'What needs doing that this person would do best?'

(b) In a relatively informal environment, where all-round knowledge, skills and experience are highly valued and suitable external labour resources scarce, for example in management consultancy, this approach would give much-needed flexibility. The organisation would try to recruit, flexible, motivated and multi-skilled people without reference to any specific job description.

However, the **selection** approach is still the most common, and is suitable for most organisations with fairly well defined goals and structures.

2 Defining the requirement

2.1 Competencies

FAST FORWARD

In contemporary organisations, recruitment and selection are often carried out within the framework of a **core competencies** model.

Many organisations now follow a contemporary Competencies Model approach. Here the HR model is closely aligned to the business model. The competencies at the diposal of the business will consciously match its mission, values and objectives.

Key generic competencies usually include areas such as communication, teamworking, business awareness, relationship management and people development.

Hence, recruitment, selection, training, appraisal and advancement will all be implemented within a consistent HR framework aligned to deliver the business strategy.

2.2 Job analysis

FAST FORWARD

The first critical stage is a **job analysis**, from which the **job specification** and/or **job description** and **person specification** can be generated. Care and attention here will ensure the manager knows the kind of person needed to suit the needs of both the task and the group.

Key concept

Job analysis is the process of examining a job to identify its component parts and the circumstances in which it is performed.

Information elicited from job analysis includes task-orientated and worker-orientated details.

(a) **Initial requirements** of the employee include aptitudes, qualifications, experience and training required.

(b) **Duties and responsibilities** include physical aspects, mental effort, routine or requiring initiative, difficult or disagreeable features, consequences of failure, responsibilities for staff, materials, equipment or cash and so on.

(c) **Environment and conditions** include physical surroundings, with particular features (eg temperature, noise, hazards), remuneration, other conditions such as hours, shifts, travel, benefits, holidays, career prospects, provision of employee services (eg canteens, protective clothing).

(d) **Social factors** include size of the department, teamwork or isolation. The sort of people dealt with (eg senior management, the public), the amount of supervision and job status.

A job analysis may cause some concern among employees from fear of standards being raised, rates cut or redundancy imposed. The job analyst will need to gain confidence; this can be done in a variety of ways.

- Communicating (explaining the process, methods and purpose of the analysis)
- Being thorough and competent in carrying out the analysis
- Respecting the work flow of the department, which should not be disrupted
- Giving feedback on the results of the appraisal, and the achievement of its objectives

2.3 Job description

Key concept

A **job description** is prepared from the job analysis. It is a broad statement of the purpose, scope, duties and responsibilities of a job. It describes the content of a job; and its relative importance in comparison with other jobs.

The job description states the principal details of the job.

- Job title
- Location of the job (department, place)
- The relationship of the job to other positions (boss, subordinates)
- The main duties and responsibilities of the job
- The limits to the job holder's authority
- Any equipment for which the job holder is responsible

In many organisations, there is no proper job analysis or person specification for a given post, but a broad job description does exist. Such a job description can be used for a number of purposes.

(a) To decide what skills (technical, human, conceptual, design etc) and qualifications are required of the job holder. When interviewing an applicant for the job, the interviewer can use the job description to match the candidate against the job

(b) To ensure that the job provides a sufficient challenge to the job holder. Job content is a factor in the motivation of individuals

(c) To determine a rate of pay which is fair for the job, if this has not already been decided by some other means, eg a separate job evaluation exercise

(d) To provide information from which particular job vacancies can be advertised

BPP LEARNING MEDIA

2.4 Person specification

Once the job has been clearly defined, the organisation can decide what kind of person is needed to fill it effectively.

Key concept

> A **person specification** identifies the **type of person** the organisation should be trying to recruit – his or her character, aptitudes, qualifications, career aspirations, special abilities and experience.

A person specification is often used as an **all-purpose selection assessment plan** for recruiting younger people in fairly large numbers into a fairly junior grade. Two designs of specification are *Professor Alec Rodger's* **Seven Point Plan** and *J Munro Fraser's* **Five Point Pattern of Personality**.

The Seven Point Plan highlights seven points about the candidate.

- **Background circumstances**
- **Attainments** such as educational qualifications
- **Disposition** or manner
- **Physical attributes** such as neat appearance, ability to speak clearly, health
- **Interests** (practical, social, intellectual and physical)
- **General intelligence**
- **Special aptitudes** such as speed and accuracy, numeracy, written communication skills

The Five Point Pattern draws the selector's attention to five important aspects of the candidate's personality.

- Impact on others
- Acquired knowledge or qualifications
- Innate ability
- Motivation
- Adjustment and emotional balance

Action Programme 2

Do you have a job description? (If you don't, draw one up.) Determine a person specification for the job.

[Key Skill for Marketers: Presenting information]

2.4.1 Example

ABC Business Machines Ltd: Job description for sales office manager		
1	Job title	Sales Office Manager
2	Branch	Head Office
3	Job summary	To provide effective office support for field sales and an efficient re-ordering system for customers.
4	Job content	Typical duties will include: (a) Ensuring staffing as needed of sales office (b) Providing telesales training to new staff (c) Dealing with customer complaints.
5	Reporting to:	Sales Director

ABC Business Machines Ltd: Job description for sales office manager		
6	Responsible for:	4 Telesales staff
7	Experience/Education	At least 4 years telesales. Some supervisory experience.
8	Training to be provided	Initial on-the-job training.
9	Hours	38 hours per week
10	Personal characteristics required	Organised, friendly, manner and enthusiastic.
11	Objectives and appraisal	Ensure smooth operation of telesales.
12	Salary	£18-22K According to experience.
Job Description prepared by: Sales Director		

3 Planning and managing the search process

> The process of **search** uses many marketing skills, to help segment the labour market and target the right sources of potential candidates.

The objective at this stage of the process is to identify candidates who are likely to be most suited to the vacancy. It is an exercise in segmentation and promotional targeting which marketers are well trained to manage. A strategic approach is needed.

There are two important demographic variables.

(a) **Long-term demographic trends.** These include the fall in the number of young people and the increase in overall labour force size because of increased female participation.

(b) **Education trends**. The proportion of school leavers going into higher education is expected to increase, but with **fewer school leavers in total**.

Equal opportunities. Any organisation that employs more than a few people should have a clear equal opportunities policy. This should promote equal opportunities in recruitment and career progression. There are three reasons for this.

(a) It is ethically desirable.

(b) Anti-discrimination legislation in most advanced countries will impose significant sanctions on organisations that do not comply.

(c) It is to the organisation's benefit to recruit using objective criteria of suitability. This widens the pool of potential recruits at all levels of ability.

 Marketing at Work

Procter and Gamble

P&G, maker of everything from Pampers nappies to Old Spice deodorant to Pringles crisps, has a huge variety of customers and wants its workforce to reflect that.

'Our success depends entirely on our ability to understand these diverse consumers' needs,' Alan Lafley, the CEO told his company last year. A diverse organisation will out-think, out-innovate and out-perform a homogenous organisation every single time. I am putting particular importance on increasing the representation of women and minorities in leadership positions at all levels.'

LEARNING MEDIA

P&G UK has a fairly good record already. Ethnic minority employees make up 6 per cent of P&G's UK workforce, compared with 5.4 per cent of the British population. 'But that is not a reason to be happy with ourselves. We primarily recruit graduates and 17 per cent of the students in this country are from ethnic minorities,' says Neil Harvey-Smith, UK Diversity Manager.

Why is PG not recruiting more of those students? 'It's not the case that people applying aren't getting in. It's that they're not applying.' Why not? 'It's probably fair to say that people perceive that we are a white company or an American company.'

Provided it fits in with their jobs, P&G staff of either sex can share jobs and change their hours. New parents can take up to a year's unpaid leave beyond their statutory maternity or paternity leave entitlements. The result is that the number of women appointed director or associate director in P&G Europe rose to eight last year from its previous rate of one or two a year.

Mr Harvey-Smith says the UK organisation has also made progress in attracting disabled recruits. It designed a computer programme that could read out the questions on a problem-solving test so that a blind applicant could complete it. The technology is now being used by P&G in the US.

Financial Times

3.1 Tapping unused labour resources

Older workers are a possible labour market. This was a feature of the mid 1980s, when some companies in the retail sector targeted older workers (over-40s and over-45s). They bring important qualities.

- Skills and experience
- High regard for customer service
- Stabilising influence on younger staff
- Contribution to better staff retention rates

Women returners. There are a number of factors determining a woman's return to work.

(a) **Child care facilities**. If these are easily obtainable, a mother is likely to use them. Employers can provide them. Private child care is expensive. Some organisations, which do not wish to provide child care facilities themselves, might offer **child care vouchers**.

(b) **Career break schemes** have been introduced in particular in the financial services sector. Women are allowed to take time off for a few years to have children and return to the same job. Some organisations require a 'satisfactory performance record'. Other factors affecting retention include equal opportunity training schemes and assertiveness courses.

It is useful to remember throughout this process that the objective is **not** to fill the post **at any cost**. The wrong appointment will always be a more costly mistake than leaving the post unfilled. But likewise the **ideal** candidate will be hard to find. The reality often means accepting a good candidate and developing his or her skills in areas of identified weakness.

3.2 Internal recruitment

FAST FORWARD

Internal applicants should be considered, but the relative advantages and disadvantages of making an internal or external appointment should be considered. It may be best to assess the internal candidate against external alternatives.

Action Programme 3

What would be the benefits of attracting an internal candidate? What would be the possible problems?

Internal candidates can be considered before advertising outside or they can be included in the process as candidates. It is worth remembering, though, that an internal candidate who fails to be offered a post requires much more sensitive handling, as there will be a strong sense of rejection and this can sour an otherwise happy team. The individual may resent the successful candidate and be unco-operative. In the worst case you might even lose what is otherwise a key member of the team, thereby creating a new search and selection problem.

Marketing at Work

Personnel Management reported an approach to **internal recruitment** at computer company Logica. As part of a more flexible and international approach (including performance-related pay, appraisal and training), Logica is implementing a global 'resource management system' in which a central database of employees' skills and experiences is being established. 'As well as holding employees' CVs, this will be the first medium to advertise vacancies on a global basis within the company.'

3.3 Job advertisements

Despite these options, in the end many posts will be advertised. The advertisement is, in a way, already part of the selection process, because it will be placed where suitable people are likely to see it, and will be worded in a way that further weeds out people who would not be suitable for the job (or for whom the job would not be suitable). Obviously, for marketing posts, the advertisement is the recruit's first sight of the firm's marketing communications.

In order for this pre-selection to be effective, the advertisement will have to contain details of the organisation and the job.

- Employer's **location** and **business**
- **Rewards**: the salary or wage benefits, training
- **The job**: title, main duties and responsibility, special factors
- **Career prospects**
- **Qualifications and experience required**/preferred, other aptitudes
- **How to apply**

It will have to present an attractive image, but also an honest one, so as not to disillusion successful applicants.

Preparation of the job information requires skill and attention in order to fulfil its objectives of attraction and preselection. It should meet a number of criteria.

(a) It should be **concise**, but comprehensive enough to be an accurate description of the job, its rewards and requirements.

(b) It should be **targeted** to attract the attention of the maximum number of the right sort of people.

(c) It should be **attractive**, conveying a favourable impression of the organisation, but not falsely so.

(d)   It should be **relevant** and appropriate to the job and the applicant. Skills, qualifications and special aptitudes required should be prominently set out, along with special features of the job that might attract or deter applicants, such as shiftwork or extensive travel.

The way in which a job is advertised will depend on the type of organisation and the type of job. A factory is likely to advertise a vacancy for an unskilled worker in a different way from a company advertising vacancies for clerical staff. Managerial jobs may merit national advertisements, whereas semi– or unskilled jobs may only warrant local coverage, depending on the supply of suitable candidates in the local area. Specific skills may be most appropriately reached through trade, technical or professional journals, like *Marketing Week*.

The choice of **advertising medium** will depend upon three considerations.

(a)   The **cost** of advertising. It is more expensive to advertise in a national newspaper than on local radio, and more expensive to advertise on local radio than in a local newspaper.

(b)   The **type and number of readers** of the medium, and its suitability for the number and type of people the organisation wants to reach.

(c)   The **frequency** with which the organisation wants to advertise the job vacancy. A monthly magazine or weekly newspaper are probably only useful for advertising a vacancy once. This is probably sufficient for a specialist or professional, or for a senior management position, since those who are interested will be on the look-out for vacancies advertised in certain magazines or newspapers.

3.3.1 Methods and media for advertising jobs

(a)   **In-house magazines and notice-boards**

(b)   **Professional and specialist newspapers or magazines**, such as *Personnel Management, Marketing* or *Computing*

(c)   **National newspapers**, especially for senior management jobs or vacancies for skilled workers, where potential applicants will not necessarily be found through local advertising. **Local newspapers** would be suitable for jobs where applicants are sought from the local area

(d)   **Local radio, television and cinema**. These are becoming increasingly popular, especially for **large-scale campaigns, for large numbers of vacancies**

(e)   **Job centres**. On the whole, vacancies for unskilled work (rather than skilled work or management jobs) are advertised through local job centres, although in theory any type of job can be advertised here

(f)   **School and university careers offices**

(g)   The **Internet**, especially for IT professionals and to attract candidates internationally

(h)   **Employment agencies and recruitment consultants** for unusual or specialist posts

3.4 Other methods of reaching the labour market

Various **agencies** exist, through whom the employer can reach the public.

(a)   **Institutional agencies** exist to help their own members to find employment: for example, the career services of educational institutions such as schools and colleges, and the employment services of professional institutions and trade unions.

(b)   **Private employment agencies** have proliferated in recent years. There is a wide range of agencies specialising in different grades of staff and areas of skill. Private agencies generally offer an immediate pool of labour already on their books, and many also undertake initial screening of potential applicants, so that the recruitment officer sees only the most suitable.

There are also more **informal recruitment methods**, not directly involving advertising.

(a)   **Unsolicited applications** are now frequently made to organisations, especially where there are few advertised vacancies. Some applicants may have heard about impending vacancies through the grapevine.

(b)   Some vacancies may be filled through **informal contacts** and on the **recommendation** of established workers.

(c)   **Head hunting** has become increasingly popular. Informal approaches are made to successful executives currently employed elsewhere.

The role of the **recruitment consultant** is to perform the staffing function on behalf of the client organisation. This involves a number of activities.

- Analysing the organisation's requirements
- Helping to draw up job descriptions and person specifications
- Designing job advertisements
- Screening applications and short-listing for interview
- Advising on the constitution and procedures of the interview

The decision whether or not to use consultants will depend on a number of factors.

(a)   **Cost** will be an important consideration when recruiting for lower grades, since an expert recruitment decision will not be so crucial, and the fees may not therefore be cost effective.

(b)   **The level of expertise and specialist techniques or knowledge which the consultant can bring to the process**. Consultants may be expert in using interview techniques, analysis of personnel specifications and so on. In-house staff, on the other hand, have experience of the particular field and of the culture of the organisation into which the recruits must fit.

(c)   **The level of expertise, and specialist knowledge, available within the organisation**. The cost of training in-house personnel in the necessary interview and assessment techniques may be prohibitive.

(d)   Whether there is a **need for impartiality** which can only be filled by an outsider trained in objective assessment. If fresh blood is desired in the organisation, it may be a mistake to have staff selecting clones of the common organisational type.

(e)   **Supply of labour**. If there is a large and reasonably accessible pool of labour from which to fill a post, consultants will be less valuable. If the vacancy is a standard one, and there are ready channels for reaching labour (such as professional journals), the use of specialists may not be cost effective.

Managing the search process can be summarised in the following steps.

1	Confirming the profile of the ideal candidate
2	Identifying possible sources of such candidates
3	Reviewing possible internal sources and external options
4	Developing an attractive but realistic advertisement
5	Determining the appropriate media
6	Placing the advertisement
7	Handling the applications.

Select any two job advertisements from a website of your choice. Note three things.

- The elements of information given
- The tone and style of the advertisement
- The visual presentation, and the impression it makes on you

Decide what sort of person each advertisement is trying to attract. How (if at all) are the advertisers going about attracting that sort of person and discouraging applications from others?

[Key Skill for Marketers: Using ICT and the Internet]

4 Recruitment interviews and selection

FAST FORWARD

It is important to prepare and plan properly for the **selection process**, especially selection **interviews**.

4.1 Application forms

Applicants who reply to job advertisements are often asked to fill in a job application form.

Application forms have two important aspects.

(a) An open-ended element, which will enable a candidate to give information about his or her abilities and achievements, including academic qualifications, work experience, activities and interests, career expectations and why the candidate thinks he or she is suitable.

(b) The closed element is much more structured. In this case the candidate is required to answer detailed questions (eg basic biographical information) which are posed in a restricted format (eg tick boxes). This element of an application form enables easier comparison between candidates.

An application form should elicit sufficient information to screen candidates into two groups.

- Those obviously unsuitable for the job
- Those who might be of the right calibre, and worth inviting to an interview

An alternative approach is simply to request applicants to send **CVs**. This will usually contain all the information needed for shortlisting and in itself is a good indication of a candidate's written communication skills.

4.2 The selection interview

The selection interview is the next stage of the selection process. Interviewing is a crucial part of the selection process.

- It gives the organisation a chance to assess applicants directly
- It gives applicants a chance to learn more about the organisation, and to decide whether or not they are still interested

Key concept

The **interview** has a three-fold purpose.

(a)   To find the best person for the job.

(b)   To ensure that applicants understand what the job is and what the career prospects are. They must be allowed a fair opportunity to decide whether or not they want the job.

(c)   To make applicants feel that they have been given fair treatment in the interview, whether they get the job or not. Current applicants may still be future employees or customers.

The interview must be prepared carefully, to make sure that the right questions are asked, and relevant information obtained to give the interviewers what they need to make their selection.

(a)   The **job description should be studied** to review the major demands of the job.

(b)   The **person specification should be studied and questions should be planned** which might help the interviewer make relevant assessments of the applicant's character and qualifications.

(c)   Each application form should be carefully studied, in order to decide on questions or question areas for the individual applicant.

The interview should be conducted in such a way that the information required is successfully obtained during the interview.

(a)   The **layout of the room** and the number of interviewers should be planned carefully. Most interviewers wish to put candidates at their ease, and so it would be inadvisable to put the candidate in a 'hot seat' across a table from a large number of hostile-looking interviewers. However, some interviewers might want to observe the candidate's reaction under severe pressure, and deliberately make the layout of the room uncomfortable and off-putting.

(b)   The **manner of the interviewers**, the tone of their voice, and the way their early questions are phrased can all be significant in establishing the tone of the interview.

(c)   **Questions should be put carefully**. The interviewers should not be trying to confuse the candidate, but should be trying to obtain the information that they need.

(d)   It is necessary to ask relevant questions, but the time of **the interview should be taken up mostly with the candidate talking,** and not with the interviewers asking questions. The more a candidate talks, the easier it should be to assess their suitability for the job. As a rule of thumb, the candidate should be talking for 70% of the time.

(e)   **The candidate should be given the opportunity to ask questions**. Indeed well-prepared candidates should go into an interview knowing what questions they may want to ask. The choice of questions might well have some influence on how the interviewers finally assess them.

(f)   Similarly the interviewer should be aware of the questions candidates are likely to ask. Candidates may well try to probe behind the statements made about the business, by asking for example why the interviewer chose or has remained with the organisation. Some candidate questioning may be a sign that the interviewer has failed to impart key information – for example the candidate's likely role within the organisation or the opportunities for advancement.

After each interview has been completed, notes should be made and, if more than one interviewer was present, impressions compared. Each candidate should be evaluated against the criteria for appointment. There are then three possible outcomes for each candidate.

BPP
LEARNING MEDIA

(a)   A job offer, possibly subject to conditions.

- Taking up references
- Obtaining evidence of educational and professional qualifications
- Medical examination

(b)   An invitation to a **second interview**. Some organisations have a two-stage interview process, whereby first stage interview candidates are reduced to a short-list for a second stage interview. The second stage of the interview might well be based on a group selection method (see below). In many instances, the recruitment consultant might carry out the first stage interview.

(c)   Rejection.

The diagram at the end of this section outlines the stages of the selection process.

4.3 The limitations of selection interviews

Interviews have often been criticised because they **fail to select suitable people** for job vacancies.

(a)   **Assessment may be unclear**. The opinion of one interviewer may differ from the opinion of another. They cannot both be right, but because of their different opinions, a suitable candidate might be rejected or an unsuitable candidate offered a job.

(b)   **Interviews fail to provide accurate predictions** of how a person will perform in the job.

(c)   **The interviewers are likely to make errors of judgement** even when they agree about a candidate. There are several reasons for this.

(i)   A **halo effect**. This is a tendency for interviewers to make a general judgement about a person based on one single attribute, which will colour the interviewers' opinions and make them mark the person up or down on every other factor in their assessment.

(ii)   **Stereotyping** candidates on the basis of insufficient evidence, for example on the basis of dress, hair style or accent of voice.

(iii)   **Contagious bias**. This is a process whereby an interviewer changes the behaviour of the applicant by suggestion. The applicant might be led by the wording of questions or non-verbal cues from the interviewer and change what he is doing or saying in response to the signals being received.

(iv)   **Incorrect assessment of qualitative factors** such as motivation, honesty or integrity. Abstract qualities are very difficult to assess in an interview.

(v)   **Logical error**. An interviewer might draw conclusions about a candidate from what is being said or done when there is no logical justification for those conclusions. For example, an interviewer might decide that a person who talks a lot in a confident voice must be intelligent, when this is not the case.

(vi)   **Incorrectly used rating scales**. For example, if interviewers are required to rate a candidate on a scale of 1-5 for a number of different attributes, there might be a tendency to mark candidates in the middle range for safety or consistently above or below average for every attribute, because of **halo effect.**

(vii)   **Misleading environment.** The interview can be a tense occasion for both parties, and as a result become very formal with interviewer and applicant on their best behaviour.

(d) The candidate may be adept at being interviewed. Many will have received training, including video debriefs, in presenting themselves.

Action Programme 5

What assumptions might an interviewer make about **you**, based on things like these.

- Accent
- School
- Clothes and hair-style
- Stated hobbies and interests
- Taste in books and TV programmes

To what extent would any of these assumptions be fair?

For objectivity, you might like to conduct this exercise in class. What assumptions do you make about the person sitting next to you?

It might be apparent from the list of limitations above that a major problem with interviews is the **skill and experience of the interviewers themselves**. Any interviewer is prone to bias, but a person can learn to reduce this problem through training and experience. Inexperienced interviewers have other problems as well.

- **Inability to evaluate** properly information about a candidate

- **Inability to compare** a candidate against the requirements for a job or a personnel specification

- Bad interview planning

- A **tendency to talk too much** in interviews, and to ask questions which call for a short answer

- A tendency to act as an inquisitor and make candidates feel uneasy.

To some extent the problems can be overcome with training.

Action Programme 6

Some careers officers give tuition in interview techniques to people looking for jobs. What do you think this says about interviewing, as opposed to testing, as a means of selection?

4.4 Selection testing

Interviews are often supplemented by some form of **selection test**. The interviewers must be certain that the results of such tests are reliable, and that a candidate who scores well in a test will be more likely to succeed in the job. The test will have no value unless there is a direct relationship between ability in the test and ability in the job. The test should be designed to be discriminating (ie to bring out the differences in subjects), standardised (so that it measures the same thing in different people, providing a consistent basis for comparison) and relevant to its purpose.

There are four types of test commonly used in practice.

(a) **Intelligence tests** aim to measure the applicant's general intellectual ability.

(b) **Aptitude tests** are designed to predict an individual's potential for performing a job or learning new skills.

(c) **Proficiency tests** are perhaps the most closely related to an assessor's objectives, because they measure ability to do the work involved. An applicant for an audio typist's job, for example, might be given a dictation tape and asked to type it.

(d) **Psychological tests** may measure a variety of characteristics, such as an applicant's skill in dealing with other people, ambition and motivation or emotional stability. To a trained psychologist, such questionnaires may give clues about the dominant qualities or characteristics of the individuals tested, but wide experience is needed to make good use of the results.

Sometimes applicants are required to attempt several tests (a **test battery**) aimed at giving a more rounded picture than would be available from a single test.

This kind of testing must be used with care and is really a job for a qualified psychologist.

4.5 References

References provide further confidential information about the prospective employee. This may be of varying value, **as the reliability of all but the most factual information must be in question.** A reference should contain two types of data.

(a) Straightforward **factual information** confirming the nature of the applicant's previous job(s), period of employment, pay, and circumstances of leaving

(b) **Opinions** about the applicant's personality and other attributes, which should obviously be treated with some caution.

4.6 The offer

Once a selection is made the candidate should be approached with a formal offer. It is best not to notify a suitable second choice until the candidate has accepted. Unsuccessful candidates should be notified as quickly as possible.

The organisation should be prepared for its offer to be rejected at this stage. Applicants may have received and accepted other offers. They may not have been attracted by their first-hand view of the organisation, and may have changed their mind about applying; they may only have been testing the water in applying in the first place, gauging the market for their skills and experience for future reference, or seeking a position of strength from which to bargain with their present employers. **A small number of eligible applicants should therefore be kept in reserve.**

 Action Programme 7

Some companies have run into trouble from disgruntled employees because the companies have given them poor references. Certain companies have therefore tried to deal with this situation by giving references along the following lines: 'You will be lucky to have this person working for you.'

What are the potential problems with that reference?

Figure 3.2: Selection process

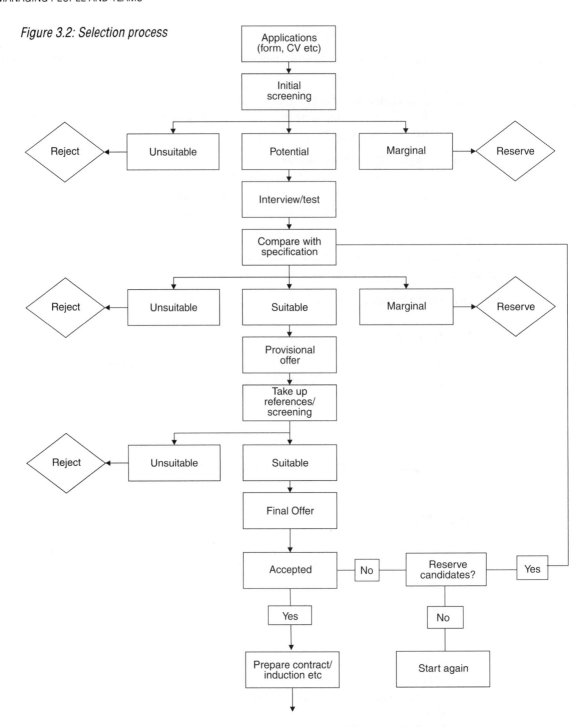

Exam tip

Questions may ask about 'recruitment and selection', but remember to look for the context. For example, the June 2005 paper contained a question on selecting a brand manager to develop an export market. In December 2006, you were recruiting new staff in a new local areas with specific skills (in hair care!).

What sort of people and skills would you need for a specific role, and how would you go about recruiting those people? What recruitment media would they consume? Are these new requirements (which need to be defined and recruited for), or well-established ones (for which job descriptions exist, and for which existing staff may be qualified)? Get used to thinking this way!

BPP LEARNING MEDIA

Chapter Roundup

- All teams will need to **recruit new members** at some time and the marketing manager will be very involved in that process, possibly supported by Human Resource specialists.

- The process of **search and selection** needs to be thoroughly planned and professionally managed if the right candidate for the post is to be identified.

- In contemporary organisations, recruitment and selection are often carried out within the framework of a **core competencies** model.

- The first critical stage is a **job analysis**, from which the **job specification** and/or **job description** and **person specification** can be generated. Care and attention here will ensure the manager knows the kind of person needed to suit the needs of both the task and the group.

- The process of **search** uses many marketing skills, to help segment the labour market and target the right sources of potential candidates.

- **Internal applicants** should be considered, but the relative advantages and disadvantages of making an internal or external appointment should be considered. It may be best to assess the internal candidate against external alternatives.

- It is important to prepare and plan properly for the **selection process**, especially selection **interviews**.

Quick Quiz

1   What is human resource planning?

2   Outline a methodical approach to recruitment and selection.

3   What goes into a job description?

4   What is a person specification?

5   List the factors included in the Five Point Pattern of Personality.

6   What long-term demographic trends must organisations consider?

7   What details should be included in a job advertisement?

8   What factors would you consider before selecting the advertising medium for a vacancy?

9   What is the purpose of an application form?

10   How should selection interviews be conducted?

11   What are the limitations of selection interviews?

12   List four types of selection test.

Answers to Quick Quiz

1   Defining the people and skills needed by the organisation to meet its objectives and how they are to be provided

2   HR planning; job analysis; identification of vacancies; evaluation of sources of labour; advertising for staff; assessing and selecting applicants; notifying applicants

3   A job description is a statement of the purpose, duties and responsibilities of a particular position. It will include:

- Job title
- Location
- Relationships

- Duties
- Authority and responsibilities
- Equipment used

4   A specification of the qualities, qualifications and experience required of a person in a particular position

5
- Impact on others
- Acquired knowledge or qualifications
- Innate ability

- Motivation
- Adjustment and emotional balance

6   Long term trends, such as the changing age distribution of western societies; and trends in education that affect the number and employability of school-leavers

7   Employer's location and business; reward package; job details; career prospects; qualifications and experience required; how to apply

8   Cost; type and number of potential respondents; desired frequency of appearance

9   To permit the selection of good candidates from those clearly unsuitable

10   To collect information about the candidate

11   Unclear assessment; inability to predict performance; errors of judgement by interviewers

12
- Intelligence tests
- Proficiency tests

- Aptitude tests
- Psychological tests

Action Programme Review

1, 2   All research is invaluable in your work and in providing context – examples offer relevant answers in the exam.

3

For Internal	Against Internal
Knows the people, systems and the business	May have pre-conceived ideas and an established and unsuitable image/reputation from current post
Fits in with the culture: knows 'how we do things here'	No new ideas, creativity or challenge to the culture and systems
Motivating to the individual and others to have an internal promotion	A post will still need filling – this person's old post!
Quicker, cheaper and less risky than an outside appointment	This person may not be the best qualified or most able candidate
The induction period will be quicker.	

BPP LEARNING MEDIA

4   You may also note your impressions of the employer through the way they present their advertisements and remember to consider the media they use, too (Press, trade mail etc). What does this tell you about the type of candidate they are trying to attract?

5   Be realistic, and if attempting this with other people, be tactful. The more people involved, the greater range of answers you are likely to find.

6   If interview techniques are taught, it might imply that, in the absence of any other selection criteria, your success at interview will have more to do with your ability to present yourself in an interview situation than you ability to do the job. On the other hand, an interview is a test of how well you perform under pressure, in an unfamiliar environment and with strangers. This might reflect some of the interpersonal skills required in a job.

7   The reference is deliberately ambiguous. The writer hopes that the subject will be satisfied with it while any potential employer is warned by it. The opposite might occur, possibly leading to protest from either party.

Now try Question 3 at the end of the Study Text

Improving team performance

Syllabus content – knowledge and skill requirements

- Response to poor performance within a marketing team. Minimising conflict, supporting team members, overcoming problems and maintaining discipline (1.6)
- Evaluation of individual and team performance against objectives or targets and provision of constructive feedback on their performance (1.8)

Introduction

Having recruited, trained and inducted a new team member we have to ensure the new member's and the team's optimal performance.

In Section 1 we discuss **different approaches to motivation** and what factors encourage people to work hard and well, and how the manager can understand and use these factors: do people have needs which managers can satisfy? Do people weigh up the options?

In Section 2, we go on from identifying the needs which people have to how they can be satisfied, using pay, the job itself, participation and empowerment to enhance motivation. **People are often motivated by things other than money**, and in times when funds are scarce, attention to the non-financial aspects can help motivate a team.

Motivation has to be translated into performance: a person can be well motivated but incompetent. Consequently we have to review **the performance of the individual or team**, the subject of Section 3. The purpose of **appraisal** is to develop a review of a person's performance, with a view to improving it. Sometimes this might be achieved by training, which we discuss in Section 4.

On occasions, performance may be such that people require **counselling or advice** outside of the normal appraisal system. In extreme cases, **disciplinary action** might be necessary. We discuss these aspects in Sections 5 and 6. You must appreciate the differences between appraisals, counselling and disciplinary interviews.

1 Motivational theory and its value to the manager

FAST FORWARD

> **Motivation** is an essential ingredient in ensuring that the individual and the team perform efficiently and effectively.

Key concept

> **Motivation** is simply reasons for behaviour. People at work display varying degrees of motivation to achieve the goals set by management. It is an important task of managers at all levels to enhance the individual's motivation to work effectively.

Managers can provide the team with the opportunity and resources to work, but without motivation, little effective work will result. Motivation is the catalyst the manager has to add to the work situation to generate results.

Earlier we considered the role and responsibilities of the leader. Responsibility for motivation is an integral part of that job. You must be aware of the theory and importance of motivation and be able to suggest solutions to motivational problems for the examiner.

Marketers may have a head start in this area of management, as they have studied motivation frequently in the context of understanding customer behaviour.

1.1 Why is motivation important?

You may be wondering why motivation is important. It could be argued that a person is employed to do a job, and so will do that job and no question of motivation arises. A person who does not want to do the work can resign. The point at issue, however, is the **efficiency** with which the job is done. It is suggested that if individuals can be motivated, by one means or another, they will produce a **better quality of work**.

1.2 Motivators and motivation

In the most basic terms, individuals share **needs** which they wish to satisfy. The means of satisfying the needs are **wants**. For example, an individual might feel the need for power, and to fulfil this need, might want money and a position of authority. Depending on the strength of these needs and wants, she/he may take action to achieve them. If successful in achieving them, she/he will be satisfied. This can be shown in a simple diagram.

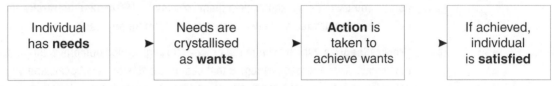

Individual has **needs** ► Needs are crystallised as **wants** ► **Action** is taken to achieve wants ► If achieved, individual is **satisfied**

Motivators can be established which act as the wants of the individual. For example, the position of sales director might serve as a want to satisfy an individual's need for power, or access to the senior executive's dining room might serve as a want to satisfy a need for status. **Motivators may exist which are not directly controllable by management;** for example, an individual might want to be accepted by work mates, to satisfy a need for friendship and affiliation with others, and might therefore choose to conform to the norms and adopt the attitudes of the work group, which are not necessarily shared by the organisation as a whole.

Management has the problem of creating or manipulating motivators which will actually motivate employees to perform in a desired way.

Action Programme 1

Before you start reading about motivation theories, answer the following questions. What factors in yourself or in your organisation motivate you:

- to turn up at work at all?
- to do an average day's work?
- to work particularly hard?

Go on – be honest!

Talk to friends and colleagues – find out what makes them tick.

2 Motivation theories

FAST FORWARD

Organisational behaviour theory has devoted considerable attention to understanding motivation because it is believed improvements here can generate competitive advantage.

What we believe motivation is and what can be done with it will influence all our attitudes to individuals in organisations and to our management style.

(a) Some suggest that a **satisfied** worker will work harder, although there is little evidence to support the assumption. Satisfaction may reduce labour turnover and absenteeism, but will not necessarily increase individual productivity. Some hold that people work best within a compatible work group, or under a well-liked leader.

(b) There is a common assumption that individuals will work harder in order to obtain a desired reward. **Incentives** can work if certain conditions are satisfied.

- The individual perceives the increased reward to be worth the extra effort
- The performance can be measured and clearly attributed to that individual
- The individual wants that particular kind of reward
- The increased performance will not become the new minimum standard

One way of grouping the major theories of motivation is by making the following distinction.

(a)   **Content theories,** which assume that human beings have a 'package' of needs which they pursue and try to define and explain them. *Maslow's* (1987) **need hierarchy** and Herzberg's (1993) **two-factor theory** are two of the most important approaches of this type.

(b)   **Process theories**, which explore the process through which outcomes are pursued by individuals. This approach assumes that people are able to select goals and choose the paths towards them, by a conscious or unconscious process of calculation. *Vroom's* **expectancy theory** and *Handy's* (1964) **motivation calculus** are theories of this type.

Exam tip

> As usual, you are unlikely to be asked detailed questions on the theories of motivation in this examination, but you need to be able to back up any recommendations you make by explaining (with reference to relevant theory) why they should work! Apart from anything else, this should give you a wider repertoire of motivational techniques than 'offering more money' – which is rarely an organisation's (or examiner's) preferred option!

2.1 Content theories

2.1.1 Maslow's hierarchy of needs

FAST FORWARD

> Maslow's **hierarchy of needs** is a commonly referred to motivation theory. It seems to have intuitive appeal.

In his motivation theory, *A H Maslow* (1987) put forward certain propositions about the motivating power of people's **needs**.

(a)   Every person's needs can be arranged in **a hierarchy of relative** pre-potency: Figure 4.1.

(b)   Each **level of need is dominant until satisfied;** only then does the next higher level of need become a motivating factor.

(c)   A **need which has been satisfied no longer motivates** an individual's behaviour. The need for self-actualisation can never be satisfied.

Figure 4.1: Maslow's hierarchy of needs

Self-actualisation   - fulfilment of personal potential

Esteem needs   - for independence, recognition, status, respect from others

Love/social needs   - for relationships, affection, belonging

Safety needs   - for security, order, predictability, freedom from threat

Physiological needs   - food, shelter

There is a certain intuitive appeal to Maslow's theory. After all, you are unlikely to be concerned with status or recognition while you are hungry or thirsty; primary survival needs will take precedence. Likewise, once your hunger is assuaged, the need for food is unlikely to be a motivating factor.

Maslow's theories may be of general interest, but they have no clear practical application.

(a) The same need may cause different behaviour in different individuals. One person might seek to satisfy his need for esteem by winning promotion whereas another individual might seek esteem by leading a challenge against authority.

(b) It is occasionally difficult to reconcile the willingness of individuals to forgo the immediate satisfaction of needs and to accept current suffering to fulfil a long-term goal (eg the long studentship of the medical or accounting professions), in terms of Maslow's hierarchy.

2.2 Herzberg's two-factor theory of job satisfaction

FAST FORWARD

Herzberg's work was important because it encourages managers to recognise the **hygiene** factors, which can cause dissatisfaction if they are absent, but are unlikely to generate positive motivation – fostered by **motivator** factors.

Frederick Herzberg (1993) saw two separate need systems in individuals.

(a) **A need to avoid unpleasantness**. This need is satisfied at work by **hygiene factors**. Hygiene satisfactions are short-lived; individuals come back for more as their expectations rise.

(b) **A need for personal growth.** This is satisfied by **motivator factors.**

Hygiene or **maintenance** factors are essentially preventative: they can be manipulated by managers to prevent or minimise dissatisfaction **but do not give satisfaction**, in the same way that sanitation minimises some threats to health, but does not ensure good health.

Action Programme 2

What factors can cause dissatisfaction at work?

The important point is that **motivation** cannot be achieved by addressing the above-mentioned factors. All that will be attained is a temporary absence of dissatisfaction, swiftly eroded once benefits are taken for granted or perceived as 'less' then those given to others.

Motivator factors, on the other hand, actively **create lasting job satisfaction** and *are* effective in motivating an individual to superior performance and effort.

- Status (may be a hygiene factor too)
- Advancement
- Recognition
- Responsibility
- Challenging work
- Achievement
- Growth in the job

Some individuals are not **mature** enough to want personal growth; they are **'hygiene seekers'**, because they are only bothered about hygiene factors. A lack of motivators at work, however, will encourage employees to concentrate on shortcomings in hygiene factors, real or imagined. The result will be an endless series of demands relating to pay and conditions of work.

Herzberg suggested various means by which motivator satisfactions could be supplied. Stemming from his fundamental division of motivator and hygiene factors, he encouraged managers to address factors in **the job itself** (the type of work done, the nature of tasks, levels of responsibility) rather than **conditions of work**.

If there is sufficient challenge, scope and interest in the job, there will be a lasting increase in satisfaction and the employee will work well; productivity will be above 'normal' levels. The extent to which a job must be challenging or creative to a motivator seeker will, in relation to each individual, depend on his ability and his tolerance for delayed success.

FAST FORWARD

> Herzberg also highlighted the motivational opportunities from **job enlargement**, **enrichment** and **rotation**, all of which are quite commonly used for both motivation and for training and development.

Herzberg specified three typical means whereby work can be revised to improve motivation.

(a) **Job enrichment**: this is the main method of improving job satisfaction and can be defined as 'the planned process of up-grading the responsibility, challenge and content of the work'. Typically, this would involve increasing **delegation** to provide more interesting work and problem solving at lower levels within an organisation.

(b) **Job enlargement**: although often linked with job enrichment, it is a separate technique and is **rather limited** in its ability to improve staff motivation. Job enlargement is the process of increasing the number of operations in which a worker is engaged This is more limited in value, since a person who is required to complete several tedious tasks is unlikely to be much more highly motivated than a man performing one continuous tedious task.

(c) **Job rotation**: this is the planned operation of a system whereby staff members exchange positions with the intention of breaking monotony in the work and providing fresh job challenge.

These ideas are discussed in more detail in Section 3.

2.3 Process theories

2.3.1 Vroom's expectancy theory

Victor Vroom (1964) stated a formula by which human motivation could be assessed and measured. He suggested that the strength of an individual's motivation is the product of two factors.

(a) The strength of his preference for a certain outcome. Vroom called this **valence**: it can be represented as a positive or negative number, or zero – since outcomes may be desired, avoided or regarded with indifference.

(b) His expectation that the outcome will in fact result from a certain behaviour. Vroom called this 'subjective probability' or **expectancy.** As a probability, it may be represented by any number between 0 (no chance) and 1 (certainty).

In its simplest form, the expectancy equation may be stated as:

$F = V \times E$

where:

F = the force or strength of the individual's motivation to behave in a particular way
V = valence: the strength of the individual preference for a given outcome or reward and
E = expectancy: the individual's perception that the behaviour will result in the outcome/ reward.

In this equation, the lower the values of valence or expectancy, the less the motivation. An employee may have a high expectation that increased productivity will result in promotion (because of managerial promises, say), but if he is indifferent or negative towards the idea of promotion (because he dislikes responsibility), he will not be motivated to increase his productivity. Likewise, if promotion was very important to him – but he did not believe higher productivity would get him promoted (because he has been passed over before, perhaps), his motivation would be low.

BPP LEARNING MEDIA

(a)   The **value** that they place on the expected outcome, whether the positive value of a reward, or the negative value of a punishment. Vroom called this '**valence**'.

(b)   The strength of their **expectation** that behaving in a certain way will in fact bring out the desired outcome. Vroom called this **expectancy**.

> Expectancy × Valence = Force of motivation.

In terms of organisation practice, *Charles Handy* (1992) suggests that several factors are necessary for the individual to complete this calculus, and to be motivated.

(a)   **Intended results should be made clear**, so that the individual can complete the calculation, and know what is expected, what will be rewarded and how much effort it will take.

(b)   Without knowledge of **actual results**, there is no check that the expenditure of energy was justified (and will be justified in future). **Feedback on performance,** good or bad, is essential, not only for performance but for confidence and prevention of hostility.

Process theories help to explain various phenomena of individual behaviour at work.

(a)   Individuals are more committed to specific goals, particularly those which they have helped to set themselves.

(b)   If individuals are **rewarded** according to performance tied to standards ('management by objectives'), however, they may well set **lower** standards: the likelihood of success and reward is greater if the standard is lower, so less expenditure of effort is indicated.

2.4 Motivating teams and individuals

FAST FORWARD

Drucker identified that motivation of individuals starts with putting the **right people in the right jobs**.

We have already talked about job satisfaction in connection with the work of Herzberg. He conducted a survey of employees in Pittsburgh and analysed their accounts of times when they 'felt good' about their jobs; this was taken to be a sign of **job satisfaction** (as opposed to **job dissatisfaction**, arising from events which made them 'feel bad' about their jobs).

P Drucker (1993) suggests that employee satisfaction comes about through encouraging employees to accept **responsibility**. There are four ingredients to this.

(a)   **Careful placement of people in jobs**. The person selected should see the job as one which provides a challenge to their abilities. There is unlikely to be much motivation for a university graduate in the job of shop assistant, whereas the same job can provide a worthwhile challenge to someone of lesser academic training and intelligence.

(b)   **High standards of performance in the job**. Targets for achievement should be challenging. However, they should not be imposed in an authoritarian way by the employee's bosses. The employee should be encouraged to set high standards of performance.

(c)   **Providing the worker with the information needed to control personal performance**. Employees should routinely receive information about their performance, but this should not come via their immediate supervisor. Being told by a boss comes as a praise or reprimand, and the fear of reprimand will inhibit performance. Access to information as a routine matter overcomes this problem of inhibition.

(d)   **Opportunities for participation in decisions that will give the employee managerial vision**. Participation means having some say and influence in the way the employee's work is organised and the targets for work are set.

2.5 Methods of improving motivation and job satisfaction

FAST FORWARD

A wide variety of options are available to motivate the individual and the team. The important thing is to develop **motivational strategies** which suit both the situation and the individual. Schemes should be simple to administer, easy to understand and perceived to be fair, and any incentives should be clear.

There are various ways in which managers can attempt to increase the motivation of their subordinates.

- Herzberg and others recommended better **job design**.

- Various writers have suggested that subordinates' **participation in decision making** will improve motivation through self-realisation and **empowerment**.

- **Pay and incentive schemes** are frequently regarded as powerful motivators.

We shall discuss each of these ways in turn.

2.5.1 Job design

Job design is similar to job analysis, but in terms of a proposed job rather than an existing one. It is concerned with the process of deciding three issues.

- The **content** of a job in terms of its duties and responsibilities

- The **methods** to be used in carrying out the job, in terms of techniques, system and procedures

- The **relationship** that should exist between job holders and their superiors, colleagues and subordinates

The objectives of the job design process are to improve productivity, efficiency and quality and to satisfy the individual's needs for interest, challenge and accomplishment.

2.5.2 Job enrichment

Key concept

> **Job enrichment** is planned, deliberate action to build greater responsibility, breadth and challenge of work into a job. A job may be enriched in a variety of ways, such as allowing the employee in the job greater freedom to decide how the job should be done.

Job enrichment attempts to add further responsibilities to a job by giving the job holder decision-making opportunities of a higher order.

 Marketing at Work

At first, a market researcher's responsibilities for producing quarterly management reports ended at the stage of producing the figures. These duties were then extended so that she prepared the actual reports and submitted them, under her own name, to the senior management. This alteration in responsibilities not only enriched the job but also increased the work-load. This in turn led to delegation of certain responsibilities to clerks within the department. These duties were in themselves job enrichment to the clerks and so a cascading effect was obtained. This highlights one of the basic elements of job enrichment – that what is tedious, mundane detail at a high level can represent significant job interest and challenge at a lower level in the organisation where a person's experience and scope is much less.

BPP
LEARNING MEDIA

The opportunity for job enrichment may be constrained.

- Technology and working conditions may dictate how work must be done.
- Jobs utilising a low level of skill may be difficult to enrich.
- Job enrichment should be wanted by subordinates.

Job enrichment alone will not automatically make employees more productive. If jobs are enriched, employees will expect to be paid fairly for what they are doing. It might be more correct therefore to say that job enrichment might improve productivity through greater motivation, but only if it is rewarded fairly.

Action Programme 3

In what ways could your work or the work of your team be enriched?

2.5.3 Job enlargement

Key concept

> **Job enlargement** is frequently confused with job enrichment. Job enlargement is the attempt to widen jobs by increasing the number of operations in which a job holder is involved.

This has the effect of lengthening the cycle time of repeated operations; by reducing the number of repetitions of the same work, the dullness of the job should also be reduced. Job enlargement is therefore a horizontal extension of an individual's work, whereas job enrichment is a vertical extension. For most **knowledge workers**, like marketing staff, this may be less useful than job enrichment.

Job enlargement is the opposite of the **micro-division of labour** approach to the organisation of work, in which a job consists of the smallest number of sequential tasks possible. Each task is so simple and straightforward that it can be learned with very little training. This is typical of mass production industries.

There are several arguments against the micro-division of labour:

- The work is monotonous and makes employees bored and dissatisfied. The consequences will be high labour turnover, absenteeism and spoilage.

- People, unlike machines, work more efficiently when their work is varied.

- Excessive specialisation isolates the individual in his work and inhibits social contacts with work-mates.

Arguably, however, **job enlargement** itself is limited in its ability to improve motivation since, as Herzberg points out, to ask a worker to complete three separate tedious, unchallenging tasks is unlikely to motivate him more than asking him to fulfil one single tedious, unchallenging task!

2.5.4 Aspects of well-designed jobs

- Scope for the individual to set work standards and targets
- Individual control over the pace and methods of working
- Provision of variety by allowing for inter-locking tasks to be done by the same person
- Opportunity to comment about the design of the product, or job
- Feedback to the individual about performance

2.6 Participation in decision making and empowerment

FAST FORWARD

Participation and **feedback** are key factors in motivating a team. **Appraisal** can help by providing a formal system of feedback which is also a useful benchmark for monitoring performance changes. Most appraisal systems require a manager to appraise a subordinate, but alternatives can be suggested.

2.6.1 Participation

Much research suggests that if a superior invites subordinates to participate in planning decisions which affect their work, if the subordinates voluntarily accept the invitation, and if results about actual performance are fed back regularly so that they can make their own control decisions, then the subordinates' **motivation will rise**.

- Efficiency may rise
- They may become more conscious of the organisation's goals
- It may be possible to raise planning targets to reasonably challenging levels
- They may be ready to take appropriate control actions when necessary

It is obvious that participation will only be feasible if the superior is willing to apply it, and if it is acceptable within the culture of the organisation.

2.6.2 What does participation mean and why is it desirable?

Merits of participation schemes

(a)   **They bring into play the employees' own experiences to decide the best methods**. Someone who is actually doing the job may be able to see where improvements can be made, and where the impact of decisions will be.

(b)   **Employees may actually set targets higher than managers expect**. In the Hawthorne experiment, a group who participated in decisions affecting them became much more productive.

(c)   **If employees can control their performance, many supervisory jobs will be removed** making supervision more effective and helping in the **delayering of organisations**.

(d)   **Improved quality of work may result where employees are interested**. A group that feels involved will perform better.

(e)   **Unexpected events will not be so traumatic**. Employees will have learned to think for themselves and will be willing to take decisions. This may have the additional effect of greater job satisfaction and reduced labour turnover and absenteeism.

The advantages of participation should also be considered from the opposite end: what would be the disadvantages of not having participation? The answer to this is that employees would be told what to do, and would presumably comply with orders. However, their compliance would not be enthusiastic, and they would not be psychologically committed to their work.

Participation can involve employees and make them committed to their task, if the following conditions are met.

(a)   Participation should be **genuine**. It is very easy for a manager to invite participation from his subordinates and then ignore their views. A culture change may be needed within management.

(b)   The efforts to establish participation by employees should be pushed over a **long period of time** and with a lot of energy. However, 'if the issue or the task is trivial...and everyone realises it, participative methods will boomerang. Issues that do not affect the individuals concerned will not, on the whole, engage their interest'. (Handy).

(c)   The **purpose** of the participation of employees in a decision is made quite **clear** from the outset. 'If employees are consulted to make a **decision**, their views should carry the decision. If, however, they are consulted for **advice**, their views need not necessarily be accepted.'

(d)   The individuals must have the **abilities** and the **information** to join in decision making effectively.

(e)   The supervisor or manager **wishes** for participation from the subordinates, and does not suggest it merely because he/she thinks it is the done thing.

Worldwide social and educational trends show that **people's expectations** have risen above the basic requirement for money. The current demand is for more interesting work and for a say in decision making. These expectations are a basic part of the movement towards greater participation at work.

2.6.3 Empowerment

Competitive pressures have encouraged processes such as **delayering** (cutting out levels of (mainly middle) management) and **downsizing**, leading to **flatter hierarchies**, with more delegation and more decentralisation of authority. All this involves **shifting responsibility** to employees further down the management hierarchy, a process recently given the broad name of **empowerment.**

The argument is that by empowering workers the job will be done more effectively.

2.7 Pay and incentive schemes

2.7.1 Pay as a motivator

Employees need income to live. The size of that income will affect the standard of living, and although they would obviously like to earn more, they are probably more concerned about two other aspects of pay.

- That they should earn **enough**
- That pay should be **fair in comparison** with the pay of others

There is no doubt that pay does have some motivating effect, but it is fundamentally a **hygiene** factor.

2.7.2 Incentive schemes

Pay as a motivator is commonly associated with payment by results or incentive schemes, where a worker's pay is dependent upon output. These are common in production settings but less appropriate for knowledge workers.

All such incentive schemes are based on the principle that people are willing to work harder to obtain more money. However, there are several constraints which can nullify this basic principle.

(a)   The average employee is not generally capable of influencing the timings and control systems used by management.

(b)   Employees remain suspicious that if they achieved high levels of output and earnings then management would **alter the basis of the incentive rates** to reduce future earnings. As a result they **conform to a group output norm.** The need to have the approval of their fellow workers by conforming is more important than the money urge.

(c)   **High taxation rates** would mean that workers do not believe that extra effort produces an adequate increase in pay.

A short-term incentive scheme involves a direct observable link between personal or team efforts and the reward gained. However a long-term scheme such as a profit sharing scheme, has a less personal relevance and a slower pay-back.

2.7.3 Common types of short-term incentive schemes

Individual payment by results, such as a sales bonus over and above a basic wage for achieving set standards of sales over a prescribed period. There is thus a direct link between performance and earnings for each individual so the motivating effect is strong. However, it has its disadvantages.

(a)   The system is complex and expensive to administer.

(b)   If **quantity** of sales is the relevant index, margins may suffer as sales staff negotiate lower prices to make sales.

(c)   Employees may **manipulate** sales, because of fears that high sales will become a new norm, with a reduction in the pay incentive.

(d)   **Employees outside the scheme may resent the wages levels of those inside:** pay differentials may be eroded. It has been known for top sales people to earn more than the Managing Director.

Group payment by results such as team bonus schemes mean that bonus pay for group performance is distributed equally among members. The cohesion of the team may then be built up in an effort to improve collective performance. This type of scheme works well where individual contributions are hard to isolate: the calculation is fairer. However, there are still disadvantages to schemes of this type.

(a)   In addition to the disadvantages of the individual system, the **larger the group, the less direct the link** between individual effort and reward – so the motivating effect may be reduced.

(b)   The system may be **unfair to harder-working individuals** within the group.

(c)   Political conflicts and rivalries **between groups** may work to the detriment of the organisation as a whole.

It has become clear from the experiences of many companies that profit sharing schemes, incentive schemes (productivity bonuses) and joint consultation machinery do not in themselves improve productivity or ease the way for work to get done. Company-wide profit sharing schemes cannot be related directly to extra effort by individuals and are probably a hygiene factor rather than a motivator.

2.7.4 Non-financial incentives

Marketing managers may already have considerable experience at developing non-financial incentives to influence sales teams and the purchase behaviour of customers. Competitions, gifts and prizes can all be utilised as the basis of specific motivation schemes. They create interest, add status for the winner and often have a higher **perceived value** than financial incentives do. Non-financial incentives can be cheaper than their cash equivalent; for example, retail vouchers can be purchased at a discount on face value.

Such incentives must satisfy two conditions.

- They must give recipients a choice.
- They must be valued by recipients.

Offering extra time off or holiday are typically very acceptable and an early finish on a Friday is the sort of incentive which can often be organised fairly informally at team level.

3 Performance appraisal

Exam tip

As well as there being an evaluation and feedback objective in Element 1 of the syllabus, there are similar objectives in Elements 3, 4 and 5. We cover them collectively here. Be aware in the exam that it may be appropriate to include material on evaluation and feedback when you are answering questions on the topics covered in Elements 3, 4 and 5. For *any* plan, there must be some way of monitoring, measuring and evaluating progress and success!

Motivation is concerned with attempts to improve the performance of groups and individuals. We saw in the last section how important regular **feedback** was to the basic concepts of motivation.

Key concept

> **Appraisal** is a systematic approach to providing feedback and for putting praise and criticism in context. It also provides an assessment of current performance against which future improvements can be measured and **training needs** established.

The general purpose of any staff assessment system is to improve the efficiency of the organisation by ensuring that the individuals within it are performing to the best of their ability and developing their potential for improvement. Within this overall objective, staff assessments have several specific purposes.

- To review **performance**, to plan and follow up training and development programmes; and to set targets for future performance

- To review **potential**, as an aid to planning career development by predicting the level and type of work the individual will be capable of in the future

- To increase **motivation by providing feedback**

- To review **salaries**: measuring the extent to which an employee is deserving of a salary increase as compared with peers

3.1 Features of a typical system

- **Identification of criteria for assessment**, perhaps based on job analysis, performance standards and person specifications

- The preparation by the subordinate's manager of an **assessment report**

- An **appraisal interview**, for an exchange of views about the results of the assessment and targets for improvement

- **Review of the assessment by the assessor's own superior**, so that the appraisee does not feel subject to one person's prejudices. Formal appeals may be allowed, if necessary to establish the fairness of the procedure

- The preparation and implementation of **action plans** to achieve changes agreed

- **Follow-up**: monitoring the progress of the action plan

There may not need to be standard forms for appraisal (and elaborate form-filling procedures should be avoided) as long as managers understand the nature and extent of what is required, and are motivated to take it seriously. Most systems, however, provide for assessments to be recorded, and report forms of various lengths and complexity may be designed for standard use, A written record of some form is essential to prevent doubts and uncertainties at a later date.

3.2 Appraisal interview

3.2.1 Approaches to appraisal interviews

(a) The **tell and sell** method. The manager gives details of the assessment to the subordinate and then tries to **gain acceptance** of the evaluation and the improvement plan. This requires unusual human relations skills in order to convey constructive criticism in an acceptable manner, and to motivate appraisees to alter their behaviour.

(b) The **tell and listen** method. The manager gives the assessment and then **invites response**. The manager no longer dominates the interview, and there is greater opportunity for **counselling**. The employee is encouraged to participate in the assessment and the working out of improvement targets and methods. Managers using this method will need to have good listening skills.

(c)   The **problem solving** approach. The manager abandons the role of critic altogether, and becomes a counsellor and helper. The discussion is centred not on the assessment, but on the employee's work problems. The employee is encouraged to think solutions through, and to commit to the recognised need for personal improvement.

Many organisations waste the opportunities for **upward communication** embedded in the appraisal process. In order to get a positive contribution from employees, the appraisal interviewer should ask positive and thought-provoking questions. Here are some examples.

- What parts of your job do you do best?

- Could any changes be made in your job which might result in improved performance?

- Have you any skills, knowledge, or aptitudes which could be made better use of in the organisation?

3.2.2 Follow-up procedures

- Having the report agreed and counter-signed by a more senior manager

- Informing appraisees of the final results of the appraisal, if this has been contentious in the review interview

- Carrying out agreed actions on training, promotions and so on

- Monitoring the appraisee's progress with agreed actions

- Taking necessary steps to help the appraisee for example by guidance, providing feedback or upgrading equipment

3.3 The effectiveness of appraisal

In practice, the system often goes wrong.

(a)   There may be a divergence between the subordinate's and interviewer's perceived and actual needs. A subordinate may **want** praise but **need** constructive criticism. The interviewer may wish to concentrate on criticising, whereas the appraisal could be used to give feedback on management practice.

(b)   Appraisal interviews are often **defensive on the part of the subordinate**, who believes that any criticism will bring sanctions. There may also be some mistrust of the validity of the scheme itself.

(c)   Interviews are also often **defensive on the part of the superior**, who cannot reconcile the role of judge and critic with the constructive intent of the interview. As a result there may be many unresolved issues left at the end.

(d)   The superior might show **conscious or unconscious bias** in the report. Systems without clearly defined standard criteria will be particularly prone to the subjectivity of the assessor's judgements.

(e)   The general level of ratings may vary widely from manager to manager.

(f)   Appraisals may deal with specific problems which should have been dealt with at the time they arose by counselling. Appraisals ought to concentrate on ongoing matters that are important to career development.

(g)   Appraisals may be seen merely as a bureaucratic form-filling exercise or as no more than an annual formality.

3.4 Peer rating

An alternative approach to individual appraisal (which also removes the link between past performance and reward) is **peer rating** in which an individual is judged and counselled by workmates or colleagues. It has been argued that peer rating will be devoid of mistrust and fear of missing promotion and will therefore be more honest and constructive, thus aiding the individual to develop in his job. It may be a useful strategy amongst professionally qualified staff.

3.5 360-degree appraisal

Another variant on appraisal schemes is the 360 degree appraisal. In this case, effectiveness is appraised by all the people with whom the subject has dealings – superiors, subordinates, peers and internal suppliers and customers.

The aim is to get an all-round picture of an employees effectiveness. An employee who achieves some objectives by alienating staff might be taking a short-term view; if this increases staff turnover in the long run. 360-degree appraisal identifies areas where an employee can do better, the employees **superior** cannot always offer the wide perspective necessary.

3.5.1 Advantages of 360-degree feedback

- It **highlights every aspect** of the individual's performance, and allows comparison of the individual's self-assessment with the views of others.

- Feedback tends, overall, to be **balanced**, covering strengths in some areas with weaknesses in others, so it is less discouraging.

- The assessment is based on the normal work environment and circumstances. The feedback is thus felt to **be fairer and more relevant**, making it easier for employees to accept.

360 degree appraisal is a key management tool within the more contemporary organisational approaches such as a boundaryless organisation or a team oriented structure where there may not be tightly drawn job descriptions. Under these circumstances it helps to identify the performance of the individual within the team or any loose *ad hoc* working scenario.

3.5.2 Potential pitfalls of 360-degree feedback

- **Negative emphasis**. Feedback on weaknesses should be balanced by positive feedback on strengths and potential, to encourage the employee to develop.

- **'Flavour of the month approach'**. The technique and its results are seen as interesting but no thought has been given to follow-up action.

- **Lack of confidentiality**. Respondents must be anonymous, or they may fear to tell the truth in an assessment.

- **Poor communication about the purpose of the exercise**. It can be daunting, and employees need to understand that it is not a political exercise, or a rod to beat anyone.

- **Lack of action and support**. The organisation must support the employee in the development suggested by the feedback.

Action Programme 4

'A skill area like "communicating", for example, might be defined as "the ability to express oneself clearly and to listen effectively to others". Typical comments would include "Presents ideas or information in a well-organised manner" (followed by rating scale); or: "Allows you to finish what you have to say".'

Rate **yourself** on the two comments mentioned here, on a scale of 1-10. Get a group of friends, fellow-students, even a tutor or parent, to write down, **anonymously**, on a piece of paper **their** rating for you on the same two comments. Keep them in an envelope, unseen, until you have collected several.

Compare them with your self-rating.

[Key Skills for Marketers: Improving own learning and performance]

4 Training and development

FAST FORWARD

> The main **purpose** of training and development is to raise competence and therefore performance standards. It is also concerned with personal development, helping and motivating employees to fulfil their potential.

Key terms

> **Development** is 'the growth or realisation of a person's ability and potential through the provision of learning and educational experiences'.
>
> **Training** is 'the planned and systematic modification of behaviour through learning events, programmes and instruction which enable individuals to achieve the level of knowledge, skills and competence to carry out their work effectively'.
>
> *(Armstrong)*

The overall purpose of employee development is:

- To ensure the firm meets current and future performance objectives by...
- Continuous improvement of the performance of individuals and teams, and...
- Maximising people's potential for growth (and promotion)

We will discuss development separately in paragraph 4.6 of this chapter.

Question

Self-appraisal

Note down key experiences which have developed your capacity and confidence at work, and the skills you are able to bring to your employer (or indeed a new employer!).

Answer

Few employers throw you in at the deep end – it is far too risky for them! Instead, you might have been given induction training to get acclimatised to the organisation, and you might have been introduced slowly to the job. Ideally, your employer would have planned a programme of tasks of steadily greater complexity and responsibility to allow you to grow into your role(s).

BPP
LEARNING MEDIA

4.1 The contribution of training

FAST FORWARD

Training offers significant **benefits** for both employers and employees – although it is *not* the solution to every work problem!

Modern business is increasingly dynamic, with changes in technology, products, processes and control techniques. The need for planned growth combined with this dynamism mean that a working organisation's competitiveness depends increasingly on the continuous reassessment of training needs and the provision of planned training to meet those needs.

Training offers some significant benefits for the organisation.

Benefit	Comment
Minimise the costs of obtaining the skills the organisation needs	Training supports the business strategy.
Increased productivity, improving performance	Some people suggest that higher levels of training explain the higher productivity of German as opposed to many British manufacturers
Fewer accidents, and better health and safety	EU health and safety directives require a certain level of training.
Less need for detailed supervision	If people are trained they can get on with the job, and managers can concentrate on other things. Training is an aspect of empowerment.
Flexibility	Training ensures that people have the variety of skills needed – multi-skilling is only possible if people are properly trained.
Recruitment and succession planning	Opportunities for training and development attract new recruits and ensure that the organisation has a supply of suitable managerial and technical staff for the future.
Retention	Training and development supports an internal job market (through transfer and promotion). It also helps to satisfy employees' self-development needs internally, without the need to change employers for task variety and challenge.
Change management	Training helps organisations manage change by letting people know why the change is happening and giving them the skills to cope with it.
Corporate culture	(1) Training programmes can be used to build the corporate culture or to direct it in certain ways, by indicating that certain values are espoused. (2) Training programmes can build relationships between staff and managers in different areas of the business
Motivation	Training programmes can increase commitment to the organisation's goals, by satisfying employees' self-actualisation needs (discussed in Part D)

Training can contribute to success, but has its limitations.

(a)   It must be the correct tool for the need: it cannot solve problems caused by faulty organisation, equipment or employee selection.

(b)   Reasons for neglecting training must be overcome: these include cost, inconvenience, apathy and an unrealistic expectation of training in the past.

(c)   Limitations imposed by intelligence, motivation and the psychological restrictions of the learning process must be understood.

4.2 A systematic approach to training

- **Identify areas** where training will be beneficial.

- **Establish learning targets**. The areas where learning is needed should be identified and specific, realistic goals stated, including standards of performance.

- Decide on the **training methods to be used**.

- **Plan a systematic learning and development programme**. This should allow for practice and consolidation.

- **Identify opportunities for broadening the trainee's knowledge and experience** such as involvement in new projects, extending the job or greater responsibility.

- **Take into account the strengths and limitations of the trainee**. A trainee from an academic background may learn best through research-based learning like fact-finding for a committee; whilst those who learn best by doing may profit from project work.

- **Implement** the scheme in full.

- **Exchange feedback**. The manager will want performance information in order to monitor the progress, adjust the learning programme, identify further needs and plan future development.

- **Validate the results** to check that the training works and benefits exceed costs.

4.2.1 Analysis of training needs

Training needs can be identified by considering the **gap** between **job requirements**, as determined by job analysis, job description and so on, and the **ability of the job holder**, as determined by testing or observation and appraisal.

The training department's management should make an initial investigation of the problem. Even if work is not done as well as it could be, training is not necessarily the right answer. We have seen that poor working standards might also be caused by other factors.

4.2.2 Training objectives

If the training department concludes that the provision of training could improve work performance, it must **analyse the work in detail in** order to decide what the **requirements** of a training programme should be. In particular, there should be a **training objective** or **objectives.** These are tangible, observable targets which trainees should be capable of reaching at the end of the course.

The training objectives should be **clear, specific and measurable**, for example: 'at the end of a course a trainee must be able to describe ..., or identify ..., or list ..., or state ..., or distinguish x from y ...'. It is insufficient to state as an objective of a course 'to give trainees a grounding in ...' or 'to give trainees a better appreciation of ...'. These objectives are too woolly, and actual achievements cannot be measured against them.

BPP
LEARNING MEDIA

4.3 Training methods and media

FAST FORWARD

There are a variety of **training methods**. These include:

- Off-the-job education and training
- On-the-job training

4.3.1 Off-the-job training

FAST FORWARD

Off-the-job training minimises risk but does not always support transfer of learning to the job.

Off-the-job training is formal training conducted outside the context of the job itself in special training rooms or off-site facilities.

(a) **Courses** may be run by the organisation's training department or may be provided by external suppliers.

(b) **Computer-based training** involves interactive training via PC. The typing program *Mavis Beacon* is a good example.

(c) **E-learning**

E-learning is computer-based learning through a network of computers or the Internet (rather than stand-alone CD-Rom or software). Learning support is available from online tutors, moderators and discussion groups. This is a major element of the UK government's Lifelong Learning initiative, through the University for Industry (UfI) and 'learndirect'.

(d) **Techniques** used on the course might include lectures and seminars (theory and information) or role plays, case studies and in-tray exercises (to simulate work activities).

4.3.2 On-the-job training

FAST FORWARD

On-the-job training maximises transfer of learning by incorporating it into 'real' work.

On-the-job training utilises real work tasks as learning experiences. Methods of on-the-job training include the following.

(a) **Demonstration/instruction:** show the trainee how to do the job and let them get on with it. It should combine **telling** a person what to do and **showing** them how, using appropriate media. The trainee imitates the instructor, and asks questions.

(b) **Job rotation:** the trainee is given several jobs in succession, to gain experience of a wide range of activities. (Even experienced managers may rotate their jobs, to gain wider experience; this philosophy of job education is commonly applied in the Civil Service, where an employee may expect to move on to another job after a few years.)

(c) **Temporary promotion:** an individual is promoted into his/her superior's position whilst the superior is absent. This gives the individual a chance to experience the demands of a more senior position.

(d) **'Assistant to' positions (or work shadowing):** an employee may be appointed as assistant to a more senior or experienced person, to gain experience of a new or more demanding role.

(e) **Action learning:** managers are brought together as a problem-solving group to discuss a real work issue. An 'advisor' facilitates, and helps members of the group to identify their interpersonal and problem-solving skills are effecting the process.

     (f)   **Committees:** trainees might be included in the membership of committees, in order to obtain an understanding of inter-departmental relationships.

     (g)   **Project work:** work on a project with other people can expose the trainee to other parts of the organisation.

4.4 Evaluating training

The effectiveness of a training scheme may be measured at different levels (*Hamblin*).

Level 1   **Trainees' reactions to the experience**. These are usually measured by post-training feedback forms ('Happy Sheets'), asking whether trainees enjoyed the course, found it relevant etc. This form of monitoring is rather inexact, and it does not allow the training department to measure the results for comparison against the training objective.

Level 2   **Trainee learning** (new skills and knowledge)**:** measuring what the trainees have learned on the course usually by means of a test at the end of it.

Level 3   **Changes in job behaviour following training**: observing work practices and outputs (products, services, documents) to identify post-training differences. This is possible where the purpose of the course was to learn a particular skill, for example. It measures not just what trainees have learned, but how far they have been able to apply their learning to the job.

Level 4   **Impact of training on organisational goals/results:** seeing whether the training scheme has contributed to the overall objectives of the organisation, in terms of quality, productivity, profitability, employee retention and so on. This is a form of monitoring reserved for senior management, and would perhaps be discussed at board level. It is likely to be the main component of a cost-benefit analysis.

Level 5   **Ultimate value**: the impact of training on the wider 'good' of the organisation in terms of stakeholder benefits, greater social responsibility, corporate growth/survival and so on.

 Marketing at Work

We can look at recent trends in marketing training, particularly its interaction with the rest of the organisation. This reflects a change in emphasis in the role of marketing in many companies, away from product management and towards anticipating and supplying customer needs.

Companies are supplying increased marketing training to operating departments in topics such as brand awareness and are giving marketing departments training which consists of two parts. The first part focuses on normal technicalities such as research and promotional techniques. The second gives marketers a wider perspective on the rest of the company, focusing on issues such as systems, distribution, customer service and financial management. Motivating operating departments to become more innovative and centred on the customer is seen as being very important.

 Action Programme 5

Devise a training programme for a new recruit who will be doing a job similar to yours.

4.5 Development

FAST FORWARD

Development includes a range of learning activities and experiences (not just training) to enhance employees' or managers' portfolio of competence, experience and capability, with a view to personal, professional or career progression.

Development is a 'wider' approach to fulfilling an individual's potential than just training. Development may include training, but may also include a range of learning experiences whereby employees are:

(a) Given **work experience** of increasing challenge and responsibility, which will enable them to other more senior jobs in due course of time

(b) Given **guidance, support and counselling** to help them to formulate personal and career development goals

(c) Given suitable **education and training** to develop their skills and knowledge

(d) Helped to **plan their future** and identify opportunities open to them in the organisation

4.5.1 Approaches to development

Approaches to development include the following.

Approach	Comment
Management development	'An attempt to improve managerial effectiveness through a planned and deliberate learning process' (*Mumford*). This may include the development of management/leadership skills (or competences), management education (such as MBA programmes) and planned experience of different functions, positions and work settings, in preparation for increasing managerial responsibility.
Career development	Individuals plan career paths. The trend for delayered organisations has reduced opportunities for upward progression: opportunities may be planned for sideways/lateral transfers, secondments to project groups, short external secondments and so on, to offer new opportunities.
Professional development	Professional bodies offer structured programmes of continuing professional development (CPD). The aim is to ensure that professional standards are maintained and enhanced through educational, development and training self-managed by the individual. A CPD approach is based on the belief that a professional qualification should be the basis for a career lifetime of development *and* adherence to a professional code of ethics and standards.
Personal development	Businesses are increasingly offering employees wider-ranging development opportunities, rather than focusing on skills required in the current job. Personal development creates more rounded, competent employees who may contribute more innovatively and flexibly to the organisation's future needs. It may also help to foster employee job satisfaction, commitment and loyalty.

Exam tip

You may need to drill down for detail on a single topic (such as motivation, say) or you may be invited to survey a range of people-management issues. In the June 2006 exam, for example, you were asked to identify a range of issues in performance monitoring, skill development and motivation (in the specific context of a multi-organisational temporary project team). In December 2006, it was issues of recruitment, induction and training (in the specific context of a completely new staff for a start-up hair salon). Note that in neither case could you get away with 'generic' answers: in the hair salon, for example, it was pointless to talk about induction as 'introducing the recruit to other staff members' – because they were all new recruits! Similarly, you couldn't talk about training needs analysis without mentioning specific training needs (eg hair care skills, customer service skills, health and safety, use of equipment/chemicals and so on). Use theoretical frameworks to *structure* your answer – add 'depth' – but continually give practical, scenario-related *examples* of each point.

5 Counselling

FAST FORWARD

In addition to appraisal people often require help. Advice is often unrequested, although it might be to do with a specific problem. **Counselling** is a more formal, long-term process with a specific objective.

To **advise** is to propose solutions to someone else's problems. To **counsel** is to assist someone through the process of finding his or her own solutions. The counselling approach involves a number of considerations.

- **Discerning the need** for counselling
- **Ensuring privacy and time**
- **Encouraging openness** and ensuring confidentiality
- **Using specific examples** to illustrate points discussed and avoiding abstract comments
- Emphasis on **constructive interaction** including personal rapport and trust
- Sensitivity to the subject's beliefs and values
- Guidance in **evolving the subject's own solutions** rather than giving advice
- **Avoiding arguments** but instead getting the subject to discuss reasons for disagreement
- **Supporting the solution** devised
- **Monitoring the progress of the solution**

You will note that **counselling** requires a systematic approach, with careful planning and a range of interpersonal skills being brought into play. Particularly important are listening skills. It requires the support of the organisation, to train counsellors, to back the solutions reached and to allow time for the counselling and monitoring period. Some organisations formalise this in a counselling programme, with qualified counsellors, while others prefer to support managers in particular counselling situations.

Advising is a much more common and on-going process. Because, unlike counselling, advising is not essentially a co-operative process, the **effectiveness of advice depends on the willingness of the recipient to accept suggestions**. It also depends on the **soundness of the advice itself**: unlike counselling, advising has very little beneficial effect **in itself**.

A counselling approach is now often applied to interviewing situations previously regarded as purely informative or judgmental, for example, disciplinary and grievance interviews, and appraisal interviews.

An open door management policy or supervisory style may encourage employees to come forward with a wide range of work and even personal problems which require counselling. Some organisations may have a welfare officer to provide counselling.

BPP
LEARNING MEDIA

5.1 The role of counselling in organisations

Effective counselling is not merely a matter of pastoral care for individuals, but is very much in the organisation's interests.

(a) Appropriate use of counselling tools can prevent underperformance, reduce labour turnover and absenteeism and increase commitment from employees.

(b) Workplace counselling recognises that the organisation may be contributing to the employees' problems and therefore it provides an opportunity to reassess organisational policy and practice.

Action Programme 6

How do you react when people try to give you advice at work? Have you ever been counselled? If so, did you feel differently about that experience?

Who (if anyone) is responsible for formal counselling in your company: a specialist or line manager? Is the availability of counselling clearly communicated to staff, and in a way that will encourage them to come forward? Do people go to informal counsellors among their colleagues instead: if so, to whom and why?

6 Discipline and grievance

FAST FORWARD

Discipline has the same end as **motivation**: to secure a range of desired behaviour from members of the organisation.

Key term

Discipline can be considered as: 'a condition in an enterprise in which there is orderliness, in which the members of the enterprise behave sensibly and conduct themselves according to the standards of acceptable behaviour as related to the goals of the organisation'.

One approach makes a distinction between methods of maintaining sensible conduct and orderliness which are essentially co-operative, and those based on warnings, threats and punishments.

(a) **Positive** (or constructive) **discipline** relates to procedures, systems and equipment in the work place which have been designed specifically so that the employee has **no option** but to act in the desired manner to complete a task safely and successfully. A machine may, for example, shut off automatically if its safety guard is not in place.

(b) **Negative discipline** is then the promise of **sanctions** designed to make people choose to behave in a desirable way. Disciplinary action may be punitive (punishing an offence), deterrent (warning people not to behave in that way) or reformative (calling attention to the nature of the offence, so that it will not happen again).

The best discipline is **self discipline**. Even before they start to work, most mature people accept the idea that following instructions and fair rules of conduct are normal responsibilities that are part of any job. Most team members can therefore be counted on to exercise self discipline.

Exam tip

Do not confuse 'discipline' with 'punishment'. There is more to it than simply punishing people for 'doing things wrong'. More generally, be aware of the importance of encouraging discipline, and using fair and systematic disciplinary procedures, so that discipline is as 'positive' as possible.

6.1 Types of disciplinary situations

There are many types of disciplinary situations which require attention by the manager. Internally, the most frequently occurring are these.

- Excessive absenteeism
- Poor timekeeping
- Defective and/or inadequate work performance
- Poor attitudes which influence the work of others or reflect on the image of the firm
- Breaking rules regarding rest periods and other time schedules
- Improper personal appearance
- Breaking safety rules
- Other violations of rules, regulations and procedures
- Open insubordination such as the refusal to carry out a work assignment.

Managers might be confronted with disciplinary problems stemming from employee behaviour *off* the job. These may be an excessive drinking problem, the use of drugs or some form of narcotics, or involvement in some form of law breaking activity. In such circumstances, whenever an employee's off-the-job conduct has an impact upon performance on the job, the manager must be prepared to deal with such a problem within the scope of the disciplinary process.

6.2 Disciplinary action

In the UK, the ACAS Code of Practice recommends the following criteria for an effective disciplinary procedure.

…good disciplinary procedures should:

- be in writing

- specify to whom they apply

- be non-discriminatory

- provide for matters to be dealt with without undue delay

- provide for proceedings, witness statements and records to be kept confidential

- indicate the disciplinary actions which may be taken

- specify the levels of management which have the authority to take the various forms of disciplinary action

- provide for workers to be informed of the complaints against them and where possible all relevant evidence before any hearing

- provide workers with an opportunity to state their case before decisions are reached

- provide workers with the right to be accompanied

- ensure that, except for gross misconduct, no worker is dismissed for a first breach of discipline

- ensure that disciplinary action is not taken until the case has been carefully investigated

- ensure that workers are given an explanation for any penalty imposed

- provide a right of appeal – normally to a more senior manager – and specify the procedure to be followed

---

BPP LEARNING MEDIA

6.3 Progressive discipline

FAST FORWARD

Progressive discipline includes the following stages.

- Informal talk
- Oral warning
- Written/official warning
- Lay-off or suspension
- Demotion
- Dismissal

Many minor cases of poor performance or misconduct are best dealt with by **informal advice, coaching or counselling**. An *informal oral warning* may be issued. None of this forms part of the formal disciplinary procedure, but workers should be informed clearly what is expected and what action will be taken if they fail to improve.

When the facts of the case have been established, it may be decided that *formal disciplinary* action is needed. The Code of Practice divides this into three stages. These are usually thought of as consecutive, reflecting a *progressive response*. However, it may be appropriate to miss out one of the earlier stages when there have been serious infringements.

6.3.1 Warnings

A *first formal warning* could be either oral or written depending on the seriousness of the case.

(a) An **oral warning** should include the reason for issuing it, notice that it constitutes the first step of the disciplinary procedure and details of the right of appeal. A note of the warning should be kept on file but disregarded after a specified period, such as 6 months.

(b) A **first written warning** is appropriate in more serious cases. It should inform the worker of the improvement required and state that a final written warning may be considered if there is no satisfactory improvement. A copy of the first written warning should be kept on file but disregarded after a specified period, such as 12 months.

If an earlier warning is still current and there is no satisfactory improvement, a *final written warning* may be appropriate.

6.3.2 Disciplinary sanctions

The final stage in the disciplinary process is the imposition of sanctions.

(a) **Suspension without pay**

This course of action would be next in order if the employee has committed repeated offences and previous steps were of no avail. Disciplinary lay-offs usually extend over several days or weeks. Some employees may not be very impressed with oral or written warnings, but they will find a disciplinary lay-off without pay a rude awakening. This penalty is only available if it is provided for in the contract of employment.

(b) **Demotion**

The employee is set back to a lower position and salary. This is not regarded as an effective solution, as it affects the employee's morale and motivation.

(c) **Dismissal**

Dismissal is a drastic form of disciplinary action, and should be reserved for the most serious offences. For the organisation, it involves waste of a labour resource, the expense of training a new employee, and disruption caused by changing the make-up of the work team. There also may be damage to the morale of the group.

Exam tip

Think of the disciplinary procedure as a progressive, six stage process:

1   Informal talk (not included in a formal ACAS procedure)
2   Oral warning
3   Written warning
4   Suspension
5   Demotion
5   Dismissal

This was examined in December 2004 and June 2005.

Question   Disciplinary policy

How (a) accessible and (b) clear are the rules and policies of your organisation/office: do people really know what they are and are not supposed to do? Have a look at the rule book or procedures manual in your office. How easy is it to see – or did you get referred elsewhere? is the rule book well-indexed and cross-referenced, and in language that all employees will understand?

How (a) accessible and (b) clear are the disciplinary procedures in your office? Are the employees' rights of investigation and appeal clearly set out, with ACAS guidelines? Who is responsible for discipline?

6.4 Disciplinary interviews

Following information-gathering and investigation of alleged infringements, a disciplinary interview may be conducted as follows.

Step 1   The manager will explain the purpose of the interview.

Step 2   The charges against the employee will be delivered, clearly, unambiguously and without personal emotion.

Step 3   The organisation's expectations with regard to future behaviour/performance should be made clear.

Step 4   The employee should be given the opportunity to comment, explain, justify or deny. If he is to approach the following stage of the interview in a positive way, he must not be made to feel 'hounded' or hard done by.

Step 5   Specific, measurable, performance-related and realistic improvement targets should be jointly agreed.

Step 6   Measures to help the employee (such as training, mentoring or counselling) should be agreed, where necessary.

Step 7   The manager should explain the reasons behind any penalties imposed on the employee. There should be a clear warning of the consequences of failure to meet improvement targets.

Step 8   The manager should explain the organisation's appeals procedures: if the employee feels he has been unfairly treated, there should be a right of appeal to a higher manager.

Step 9   Once it has been established that the employee understands all the above, the manager should summarise the proceedings briefly.

Step 10   Records of the interview will be kept for the employee's personnel file, and for the formal follow-up review and any further action necessary.

BPP
LEARNING MEDIA

6.5 Grievance

Key concept

> A **grievance** occurs when an individual feels that (s)he is being wrongly or unfairly treated by a colleague or supervisor and wishes to assert his or her rights.

FAST FORWARD

> **Grievance procedures** embody the employee's right to appeal against unfair or otherwise prejudicial conduct or conditions that affect him and his work.

Formal grievance procedures are usually based on appeals to progressively higher levels of authority, if necessary, until the problem is fairly resolved.

The dynamics of a **grievance interview** are broadly similar to a disciplinary interview, except that it is the **subordinate** who primarily wants a positive result from it.

Prior to the interview, the manager should have some idea of the complaint and its possible source. The meeting itself can then proceed through a number of stages.

(a)   **Exploration**. What is the problem: the background, the facts, the causes, manifest and hidden? At this stage, the manager should simply try to gather as much information as possible, without attempting to suggest solutions or interpretations.

(b)   **Consideration**. The manager should do three things.

- Check the facts

- Analyse the causes – the problem about which the complaint has been made may be only a symptom

- Evaluate options for responding to the complaint, and the implication of any response made

It may be that information can be given to clear up a misunderstanding, or the employee will, having aired the matter, withdraw the complaint. However, the meeting may have to be **adjourned** while the manager gets extra information and considers extra options.

(c)   **Reply**. The manager, having reached and reviewed conclusions, reconvenes the meeting to convey and if necessary justify a decision, and to hear counter-arguments and appeals. The outcome (agreed or disagreed) should be recorded in writing.

Grievance procedures should be seen as an employee's right. To this end, managers should be given formal training in the grievance procedures of their organisation, and the reasons for having them. Managers should be persuaded that the grievance procedures are beneficial for the organisation and are not a threat to themselves (since many grievances arise out of disputes between subordinates and managers).

6.6 Exit interviews

Employees may resign for any number of reasons, personal or occupational. Some or all of these reasons may well be a reflection on the structure, management style, culture or personnel policies of the organisation itself. When an employee announces the intention to leave, verbally and/or by letter, it is important for the manager to find the real reasons why they are leaving, in an exit interview. This may lead to a review of existing policies on pay, training, promotion, the work environment, the quality and style of supervision and so on.

Chapter Roundup

- **Motivation** is an essential ingredient in ensuring that the individual and the team perform efficiently and effectively.

- **Organisational behaviour theory** has devoted considerable attention to understanding motivation because it is believed improvements here can generate competitive advantage.

- Maslow's **hierarchy of needs** is a commonly referred to motivation theory. It seems to have intuitive appeal.

- **Herzberg's** work was important because it encourages managers to recognise the **hygiene** factors, which can cause dissatisfaction if they are absent, but are unlikely to generate positive motivation.

- Herzberg also highlighted the motivational opportunities from **job enlargement**, **enrichment** and **rotation**, all of which are quite commonly used for both motivation and for training and development.

- **Drucker** identified that motivation of individuals starts with putting the **right people in the right jobs**.

- A wide variety of options are available to motivate the individual and the team. The important thing is to develop **motivational strategies** which suit both the situation and the individual. Schemes should be simple to administer, easy to understand and perceived to be fair, and any incentives should be clear.

- **Participation** and **feedback** are key factors in motivating a team. **Appraisal** can help by providing a formal system of feedback which is also a useful benchmark for monitoring performance changes. Most appraisal systems require a manager to appraise a subordinate, but alternatives can be suggested.

- The main **purpose** of training and development is to raise competence and therefore performance standards. It is also concerned with personal development, helping and motivating employees to fulfil their potential.

- **Training** offers significant **benefits** for both employers and employees – although it is *not* the solution to every work problem!

- There are a variety of **training methods**. These include:
  - Off-the-job education and training
  - On-the-job training

- **Off-the-job training** minimises risk but does not always support transfer of learning to the job.

- **On-the-job training** maximises transfer of learning by incorporating it into 'real' work.

- **Development** includes a range of learning activities and experiences (not just training) to enhance employees' or managers' portfolio of competence, experience and capability, with a view to personal, professional or career progression.

- In addition to appraisal people often require help. Advice is often unrequested, although it might be to do with a specific problem. **Counselling** is a more formal, long-term process with a specific objective.

- **Discipline** has the same end as **motivation**: to secure a range of desired behaviour from members of the organisation.

- **Progressive discipline** includes the following stages.
  - Informal talk
  - Oral warning
  - Written/official warning
  - Lay-off or suspension
  - Demotion
  - Dismissal

- **Grievance procedures** embody the employee's right to appeal against unfair or otherwise prejudicial conduct or conditions that affect him and his work.

Quick Quiz

1   What is motivation and why is it important?

2   What are the levels in Maslow's hierarchy?

3   Briefly describe Herzberg's 'two-factor' theory.

4   Drucker suggested that, in order to persuade employees to accept responsibility, four ingredients are needed. What are they?

5   What are the benefits of non-financial incentives?

6   What is the purpose of appraisal?

7   What is the difference between advice and counselling?

8   What is the heart of discipline?

Answers to Quick Quiz

1   Motivation is the spur that produces visible behaviour: managers must promote motivation towards action that furthers the aims of the organisation.

2

3   Job satisfaction is caused by the presence of motivator factors; hygiene or maintenance factors merely prevent dissatisfaction when they are present. They cannot create satisfaction.

4   • Careful placement of people in jobs
    • High standards of performance in the job
    • Providing the worker with the information needed to control personal performance
    • Opportunities for participation in decisions

5   They can have a higher perceived value than a financial incentive while actually being cheaper in many cases

6   To review performance, salary and potential and to increase motivation by increasing feedback

7   To advise is to propose solutions. To counsel is to assist with the finding of solutions

8   The promotion of order and good behaviour by the enforcement of acceptable standards of conduct

Action Programme Review

1   As you work through the chapter, relate your motivating factors to the levels described by Maslow and Herzberg's two factor theory.

2   Hygiene factors, which can cause dissatisfaction at work

- Company policy and administration
- Salary
- The quality of supervision
- Interpersonal relations
- Working conditions
- Job security

3   Typical features of enrichment are challenge; a whole job rather than part of one; responsibility for results; trust in small matters such as access to stores and making small purchases; and the power to take decisions, even if only small ones.

4   Your own research.

5   Don't forget administrative items like where the lavatories are, nor health and safety issues. Allow time for the recruit to ask questions and make some allowance for checking that the training has achieved its objectives. You did start with objectives, didn't you?

6   How easily you found out this information will tell you something about your organisation. If you have difficulty answering these self-reflective questions, try to develop your awareness so that you can assess your reactions to this type of situation in the future.

Now try Question 4 at the end of the Study Text

5

Managing change

Syllabus content – knowledge and skill requirements

- The sources and nature of change affecting organisations and the techniques available for managing change (1.7)

Introduction

The world is constantly changing and there regularly appear new factors in the environment that managers have to cope with. They offer challenges to all marketing managers, who might have to implement change.

In Section 1 we identify the **types of changes that might be necessary** and where change comes from – the environment, technology and so forth. Organisations therefore have to innovate to grow or even to survive (and we discuss this in Section 2). Organisations have to respond to these changes by changing themselves – a change in organisation structure, discussed in Section 3, is sometimes needed.

Change inevitably affects established ways of working which individuals have grown used to and feel comfortable with. The ease with which change is implemented in part depends on **how individuals respond to it**. Their possible reactions are discussed in Section 4.

As a marketing manager, you may be responsible for making changes yourself, or implementing changes which your superiors have decided. The **broad outlines** of what a manager has to do, including a brief model of how to implement a change process, are discussed in Section 5.

Finally, as a marketer, you may find yourself involved in internal communications and **internal marketing**, and you can use sound marketing principles, as elaborated in Section 6, to communicate to the people affected by change. Sometimes the changes you have to market will affect the company's whole way of doing things, at other times it will be a change in a specific aspect of operations, maybe even the company's system of internal communications.

1 The need for organisational change

FAST FORWARD

Change is a constant challenge and requirement for business and its managers. Those who fail to respond to change will fail to survive.

The business environment is constantly changing and businesses must respond if they are to survive and prosper. Environmental change thus drives internal change.

- **Changes in the market** include competitors' responses, changes in customer requirements and changes in promotional methods.
- **Technological change** can introduce new product possibilities and more efficient ways of working.
- **Social, legal and political developments** can extend or constrain the acceptability of products and business practices.

The organisation must respond by instituting its own **internal changes**.

- New or developed **products or services**
- Changed **working practices**
- Entry into **new markets** or withdrawal from old ones
- New **organisational structures and philosophies**

There is a distinction between **change**, which is gradual and small and **transformation**, which is change on a significant scale: Figure 5.1

Figure 5.1: Transformational change

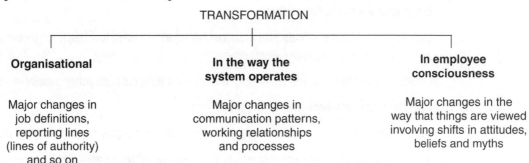

2 Innovation, growth and decline

FAST FORWARD

Innovation and **growth** are key aspects of contemporary business activity.

Key concept

Change management is the process of planning and implementing change within organisations.

2.1 Innovation

Innovation is a term that is often associated with change. Innovation is something completely new. Some changes might result in going back to something that was done before.

The rate of change might be fast or slow, depending on the organisation's circumstances, and the environment in which it operates. Organisations which operate in a rapidly changing environment need to be highly innovative and responsive to change if they are to survive and grow.

2.1.1 The value of innovation

The chief object of being innovative is to ensure that organisation's **survival** and **success** in a **changing world**. It may develop prompt and imaginative **solutions** to problems (through use of project teams), and generate greater **confidence** inside and outside the organisation in its ability to cope with change.

2.1.2 Encouraging innovation

To encourage innovation management should aim to create a more outward looking organisation which actively seeks new products, markets, processes and ways to improve productivity.

 Marketing at Work

Team creativity

What have we discovered about how to promote creativity and innovation in teams at work? Here are six tips.

1   **Recognise that creativity and innovation are not easy**

Conflict is a common characteristic of innovation, observable principally in resistance to change.

Innovation, by definition, represents a threat to the status quo. For a team to implement innovation successfully, its members must manage conflict, with the attendant emotional pain and difficulty. They must overcome resistance to change. They must persist in ensuring the successful implementation of their innovative proposal. And they must accept that, after all that, the innovation may turn out to have been a mistake.

2   **Pick creative people with wide experience and knowledge, put them in a supportive environment and challenge them**

Creativity requires individuals with creative characteristics who feel free from threat and pressure and who work in a supportive environment.

Learning and innovation will occur only when team members trust other members' intentions.

3   **Give the team members interesting jobs**

Jobs that stimulate individual innovation are likely to score highly on the following characteristics.

- **Skill variety**. The degree to which a job requires different activities in order for the work to be done, and the degree to which the full range of skills and talents of the person working in the role is used.

- **Task identity**. The extent to which a job is not a small part of a larger task.

- **Task significance**. The job's impact upon other people within the organisation or in the world at large.

- **Level of autonomy**. The amount of discretion vested in employees.

- **Task feedback**. People who receive feedback on their performance are more likely to become aware of the performance gaps. This also implies that they have clear job objectives.

4   **Emphasise team creativity, not only productivity, and make them stop work**

One of the implications of our findings is that organisations need to encourage teams by focusing on creativity and innovation as important performance outcomes, rather than only on productivity.

5   **Encourage constructive conflict and dissent and treasure team errors**

Dissent can stimulate team innovation when it occurs in a co-operative context. It allows individuals in small teams to change the views of the majority by being consistent and persistent.

Learning about the causes of errors as a team – and then devising innovations to prevent future errors – were possible only in those teams that discussed them.

6   **Does the organisation inspire the team?**

Organisations can create an ethos within which creativity is either nurtured and blooms into innovation or is starved of support.

Across the world, companies use a range of schemes to support team innovation. The US-based firm 3M, which produces Post-it Notes and adhesive tape, has 30,000 employees. Its technical staff are encouraged to spend 15 per cent of their time 'bootlegging' – working on pet projects that they hope will become new products for the company. They are given the time to pursue these ideas and, if necessary, they can apply for money to buy equipment or hire extra help.

For an idea to be taken further at 3M, it must win the backing of one member of the board. Once this occurs, an inter-disciplinary venture team of researchers, engineers, marketing people and accountants is set up to push the idea further. If a director is not willing to support the idea, it returns to the drawing board. But teams are not penalised for failure.

Michael West, *People Management,* 8 March 2001

BPP LEARNING MEDIA

2.1.3 Creativity

Creative ideas can come from anywhere and at any time and management should try to provide an organisation structure in which innovative ideas are encouraged.

(a) Creative ideas must then be rationally analysed to decide whether they provide a viable commercial proposition.

(b) A system of organisation must exist whereby a viable creative idea is converted into action. In marketing terms constructive new product development frameworks would need to be established.

Management can also create conditions in which risk taking, creativity and enthusiasm for change is **impossible**.

1	Regard any new idea from below with suspicion.
2	Insist that people who need your approval first go through several other levels of management.
3	Get departments/individuals to challenge each other's proposals.
4	Express criticism freely, withhold praise, instil job insecurity.
5	Treat identification of problems as signs of failure.
6	Control everything carefully. Count everything in sight – frequently.
7	Make decisions in secret, and spring them on people.
8	Do not hand out information to managers freely.
9	Get lower-level managers to implement your threatening decisions.
10	Above all, never forget that you, the higher-ups, already know everything important about the business.

Action Programme 1

Fishpaste Ltd is a business making adhesives. One of the employees, during the course of some research into adhesives, discovers a dryish glue that will not quite stick properly. It holds things in place, but two pieces of paper stuck together with this glue can be easily separated without damage to either. What do you do with the tub of glue and the employee?

2.2 Growth

An organisation will usually seek to grow by increasing its **range of products** and **markets**, its **sales turnover** and its **profits**. Companies might seek to grow **organically**, by developing their own internal resources, or else to grow by merger and acquisition. Many companies seek growth through a combination of the two strategies.

2.2.1 Innovation and growth

If a company operates in a market with a good prospect for growth, it can grow **organically** either by exploiting existing product-market opportunities or by diversifying. However, **because existing products have a finite life, a strategy of organic growth must include plans for new product development**.

2.2.2 Innovation and stability

Stability calls for innovation too. An organisation cannot rely on its existing products and markets for ever. An organisation which wants to maintain its sales and profits must also, therefore, develop new or improved products, or new markets, to replace the old ones in decline. Product development involves R&D costs and, often, heavy capital expenditure to set up a new product or new market opinion.

An innovation strategy should take a broad view of what sort of innovations should be sought. A product might be completely new, or just a different quality version of an existing product. A new product is not necessarily much different from existing products; rather, the essential characteristic is that it should be distinguishable from its predecessors **in the eyes of its customers**.

The car industry provides a very good example of the different types of product innovation. Some years ago, the hatchback was a fairly major innovation. Modifications to existing models are made regularly, to keep consumers interested and wanting to buy.

2.2.3 Leaders and followers

Some firms **lead the way** with technological innovation, and actively seek new products for their markets. Other firms **react to what the leaders do**. Either approach can be a successful strategy for innovation, but later entry is a more successful approach than leadership, because the leader will make mistakes that the followers can learn from and avoid. Research shows that the eventual leaders in high-technology industries usually enter several years after the pioneers. The failure rate for pioneers is almost 50%.

2.2.4 New product strategies

Innovation can mean creating new markets as well as new products, creating extra demand from existing customers or creating new demand from new customers.

2.2.5 Motives for growth

There are various motives for organisational growth

(a)   Organisations attempt to realise their ultimate **objective**. This may involve providing **a more complete service** to customers, perhaps by expanding geographically or by vertical integration.

(b)   Executives might like the **challenge and adventure** of a new gamble. Boredom with the existing situation might prompt changes.

(c)   The **status, power and job security** of individuals may be enhanced by growth.

(d)   Executive **salaries** are likely to rise as a result of increasing **turnover** (rather than by increasing profits).

(e)   Growth may lead to **profit maximisation**.

(f)   Growth may lead to **economies of scale**.

(g)   Large organisations tend to be more **stable** than small ones. The desire for stability may lead to growth.

2.3 The management of contraction

Change might involve a contraction of the organisation and its business, rather than growth. **Divestment** means getting rid of something. In strategic planning terms, it means selling off a part of a firm's operations, or pulling out of certain product market areas.

BPP *)))*
LEARNING MEDIA

One reason for divestment is economic recession. A more common reason is to **rationalise** a business as a result of a strategic appraisal. A company might decide to concentrate on its **core businesses** and sell off fringe activities to **sell off subsidiaries** where performance is poor, or where growth prospects are not good.

2.3.1 Advantages of divestment

(a)   By selling off parts of the business that are not performing as well as others, a firm can concentrate on areas of its business that provide better results.

(b)   Selling off a subsidiary will bring in funds that can be invested in other projects.

If a firm goes into a product market area and finds that it has made a mistake or that, after some years of good returns, the market is declining, it makes good commercial sense to pull out. There is no point carrying on with an operation just through reluctance to let things go. However, divestments will probably mean significant redundancies among staff, which might meet strong resistance from employees and their trade unions.

Action Programme 2

In what way is your business changing? How is this change being managed?

3 Changing organisation structure

FAST FORWARD

Customer led businesses are often driven by changes in their **corporate environment**.

Changes in what an organisation **does** could lead to a need for **restructuring**.

However, this is not the only reason why a new structure might be needed.

(a)   **Changes in the environment** such as **greater competition** might create pressures for:

- Streamlining, enhanced flexibility and speed of response including thinning out of layers of middle managers, organisational gatekeepers etc, ie disintermediation

- Improved cost efficiency including reductions in personnel

(b)   **Diversification into new product market areas** might have caused the structure to become fragmented. There is a need to make it more integrated or joined-up.

(c)   **Growth** of staff numbers creates problems of extended management hierarchies and poor communication.

(d)   **New technology** often involves new operational processes and hence the structure might need to adapt and facilitate efficient operation of processes.

(e)   The organisation might be making a **transition** from a production or product focus into a **market or customer focus**. There may be a change from a more hierarchical and bureaucratic structure to a structure more based on teamwork and fewer boundaries.

(f)   **Greater managerial transparency**. The chief executive prefers to **look through the organisation** without layers of management blocking or distorting the view.

Change might be triggered either by financial results and/or market forces or by a recognition of the potential for business improvement, ie:

(a)   Financial results are declining or showing unacceptable levels of growth

(b)   Financial results are currently acceptable but there is obvious scope for improvement if changes are implemented. The situation is assessed as not bad, but could be better.

Sometimes, change is in response to internal operational difficulties such as:

(a)   Conflict and dysfunctional relations between departments.

(b)   Excessive bureaucracy, internal controls and paperwork and there is a need for streamlining. Alternatively, there may be a lack of controls, slippages and excessive waste requiring tighter systems.

(c)   Too few or too many managers/staff.

(d)   Over-complex or over-formal communications channels resulting in ineffective communication eg e-mailing somebody quite close by rather than just speaking to them.

(e)   Lack of innovation.

(f)   Need to introduce **fresh blood** into the organisation. Some companies set target staff turnover rates so that staff turnover is not too high so as to disrupt performance nor too low so as to cause stagnation and complacency.

A major restructuring is not always necessary every time changes take place in an organisation's circumstances. However, contemporary organisations often work on a continuous restructuring basis, responding to continuous changes in the marketplace. By making small ongoing changes in structure, the organisation avoids costly and disruptive major changes. Continuous restructuring also provides the organisation with the opportunity to promote talented staff and allow underperforming staff to leave. Also, ambitious staff are less likely to find themselves in **dead-end jobs**.

3.1 The stages in a programme of organisational change

FAST FORWARD

Key steps in the **change management process** include:

–   Problem identification
–   Business case building
–   Consultation and consensus building
–   Impact analysis
–   Planning
–   Roll out
–   Monitoring
–   Success measurement
–   Success celebration

3.1.1 Basic stages

(a)   The first step in the process is to **acknowledge** that there is a **problem** and that change is necessary. In practice, it is often psychologically difficult for management to admit that something is wrong in the organisation which they have been responsible for running.

(b)   Having **'grasped the nettle'** for change it is necessary to:

   •   Identify the **problem areas** and the **issues** involved

   •   Make an honest estimate of how much it will **cost** to make the change and also estimate **how long** it will take to implement

- Identify any **gaps in resources** (managers, knowledge, skills etc) available to utilise in the change process and afterwards

- Define the **benefits** that will be derived from the change

- Articulate the **criteria** or **benchmarks** that will be used to **measure the success** of the implementation

In practice, planning is vital. Lack of planning is likely to lead to a lack of focus as well as a lack of direction.

(c) **Consult and communicate internally**. These are perennial principles of **good management**. Consultation helps to ensure that the **right problem** is actually **solved**. The process of consultation itself helps to **build consensus** and **commitment** to the solution. As always it is better to overcommunciate than undercommunicate. Where there is a **communication vacuum**, inaccurate and potentially damaging **rumours** are likely to flourish! Management must clearly define its **messages** and maintain control of the **communication agenda**.

(d) Consideration should be given to the way information is to be gathered. It is usually difficult to make good quality decisions without having good quality information. Information may be gathered by various approaches.

- Group or departmental meetings
- Small interactive workshops
- One-to-one discussions/interviews
- Internal focus group meetings
- Use of questionnaires
- A mixture of the above

The information should be properly summarised and fed back to staff so that it can be seen that they have not wasted their time and effort in providing input to the business. It should then be explained how the input will be used to develop a business solution for managing change. This is likely to be considered in conjunction with the market research information discussed below.

(e) **External communication and research**. In practice, this is likely to be the original driver or trigger for change. For example, market research might have indicated that customers feel their queries were being bounced around the company and that the people handling the queries lacked product knowledge and service skills. Such information will be a key input to the reorganisation and change plans.

(f) In formulating the reorganisation plans, an **impact analysis** should be drawn up to identify the implications in various key areas.

- Personnel **headcount**
- Revision of employment **contracts**
- Skills deficiencies and **training** required
- **Operations process** improvements
- **Logistics** and **facilities**; office space, location, IT facilities, travelling for key people
- **Motivation** and morale
- **Career development** opportunities
- Financial **budget** and **cash flow**
- Employee **attitudes** and **service style** improvements
- **Customer perceptions** and **experience**

(g)   **Roll out**. In practice, there are a variety of ways change may be implemented. These depend on factors such as corporate culture, the attitudes of management towards change and the skills and experience of the managers involved in delivering change. Some of the approaches are more sophisticated than others and some are more effective in the long term than others.

- **Big bang approach**. This usually entails a **one-off launch**, often accompanied by **meetings** and **brochures**. The underlying idea is to create some **excitement** and enthusiasm. This approach was popular in practice in the 1980s but suffered from its **lack of ability to 'achieve buy-in'**, ie staff felt it was an attempt to **hard sell** changes in which they had not adequately participated in developing

- **Phased implementation**. This is a response to the weaknesses of the big bang approach. Hence, the changes are released in **smaller** more **manageable chunks**. The **programme** is usually **trailed** or **communicated in advance** so that staff know what is coming from around the corner

- **Fait accompli**. This is a development made more convenient by the increased use of e-mail and entails mailshotting change initiatives electronically to peoples' desks. The weakness of releasing a *fait accompli* is there is no way of gauging the **recipient's reaction**. A variation is to send a brochure accompanied by a letter from the chief executive or chairman through the postal system. The weaknesses of this approach is that it has to compete for attention with 'junk mail' a person receives, it intrudes on the employee's non-work time, and perhaps most importantly, there is no way of ensuring that the messages are properly **understood** and have been **taken on board**.

- **Continuous interactive change**. This is a contemporary approach that epitomises the idea that **change is ongoing** and happens on a day-to-day basis. The company is sensitive to **signals from the market and its customers**; these are discussed as part of the ongoing day-to-day management activities of a business. This approach possesses the **responsiveness** and **flexibility** to identify and implement any necessary changes on an ongoing basis and as part of its **normal business activity**. Change is continuous rather than being one-off special events.

(h)   **Monitoring**. The process of implementation of change does not cease at the end of the launch phase. Traditionally, it was necessary to monitor or 'police' the actioning of the new procedures. The more contemporary approach is to treat change as part of an **ongoing process** and manage the new situation in the **normal course of business**.

(i)   **Celebration of success**. In practice, this is an important consideration. Change usually involves a lot of disruption of work and extra effort by employees. It is wise and clever for management to say **'thank you'** and psychologically reinforce a **winning mentality**.

The above process may be summarised as follows: Figure 5.2.

Figure 5.2: Change management process

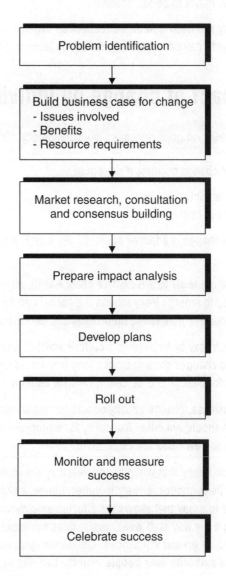

3.2 External consultants

3.2.1 Benefits of using external consultants

- They will use specialist analytical techniques and knowledge.

- They bring experience of similar problems in other organisations.

- They can resolve internal conflicts by acting as an independent referee.

- They are neutrals, outside departmental politics.

- They are not tied by status or rank, and can discuss problems freely at all levels within the organisation.

- They can look at problems objectively and don't have to worry about the consequences of their recommendations for their career prospects.

3.2.2 Disadvantages of using consultants

- They might be seen as mere agents of top management.

- They might try to impose a standard solution on a unique problem.

BPP LEARNING MEDIA

- They might to be too academic.

- They will need time to learn about an organisation themselves. The client organisation will have to pay consultancy fees for this learning process.

4 The impact of change on individuals

The **impact of change** on personnel are a key consideration in change management.

People are wary of change because it can cause:

- Uncertainty
- Loss of control

However, because change is a fact of business life, a task of management is to manage these impacts on their staff.

Potential problems are likely to arise where change is thrust on people as a **surprise**. If people do not know what is going to emerge from around the corner and hit them, they inevitably become **insecure**. In consequence, employees may **loose their focus** and performance may suffer.

A sensible approach may be to develop a **culture** which is **change oriented**; there is an **openness** and staff can see impending changes coming from a long way off. Ideally, the staff themselves will spot the need and opportunities for change and be **champions for change**.

In a successful business, change usually occurs to take advantage of **opportunities** to improve and grow the business. This should not entail insecurity for employees but should instead provide **opportunities for job advancement** as **new roles** are established.

It is a psychological reality that when people feel they are **losing control** of the situation, they begin to feel **anxious** and their performance is likely to suffer. Hence, a skilled professional manager is more likely to implement change in a way that allows the affected employees to have **some say in the outcome**. Often, it may be that doing it the way staff would prefer does not make the outcome more inefficient, but perhaps might instead produce greater efficiencies. Good managers tend to be able to balance the need to exert their **own sense of authority over people** with the benefits of allowing employees to feel they have some **ownership** of the **new processes and procedures**.

An internal marketing approach may be used. Managers should put themselves into employees' shoes and look at change from their perspective. Changes which appear relatively minor from a strategic vantage point can have considerable **implications at the operational level**.

As we will see later in this chapter when we consider developing **internal marketing plans** to help promote change, there is a price to change. Individuals must perceive they will benefit to an extent which outweighs the cost. Once managers have stood in the employees' shoes they will have a greater appreciation of the cost of change to them and so be able to present plans and strategies in a way which emphasises **relevant benefits**.

Action Programme 3

Think about the following situations and how might you feel as the employee. What is the possible cost to you?

(a)   As manager of a retail branch you are faced with a change of opening times to take advantage of Sunday trading.

(b) You have been assistant manager in the marketing department for four years. The existing manager is retiring in three months.

- You have been offered her job
- A new younger manager has been appointed from outside the company.

(c) A reorganisation of sales territories means that you are now only looking after 20% of your old customers – 80% of your territory is new.

Managers need to think about how individuals in their teams will respond to change. Reaction may vary widely.

- **Acceptance**, whether enthusiastic espousal, co-operation, grudging co-operation or acquiescence.

- **Indifference**, usually where the change does not directly affect the individual: apathy, lack of interest and inaction

- **Passive resistance** including refusal to learn, working to rule, pleas of ignorance and delayed judgement

- **Active resistance** such as go-slows, deliberate errors, sabotage, absenteeism or strikes.

Adaptability is a trait which can be considered in the selection process, and perhaps developed through training and encouraged by the culture and organisational systems. **Job rotation** can give individuals experience of change. For example, Hewlett Packard move their trainees around the various functions of the business so as to create cross-functional individuals who then can be easily drafted into cross-functional teams when required.

When change is significant or particularly distressing, managers need to take account of the fact that it will affect individuals in the team differently. Monitoring individuals for evidence of stress caused by change should be a routine part of the feedback and control process.

Where stress is apparent, counselling and coping strategies should be provided. Individuals should **not** be made to feel they have failed but given every support to help them through. It will be a lot cheaper to work with valued staff members than to replace them.

Generally, a significant element of how employees adapt to change may well depend on the skills which management demonstrates in managing change. Managers might induce an atmosphere of stress and uncertainty or inspire enthusiasm, hope and confidence.

4.1 Change and the manager

Managers often suffer from a degree of divided loyalty when implementing change. Like the team, the manager may resent or be scared of the implications of change, but is forced to implement it. It is hard to deliver something you have no confidence in, so a manager should try to talk through concerns about the change with his or her own line managers.

Generally, where the organisation itself is change oriented, change is a part of day-to-day organisational life and the impact of change is less dramatic. Ideally, in an **open organic organisation**, employees share information and ideas and **everyone is responsible** for and participates in **continuously changing** the organisation.

5 The role of the manager in facilitating change

FAST FORWARD

Change management is an ongoing process. Ideally, the **manager** should build a change oriented organisation where change takes effect on a day-to-day basis.

5.1 Building a change oriented organisation

A business that does not change will **stagnate** and fall behind its competitors. A manager should ensure that the company's **culture, processes, systems** and **practices** are geared for **sensing external changes** and responding quickly and effectively.

The organisation's **work practices** should be designed to keep in touch with developments in the **marketplace** and has processes to ensure that appropriate **responses** are actioned.

- Processes to ensure that there is **adequate market research** carried out

- Review of **media**; magazines, newspaper ads, TV ads etc.

- **Regular meetings** to discuss what is going on in the marketplace, what **competitors** are doing and developments in **consumer behaviour**.

5.2 Looking after the team

During any discussions and planning for change, the manager is responsible for identifying the **implications for the team**, and where necessary negotiating for adjustments to the plan. The manager should also recognise the implications of change on **individuals** and identify coping strategies which will help smooth the process of change.

The manager must consider the most effective time, place and manner to present the change to the team. This should emphasise the positive aspects of change, whilst acknowledging the costs. By involving the team in the decision making about how best to implement the change, the manager can make the change feel less threatening and such participation can be a positive motivator in the acceptance of change.

5.3 Rebuilding morale and motivation

Marketing departments are often the first to suffer the effects of cost-cutting if a company falls on hard times. (This may not be the wisest strategy from the company's point of view, of course.)

This may result in a cut-back in marketing plans or even redundancy, and this can be quite traumatic for a team. Other changes can also hurt morale. A number of stages characterise this process.

Shock → Denial → Frustration → Depression → Experimentation → Acceptance → Integration

Exam tip

Questions on the management of change may ask you to produce a report for senior management, describing the problems associated with change, including the effects on employees, and how they may be overcome.

The scenario will place you in a practical marketing context, so the changes taking place in the company are likely to be concerned, for example, with encouraging a more customer focused approach, or (as in December 2006) with expansion of a business into new locations and markets. In such examples, there will be 'soft' change management issues (covered by the theory) such as the need for a different management style or culture, and the need to overcome staff resistance. There will also be 'hard' issues – logistical challenges, structural changes, need for new technology and systems and so on – and these provide a great opportunity to relate your answer to the specifics of the scenario. Use the theory but nail it firmly to the question setting.

Team leaders and managers can help the process of change. *Marketing Success* (May 2002) suggests a handy checklist, that you might use in exam questions.

- **Inform** – let people know what is happening and why
- **Include** – make sure everyone knows their role
- **Investigate feedback** – let people know how well they are doing
- **Identify** – team members may have ideas for improvements
- **Inspire** – lead by example
- **Implement** – try to encourage new ways of implementing useful ideas.

6 The internal marketing of plans and change

FAST FORWARD

Internal marketing is a useful tool in helping change management.

Managers have come to recognise a number of things about change.

- It is inevitable.
- It is easy to **plan** to change.
- It is often difficult to **implement** change as people may potentially resist.

Recognising that success of a plan depends on the level of skill applied to the implementation, increasing attention and support is being given to those managers charged with implementation. Amongst the tools and techniques available is **internal marketing**. In this context, we mean the use of a **marketing approach to help in the presentation of change to those it affects**.

The following, as a recipe for change management, suggests a marketing approach.

Suggested approach	Comment
Tell	The people: clearly, realistically, openly
Sell	The pressures which make change necessary and desirable
	The vision of successful, realistically attainable change
Evolve	The people's attitudes, ideas, capacity to learn new ways
Involve	The people where possible in planning implementation

Marketing can play an important part in the **selling** activity. It should also be aware of how the company can benefit by matching corporate needs with individual needs. Remember that in practical terms, salesmanship skills usually entail asking the potential customer a lot of open ended questions with the objective of tailoring the sales offering accordingly and thereby sealing the deal.

6.1 Principles of internal marketing

(a)   A plan's implementation itself needs planning.

(b)   Staff needs must be identified and the benefits of the plan must be agreed.

(c)   It is sensible to identify those employees who carry influence in the organisation. They can help the change management process by being **champions for charge**.

(d)   Plans need **packaging and promoting**. Resources may be needed to achieve this.

(e)   Managers might utilise **informal networks of communication** within the organisation. In practice, it is usually insufficient to rely wholly on the formal networks which are the result of the prevailing organisation structure.

Internal marketing plans should be based on research to identify the relevant decision making unit and their needs and concerns.

The **internal marketing mix** can be described in terms of the 4Ps.

(a)   **Product**: this is the plan or change which management wants to implement.

(b)   **Price**: there will be a perceived price tag. The costs and benefits to staff must be clearly assessed. As with any product, there may need to be negotiation, but managers must be clear what the costs and benefits are. For example, a move to a new office block may entail a longer journey to work, but it may offer improved working conditions. A change in the sales commission package may depress potential earnings in exchange for a higher average salary overall; employees must feel that the change is to their benefit.

(c)   **Place**: in marketing, place represents when and where the product is available. The method and timing of the announcement of plans can have a dramatic effect on the way they are received.

(d)   **Promotion**: poor communication is probably the biggest single internal company problem. The grapevine tends to work quickly and not always very accurately. Therefore, when plans are announced they are often met by hostility and antagonism. Improving the communication of plans is an **essential** step to ensuring that they are owned and supported by those who have to implement them. Communication should be two way and meetings and discussions to take account of staff's views and thoughts at an early stage will help implementation later. It is always better to over-communicate than to under-communicate.

Internal marketing is about the **manner** in which plans and change are presented to those they affect. The right manner is important in creating a motivated and successful team at whatever level the plan is being implemented.

6.2 The internal marketing plan

Just as the normal processes of marketing outside the organisation are driven by a marketing plan, so to should the process of internal marketing be the subject of an **internal marketing plan**. Clearly, you must be familiar with marketing plans generally (the BPP Study Text *Marketing Planning* will help you here), but for convenience we will outline the essentials of an internal marketing plan.

We commence by considering where we are now and where we would like to be; that is, what we consider to be our **objectives**. These must be stated as clearly as possible For example, if we are embarking on a change programme, our overall objective might be to achieve a culture change which will support a new commitment to customer service.

When we are sure of our aims we may consider our **strategy**. This may be assisted by establishing a number of secondary aims, given in terms of outcomes. For instance, we might set a specific objective to

BPP
LEARNING MEDIA

communicate and consult with every employee by a certain date to deliver the messages about the need for change and to discuss the implications for all concerned; customers, company and employees. This may involve setting up meetings or workshops.

The determination of the targets for our communication effort will be assisted by **segmenting the market**, just as in external marketing. When *British Aerospace* embarked on its major culture change strategy, it identified senior managers who had to be convinced of the need for the new approach. This approach will also make it easier to identify the most effective communication techniques.

In the context of organisational change, **training** will be of particular importance. Training policy is usually a Human Resources responsibility, but if the Marketing Department is in overall charge of change management, they will have to work closely with the HR specialists. In most contemporary organisations, change management is most likely to be a multi-departmental effort.

The final element of the internal marketing plan is **control**. A timetable should be established, announced and the progress of the various activities monitored and action taken so that the milestones are met. A **double loop** approach may be necessary. This means that feedback in the control system is not just used to control outcomes; it may indicate that the **plan itself** is unrealistic and needs amendment. The plan itself should be flexible and organic.

6.3 Evaluating change management

The effectiveness of change management can be evaluated in a number of ways.

(a) Has a **sound business case** been made supporting the proposed change?

(b) Have the **financial** and **non-financial benefits** to be derived from the change been fully defined?

(c) Has a detailed and **professionally prepared plan** been developed?

(d) Has proper consultation and consensus building been conducted? Are the people who have to ultimately do the work *on side* and fully committed to the success of the charges?

(e) Are the **change objectives** against which **success** will be **measured** been clearly identified? Is the measurement **scale** sufficiently precise and informative?

(f) The behaviour of people in the organisation: **has the change programme resulted in the behavioural changes planned** (for example higher output, better teamwork, greater customer focus).

(g) The **reaction of the people** in the organisation: has the change programme been implemented without arousing hostility or fear with their symptoms of absenteeism, labour turnover and conflict? [see (d) above]

6.3.1 Problems in change management

(a) Failure to identify the **need** to change (typically a failure of sensitivity to change in the environment). The business lacks the tools and processes to be able to detect the need for change.

(b) Failure to identify the **objectives** of change, so that the wrong areas are addressed.

(c) Failure to identify a suitable **strategy** to achieve the objectives. The result is that change takes place, but not in the relevant direction. New technology, for example, is sometimes regarded as a universal solution to organisational problems, but it will not necessarily improve productivity or profitability if the product/market strategy or the workforce is the real problem. For example, a railway network may spend a lot of money trying to improve

 123

its equipment to prevent train delays when what may be needed is to improve its customer communications and people handling skills.

In general, managers often opt for expensive technology based solutions when a change of employee attitudes and an improvement in skills might be more appropriate.

(d)   Failure to commit **sufficient resources** to the strategy.

(e)   Failure to identify the **appropriate method** of implementing change, for the situation and the people involved (typically, failing to anticipate resistance to change).

(f)   Failure to implement the change in a way that **secures acceptance**, because of the **leadership style** of the person managing the change (typically, **failure to consult** and involve employees).

The first four of the above reasons for failure are to do with **strategic planning** generally: they are potential shortcomings in any planning exercise. The peculiar difficulties of introducing change, however, are human factors. When implementing plans or changes, managers must never lose sight of the fact that their success depends on people.

In practice, managers are often tempted to implement change quickly without due consultation and consensus building. The risk of a 'tell' or 'sell' approach is that staff may not understand the new processes and are not really committed to their successful implementation. As a result, a lot of time and resource has to be devoted to 'policing' the new procedures and dealing with people who do not put their hearts into carrying them out.

Ideally, the change management process should be skilfully managed so the company derives the efficiencies of having staff who are motivated, eager and enthusiastic to deliver the changes.

7 Skills of the change agent

In addition to organisational and cultural support for change, the success of any change programme (and indeed, any marketing management initiative) depends on **skill**: in this case, the skills of the manager or change agent.

Crainer has emphasised seven key skill areas for managing change.

(a)   Managing conflict (while stimulating diversity and expression of concerns)

(b)   Interpersonal skills

(c)   Project management skills (complex planning, control and stakeholder management)

(d)   Leadership *and* flexibility (giving clear direction, but being willing to respond to contingencies and input)

(e)   Managing processes (not just the 'content' of change)

(f)   Managing strategy (aligning change objectives to corporate/business goals)

(g)   Managing personal development (aim learning and growth)

Chapter Roundup

- **Change** is a constant challenge and requirement for business and its managers. Those who fail to respond to change will fail to survive.

- **Innovation** and **growth** are key aspects of contemporary business activity.

- Customer-led businesses are often driven by changes in its **corporate environment**.

- Key steps in the **change management process** include:

    - Problem identification
    - Business case building
    - Consultation and consensus building
    - Impact analysis
    - Planning
    - Roll out
    - Monitoring
    - Success measurement
    - Success celebration

- The **impact of change** on personnel are a key consideration in change management.

- Change management is an ongoing process. Ideally, the **manager** should build a change oriented organisation where change takes effect on a day-to-day basis.

- **Internal marketing** is a useful tool in helping change management.

Quick Quiz

1   Distinguish between change and transformation

2   Does an organisation have to innovate in stable conditions?

3   Why is late entry usually a more successful strategy then leading the way?

4   What is the role of the champion of change?

5   What are the advantages of involving external consultants in the process of organisational development?

6   Why might an individual resist change?

7   Why might the manager find it particularly difficult to implement change?

8   What is the seven point plan for implementing change?

9   What is the dual responsibility of the manager in the process of change?

10 What should managers consider under the headings of the internal marketing mix, when preparing a plan for change?

Answers to Quick Quiz

1   Transformation is much more significant, all-embracing and extensive than change, which can be on quite a small scale

2   Yes. Even in stable conditions products and brands will decline. Also, new ideas will inevitably emerge from competitors

3   The followers learn from the leaders' mistakes

4   To promote and organise change

5   Specialist knowledge, techniques and experience; independence; access to all levels; objectivity

6   Insecurity; fear; uncertainty; social disruption

7   Divided motivations: to the organisation's plan on the one hand and innate conservatism on the other

8   • Determine need or desire for change
     • Develop possible strategies
     • Assess likely reactions
     • Select a strategy
     • Set a timetable
     • Communicate the plan
     • Implement

9   Efficient change management and protection of the interests of the team

10   Product: the change
     Price: costs and benefits to staff
     Place: method and timing of announcements
     Promotion: early, frequent and sincere communication of plans and discussion of problems

Action Programme Review

1   You could have simply ignored the product, on the grounds that a glue which does not stick things together is not a glue that is worth making or selling. This is one response.

     Another response would be to discuss with the employee, and other employees, the possible use for such a glue. In this case, you might come up with a revolutionary idea – the 'Post-It' note. Then you reward the employee.

2   You can relate this activity back to the exercise you did in Chapter 1.

3   (a)   There may be staff (possibly including yourself) who object to this change. You will certainly have to be present on at least some Sundays, assuming you have a deputy with whom you can share the work. You will also have the task of dealing with staff's objections and motivating them to accept the change, because that is part of your management role.

     (b)   (i)   Your responsibility, status, pay and prospects will all increase. You may have to work longer hours and deal with more demanding tasks. How do you feel about this?

            (ii)   All the considerations above apply, but in reverse. Also, you may experience frustration and disappointment if you thought you were ready for the job.

     (c)   You are faced with a major change in your work role and duties. Instead of building on existing successful relationships, you have to start from scratch. However, if your territory was a particularly difficult one, you may be better off.

Now try Question 5 at the end of the Study Text

International influences on management

6

Syllabus content – knowledge and skill requirements

- The key challenges of managing marketing teams in a multinational or multicultural context (1.3)

Introduction

The aim of this part of the syllabus is for you to acquire an appreciation of some of the problems of managing internationally and their implications for management practice.

Section 1 deals with the trade background to international management and the idea of the global company. This is not an entirely satisfactory theory, as the section discusses, but it helps to put the rest of the chapter in context.

Section 2 introduces the international environment and its complexity compared with the much simpler business environment in a single country. The social and cultural aspects of international business are particularly relevant for management and so we devote section 3 to these topics.

Section 4 focuses our consideration of culture on the organisation and cultural influences on management style.

Section 5 considers a number of practical issues including structure and control systems, and Section 6 discusses the special features of human resource management in an international setting.

Exam tip

As with change management, there are 'soft' aspects to international management (cultural differences etc) and 'hard' aspects (different time zones, exchange rates, logistical infrastructure and so on). Don't forget to consider both. As with any environmental analysis, the 'PEST' or 'PESTLE' framework may provide a clear way of structuring your answer giving you a checklist of environmental issues/factors to consider – in relation to the specifics of the scenario!

Don't panic: questions will generally allow you to situate scenarios in a country of your choice – so just ensure that you are familiar with the marketing environment in your own country, and perhaps one other (with discussable differences!).

1 Globalisation

FAST FORWARD

The processes of **globalisation** have massively expanded international trade, but there are still areas of protection. In particular, regional trading groups have emerged that are to some extent opposed to one another.

Since 1945, the volume of world trade has increased. This has meant a proliferation of suppliers exporting to, or trading in, a wider variety of places. However, the existence of global markets should not be taken for granted in terms of all products and services, or indeed in all territories.

(a) Some **services** are still subject to managed trade (for example, some countries prohibit firms from other countries from selling insurance). Trade in services has been liberalised under the auspices of the World Trade Organisation.

(b) **Immigration.** There is unlikely ever to be a global market for labour, given the disparity in skills between different countries, and restrictions on immigration.

(c) The market for some goods is much more globalised than for others.

(i) Upmarket luxury goods may not be required or afforded by people in developing nations.

(ii) Some goods can be sold almost anywhere, but to limited degrees. Television sets are consumer durables in some countries, but still luxury or relatively expensive items in other ones.

(iii) Other goods are needed almost everywhere. In oil a truly global industry exists in both production (e.g. North Sea, Venezuela, Russia, Azerbaijan, Gulf states) and consumption (any country using cars and buses, not to mention those with chemical industries based on oil).

1.1 Global production

Global production implies that a firm's production planning is considered on a global scale.

(a) **Global manufacture**. A company can **manufacture** components for a product in a number of different countries. China is becoming the workshop of the world.

(b) **Global sourcing**. Sub-components may be purchased from countries overseas. As the case example below demonstrates, companies can exploit the comparative advantages of different countries.

The extreme form of global production has been referred to by *Kenichi Ohmae* (1990) as **insiderisation**. In other words, in each of your markets you build up a production and distribution organisation from scratch or in conjunction with local suppliers, even though there may be few variants to the product from market to market.

While more and more companies are competing in the world market place, most of them tend to focus on the developed markets of North America, Europe and Japan. A vast majority (86%) of the world's population resides in countries where GDP is less than $10,000 per head. Such countries offer tremendous marketing opportunities if the offering is presented correctly.

Going international can add to profitability. Integrating the supply chain across several countries can lead to considerable cost savings. Increased levels of customer service allied with these cost savings can lead to a dominant market position. This needs an organisational culture that is aware of the supply chain and customer service whatever the country (or countries) of operation.

1.1.1 Other factors encouraging the globalisation of world trade

(a) **Financial factors** such as Third world debt. Often the lenders require the initiation of economic reforms as a condition of the loan.

(b) **Country/continent** alliances, such as that between the UK and USA, which fosters trade and other phenomena such as tourism.

(c) **Legal factors** such as patents and trade marks, which encourage the development of technology and design.

(d) **Markets** trading in international commodities. Commodities are not physically exchanged, only the rights to ownership. A buyer can, thanks to efficient systems of trading and modern communications, buy a commodity in its country of origin for delivery to a specific port. There is also a market in **futures**, enabling buyers to avoid the effect of price changes by buying for future delivery at a set price. This smoothes the process of international trade and lowers risk.

1.2 Do global firms really exist?

Some writers believe that there is an increasing number of 'stateless corporations', whose activities transcend national boundaries, and whose personnel come from any country.

This theory looks attractive on the surface, particularly in a relatively open economy like that of the UK, which is host to a number of multinational corporations and has attracted a fair degree of inward investment.

Do these global or stateless corporations really exist?

(a) Most multinationals, other than those based in small nations, have **less than half of their employees abroad.**

(b) **Ownership and control** of multinationals remain **restricted**. This is partly because of the way in which capital markets are structured. Few so-called global companies are quoted on more than two stock markets.

(c) **Top management** is rarely as multinational as the firm's activities. This is particularly true of Japanese companies. A foreigner is rarely seen on the Tokyo-based board of a Japanese multinational.

(d) **National residence and status** is important for tax reasons. Boundary-less corporations are not recognised as such by lawyers or tax officials.

(e) The bulk of a multinational's **research and development** is generally done in the home country. Indeed *M Porter* (1996) says that the home market is important for product development in the information it gives about consumers.

(f) Where capital is limited, 'global' companies stick to the home market rather than developing overseas ones.

(g) Finally, **profits** from a global company must be **remitted** somewhere.

However, it may be the case that firms will become more globally orientated if they are able to specialise and if it becomes easier to trade.

2 International environmental influences

FAST FORWARD

The social, legal, economic, political and technical **(SLEPT) business environment** differs widely across the globe. **Demographic differences** are particularly important for business.

Managers responsible for international operations must be aware of the environmental differences they will encounter. In particular, the cultural aspect of the social environment is vitally important.

Action Programme 1

You should be aware of the PEST, SLEPT, PESTLE or STEEPLE framework for analysing factors in the external environment of an organisation. In its fullest form (STEEPLE), it includes:

- Socio-cultural
- Technological
- Economic
- Environmental (ecological)
- Political
- Legal
- Ethical factors

Before reading on, see if you can list some factors under each heading that would pose challenges in international marketing and managerial contexts.

2.1 Law and politics

The **system of courts and the legal profession** may be unfamiliar. The very existence of the **rule of law** and an **independent judiciary** may be in doubt. Rules relating to corporate status, property, the regulation of business, and financial reporting may all be very different. There may be significant **political risk**. The government may be unstable; its ideology may be unsympathetic to Western business methods or it may have poor relations with the rest of the world. In many countries there is a need for political contacts and extensive lobbying before business can be done.

2.2 Economy

Economic factors affecting international businesses:

- Is there **growth** or is the economy stagnating?
- Is the **exchange rate** stable?
- How does the **interest rate** compare with other countries? Is it stable?
- What is the rate of **inflation**? What is the government's policy? Is it realistic?
- What are the existing **price structures** in the target markets?

Various forms of **protectionism** hamper international trade. Formal tariff barriers have been much reduced and are now policed by the World Trade Organisation, but non-tariff barriers are still a problem. These all protect the home producer and include licences, quotas, size and weight regulations, environmental protection standards and hidden domestic subsidies.

2.3 Regional trading groups

Currently, a number of **regional trading arrangements** exist, as well as global trading arrangements. These regional trading groups take three forms: Figure 6.1.

- Free trade areas
- Common markets
- Customs unions

Figure 6.1: Regional trading arrangements

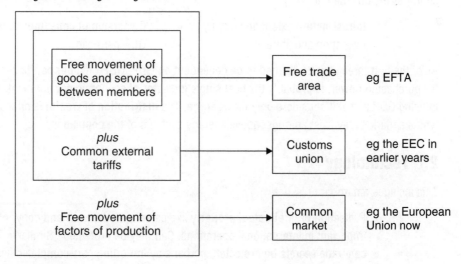

2.3.1 Free trade areas

Members in these arrangements agree to lower barriers to trade amongst themselves. They enable free movement of **goods** and **services,** but not always the factors of production.

2.3.2 Customs unions

Customs unions provide the advantages of free trade areas and agree a common policy on tariff and non-tariff barriers to **external countries.** Internally they attempt to harmonise tariffs, taxes and duties amongst members.

2.4 Economic unions/common markets

In effect the members become one for economic purposes. There is free movement of the factors of production. The EU has economic union as an aim, although not all members, including the UK, necessarily see this goal as desirable. The EU has a 'rich' market of over 300 million people and could provide a counterweight to countries such as the USA and Japan.

The major regional trade organisations are as follows.

(a)   North American Free Trade Agreement (NAFTA) – US, Canada and Mexico.

(b)   European Free Trade Association (EFTA) – Norway, Switzerland, Iceland, Liechtenstein.

(c)   European Union (EU) – Ireland, Britain, France, Germany, Italy, Spain, Portugal, Finland, Sweden, Denmark, Luxembourg, Belgium, the Netherlands, Austria, Greece. A number of other countries have applied to join.

2.5 Economic development

Economic factors affect both the demand and the ability to acquire goods and services. Even in lesser developed countries (see below) there often exists a wealthy elite who provide a significant demand for sophisticated consumer goods.

Countries generally have larger agricultural sectors in the earlier stages of economic development (for example India and Africa). As the economy develops, the manufacturing sector increases.

Commonly, economists and marketers categorise countries into five broad types. Each type then exhibits a fairly consistent pattern of demand for goods and services. Commonly used factors in classifying countries include the following.

- **Infrastructure** extent and quality
- Education and literacy
- Ownership of **consumer durables**
- GDP per head

All of the first three may be claimed to be dependent on GDP. GDP on a **per capita** basis, suitably adjusted for purchasing power, is probably the best single indicator of economic development. However, a danger in using GDP is that it considers only the **average**. The **distribution of wealth** is critical in poor countries, where a market may exist amongst above average sections of the population.

2.6 Technology

This includes a number of issues.

(a)   Protection of **intellectual property** like patents, trademarks and copyright is particularly important in international operations. Can they be protected? Similarly, in manufacturing, can trade secrets be protected, perhaps by importing part-completed assemblies? Sometimes technology transfer to local businesses is required before permission can be obtained to do business.

(b)   If advanced technology is involved, it will be necessary to consider local **standards of education and technical infrastructure**.

(c)   Reliance on **'e' methods** for marketing communications and product delivery (eg information or music downloads) depends on potentially differing levels of infrastructure

BPP LEARNING MEDIA

(eg availability of broadband Internet connections) and adoption (eg mobile phone ownership).

(d) Ease of **communication** with overseas markets (eg via email and e-commerce) creating potential **fulfilment/delivery** problems (given distance and infrastructure).

Action Programme 2

You are required to have up-to-date awareness of 'e'-marketing and e-commerce tools, by browsing the marketing press and relevant websites.

(a) Compile a list of examples of e-marketing and the use of ICT tools (mobile telecom, Internet, interactive and virtual media and so on).

(b) For each example, consider whether it would 'translate' to a different overseas country of your choice. What further information might you require to decide on its feasibility? What might the challenges be?

3 Social and cultural considerations

FAST FORWARD

Cultural factors influence the ways of doing business, as well as management style and methods.

3.1 Demographic issues in overseas markets

Key concept

Demography is the study of populations. It deals largely in statistics such as birth rates, death rates, incidence of disease and distribution densities.

The **purpose** of studying a country's population and trends within it is as follows.

(a) People create a demand for goods and services.

(b) If economic growth exceeds population growth you would expect to see enhanced **standards** of living. **Quality of life** measures would also include pollution measures, life expectancy rates, infant mortality and so on.

(c) Population is a source of labour, one of the **factors of production.**

(d) Population creates demands on the physical environment and its resources, a source of increased international political concern. (the Kyoto conference in Japan at the end of 1997 agreed reductions in carbon dioxide).

Demographic factors will affect both management in general and marketing in particular. A local workforce can only be recruited if the labour is available; **working practices** may have to conform to local norms. Demand for many categories of consumer goods is heavily influenced by social factors like **fashion and status**. The age structure, geographic distribution and class system of the target population will partly determine what can be achieved.

The higher rate of population growth in **less-developed countries** compared with developed countries has arisen due to a continuing high birth rate and a declining death rate although some populations are being threatened by the HIV virus (for example in South Africa). Social changes (eg attitudes to large families) have not accompanied medical advances imported from developed societies. People are living longer.

(a)   **Growing populations**

- Require fast economic growth just to maintain living standards
- Result in overcrowding on land and/or cities and a decline in the quality of life
- Require more resources for capital investment
- Stimulate investment (as the market size is increasing)
- Lead to enhanced labour mobility

(b)   **Falling populations**

- Require more productive techniques to maintain output
- Make some scale economies harder to achieve
- Put a greater burden on a decreasing number of young people
- Exhibit changing consumption patterns

3.1.1 Age structure and distribution

We should now discuss the **age structure** of the population.

(a)   The effect of greater life expectancy is that a larger proportion of the population will be senior citizens and unlikely to be working. These offer significant opportunities to international marketers. The UK, Europe and Japan all face an ageing population.

(b)   The proportion of old people is lower in developing countries. In Egypt and Iran, over half the population is below the age of 30.

3.1.2 Geographic distribution

Where we live is another important feature of demography. The above arguments have taken the individual country as a homogenous unit. In practice, however this is a vast oversimplification. A country may suffer the problems of overpopulation in some areas and underpopulation in others.

Demography also deals with the effect of concentration and dispersal of population in particular areas. Industrialisation has traditionally meant a shift from the countryside to the towns and can be seen in the explosive growth of **mega-cities** in Latin America (Mexico City, Sao Paolo in Brazil), and Asia (eg Bombay, Shanghai, Jakarta).

3.1.3 Gender

There is often an imbalance in the population between the numbers of men and the numbers of women. This has arisen for a number of reasons.

(a)   Males tend to die younger.

(b)   In some countries male children are more valued than female children, and female children are more likely to suffer infanticide.

The **work roles** played by males and females in different societies vary, even within the industrial world. In different societies, women and men have distinct purchasing and social powers. This is a key cultural issue.

3.1.4 Ethnicity

Only a few societies are homogenous, with populations of one culture and ethnic background. Japan is an example, although the population includes descendants of Koreans. On the other hand, societies like the USA and the UK have populations drawn from a variety of different areas.

3.1.5 Buying patterns

Buying behaviour is an important aspect of marketing. Many factors influence the buying decisions of individuals and households. Demography and the **class structure** (the distribution of wealth and power in a society) are relevant in that they can be both **behavioural determinants** and **inhibitors**.

(a)   **Behavioural determinants** encourage people to buy a product or service. The individual's personality, culture, social class, and the importance of the purchase decision (eg a necessity such as food or water, or a luxury) can predispose a person to purchase something.

(b)   **Inhibitors** are factors, such as the individual's income, which will make the person less likely to purchase something.

Socio-economic status can be related to buying patterns in a number of ways, both in the amount people have to spend and what they spend it on. It affects both the quantity of goods and services supplied, and the proportion of their income that households spend on goods and services.

 Marketing at Work

Demographics

(a)   India has a large peasantry and an industrial proletariat, but its huge population size means that its wealthy middle class is bigger than the populations of many developed countries. With import liberalisation and economic deregulation, this should be an attractive segment for marketers.

(b)   The level of inequality in society also influences its attractiveness to the marketer. Brazil has the greatest degree of inequality in the world. Japan, famously, has low inequality.

   (i)   In societies of high inequality, wealth is concentrated, hence the buying power of the majority is limited. This might suggest more success in selling luxury goods.

   (ii)   Where equality is higher, there may be a higher demand for mass market goods as more people will have access to them.

3.1.6 Family structure

The role of the family and family groupings varies from society to society.

(a)   In societies such as India, the **caste system** still exists and family structures can be part of this wider network.

(b)   **Extended families** are still strong in many countries, especially where the family is to assume most of the burden of looking after the elderly: many countries do not have a welfare state.

(c)   Family size varies.

Marketers have often used the model of the **family life cycle** model purchase and consumption patterns. You will have encountered it before.

- Bachelor – single people
- Newly-weds – household and childcare products
- Full nest
- Empty-nest: children have left home
- Solitary survivor

This model may not hold.

(a)   Quite often, households contain three generations (grand-parents, parents, children).

(b)   People leave home later in life. In countries such as Italy and Spain it is common for adult children to live at home.

(c)   Purchase and consumption decisions vary.

3.2 Culture

Culture is inherent within the group and taken for granted. A national culture will be very difficult to change; if change occurs it will take place very slowly. National culture influences the perceptions and behaviour of consumers as well as employees and managers. We should beware of interpreting marketing research, in particular, according to our own cultural norms.

Language is an important aspect of culture. While English is more and more the international language of business, there are many areas where it is not commonly understood, sometimes as a matter of local pride. Mistaken use of a foreign language will undermine otherwise competent marketing operations.

The national way of doing things pervades society. Business practice is part of the structure of society and therefore subject to cultural influences.

4 Culture and the organisation

We have discussed culture in a society and as a factor of a firm's environment and market for its products or services. The issue of corporate culture is quite important for multinational businesses. This is because many companies have their own culture.

Key concept

> **Culture** embodies the common set of values: 'the way things are done around here'.
>
> Culture is embodied in rituals and behaviour.
>
> Culture is an important filter of **information** and an **interpreter** of it. For example, a firm might have a cultural predisposition against embarking on risky ventures. Finally existing behaviour patterns may make a proposed strategy incompatible with the culture and so impossible to implement.

An organisation's culture is influenced by many factors.

(a)   The organisation's **founder**. A strong set of values and assumptions is set up by the organisation's founder, and even after he or she has retired, these values have their own momentum.

(b)   The organisation's **history.** The effect of history can be determined by stories, rituals and symbolic behaviour. They legitimise behaviour and promote priorities. (In some organisations certain positions are regarded as intrinsically more 'heroic' than others.)

(c)   **Leadership and management style**. An organisation with a strong culture recruits managers who naturally conform to it.

(d)   **Structure and systems** affect culture as well as strategy.

(e)   The industry (eg computer software firms in the 'silicon valley' had a reputation for being laid back on office dress).

(f)   Location of head office – and its acquired culture

(g)   Of most significance in this chapter, the wider **society**, discussed below.

4.1 Management culture

FAST FORWARD

Management culture drives management practice. The **Hofstede model** of national cultures indicates how far imported methods of management may be applicable in different countries.

A factor which has an impact on the culture of transnational organisations, or organisations competing in global markets, is **management culture**. This is the views about managing held by managers, their shared educational experiences, and the 'way business is done'. Obviously, this reflects wider cultural differences between countries, but national cultures can sometimes be subordinated to the corporate culture of the organisation (eg the efforts to ensure that staff of EuroDisney are as enthusiastic as their American counterparts).

Key concept

Management culture is a part of overall organisational culture and relates to the prevailing view within management about how to do its job.

Important aspects of management culture include:

- The relative priorities accorded to such matters as technical excellence, customer service, workforce development and innovation.

- The relative value managers place on personal attributes such as people skills, creativity, leadership, drive and professional competence.

4.2 The Hofstede model of national cultures

Hofstede (1984) carried out cross-cultural research at 66 national offices of IBM and formulated one of the most influential models of work-related cultural differences.

The Hofstede model describes four main dimensions of difference between national cultures, which impact on all aspects of management and organisational behaviour: motivation, team working, leadership style, conflict management and HR policies.

(a) **Power distance**: the extent to which unequal distribution of power is accepted.

   (i) *High* PD cultures (as in Latin, near Eastern and less developed Asian countries) accept greater centralisation, a top-down chain of command and closer supervision. Subordinates have little expectation of influencing decisions.

   (ii) *Low* PD cultures (as in Germanic, Anglo and Nordic countries) expect less centralisation and flatter organisational structures. Subordinates expect involvement and participation in decision-making. (Japan is a medium PD culture.)

(b) **Uncertainty avoidance**: the extent to which security, order and control are preferred to ambiguity, uncertainty and change.

   (i) *High* UA cultures (as in Latin, near Eastern and Germanic countries and Japan) respect control, certainty and ritual. They value task structure, written rules and regulations, specialists and experts, and standardisation. There is a strong need for consensus: deviance and dissent are not tolerated. The work ethic is strong.

   (ii) *Low* UA cultures (as in Anglo and Nordic countries) respect flexibility and creativity. They have less task structure and written rules; more generalists and greater variability. There is more tolerance of risk, dissent, conflict and deviation from norms.

(c) **Individualism**: the extent to which people prefer to live and work in individualist (focusing on the 'I' identity) or collectivist (focusing on the 'we' identity) ways.

   (i) *High* Individualism cultures (as in Anglo, more developed Latin and Nordic countries) emphasise autonomy and individual choice and responsibility. They prize individual initiative. The organisation is impersonal and tends to defend business interests: task achievement is more important than relationships. Management is seen in an individual context.

(ii) *Low* Individualism (or Collectivist) cultures (as in less developed Latin, near Eastern and less developed Asian countries) emphasise interdependence, reciprocal obligation and social acceptability. The organisation is seen as a 'family' and tends to defend employees' interests: relationships are more important than task achievement. Management is seen in a team context. (Japan and Germany are 'medium' cultures on this dimension.)

(d) **Masculinity**: the extent to which social gender roles are distinct. (Note that this is different from the usual sense in which the terms 'masculine' and 'feminine' are used.)

(i) *High* Masculinity cultures (as in Japan and Germanic and Anglo countries) clearly differentiate gender roles. Masculine values of assertiveness, competition, decisiveness and material success are dominant. Feminine values of modesty, tenderness, consensus, focus on relationships and quality of working life are less highly regarded, and confined to women.

(ii) *Low* Masculinity (or Feminine) cultures (as in Nordic countries) minimise gender roles. Feminine values are dominant – and both men and women are allowed to behave accordingly.

Action Programme 3

According to the *Hofstede* model, what issues might arise in the following cases?

(a) The newly-appointed Spanish (more developed Latin) R & D manager of a UK (Anglo) firm asks to see the Rules and Procedures Manual for the department.

(b) A US-trained (Anglo) manager attempts to implement a system of Management by Objectives in Thailand (less developed Asian).

(c) A Dutch (Nordic) HR manager of a US (Anglo) subsidiary in the Netherlands is instructed to implement downsizing measures.

4.3 The Hall model of national cultures

Hall discussed the different role of 'context' in communication in different cultures.

Context has a number of aspects. Here are some examples.

- Where the communication takes place
- The people involved and their age, sex and status
- The general subject area of the conversation, such as work, appraisal or leisure

According to Hall, in **low context** cultures, the context is of little importance to communication. A message means what it says, and people take it at face value. Examples are Germany, Scandinavia and North America.

In **high context** cultures, the message can only be understood by reference to its context and must not be taken at face value. Important topics like motivation, trustworthiness and co-operation are subject to much non-verbal communication. Examples are Latin America, Arabia and Japan.

The UK, France, Italy and Spain fall into an intermediate, medium context category.

4.4 Relevance to international marketing

What is the relevance of this issue for international marketers and managers? Many argue that a corporate culture depends more on the **industry sector** than on the **country**. That said, to ease communication between managers, many firms rely on corporate cultures to ensure a common value system throughout the organisation as a whole.

For example, performance related pay for individuals might be applied either in the UK or the USA, but it may have adverse consequences in cultures skewed towards collectivism such as Japan.

Some cultural problems can be solved if there is some **interchangeability of personnel**. Regular meetings, conferences, summaries, secondments and so on can help instil a sense of corporate loyalty, and also give executives skills in dealing with different cultures. The senior managers of many large companies need to be skilled in negotiating the many cultural minefields which exist in international businesses.

Exam tip

You could get a question on the problems associated with international cultural differences. This is a very wide ranging topic, covering both behaviour in the workplace and environmental aspects. Marketing mix issues can be specifically mentioned. As always, what the examiner calls a 'theory dump' would be useless: a mention of the differences observed by Hofstede might be useful as a framework for analysis or examples from the case study, but a detailed description would not.

To answer this question well it would be necessary to review the information in this chapter through the lens of the question requirements, selecting and arranging to emphasise the **cultural** issues of greatest relevance to marketing management. Here are some examples.

Environmental issues

Language
Business practices eg credit and negotiation
Status of women
Context
Attitude to advertising
General educational level

Internal issues

Attitude to management and authority generally
View of appraisal systems
Status of women
Negotiating customs
Attitudes to customers

5 Managing across borders

FAST FORWARD

> **Organisational structure** must suit both the global **need for control** and **local sensitivities**.

5.1 Management effectiveness

A problem is that there are often severe cultural differences as to what constitutes 'management' in the first place. Are **management** principles universally applicable? The marketing function needs awareness of effective management approaches in different cultures.

R N Farmer and B M Richman (1990) emphasise the importance of the external environment in which an organisation operates. They developed a model to illustrate the distinction between the management process and the environment of managing: Figure 6.2.

Figure 6.2: The Farmer-Richman model

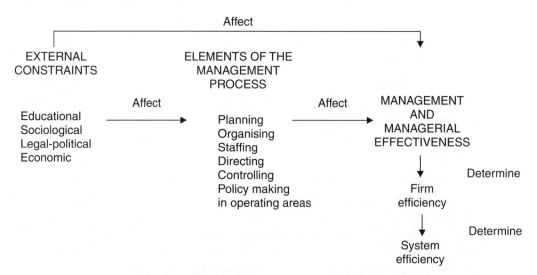

Farmer and Richman elaborate on the four categories of external constraints identified in the model.

(a)   **Educational** constraints include the level of literacy in the environment (country) and the availability of secondary education, vocational training and higher education. Poor educational facilities will inevitably result in poor management.

(b)   **Sociological** constraints are the most numerous category. For example, one country may have a tradition of antagonism between trade unions and management whereas another might have a history of mutual trust and co-operation.

(c)   **Legal and political constraints.** It is much more difficult to reduce headcount in France than in the UK because of more restrictive French legislation, for example.

(d)   **Economic constraints.** Some countries suffer from high rates of inflation and other symptoms of economic instability. The availability of capital is another important factor which varies from one environment to another.

5.2 Management structure

Local conditions and the scale of operations will influence the organisation structure of companies trading internationally. Structures vary from the inclusion of an export department into the usual pyramid, through variations on a combination of functional and geographic responsibility areas, to a matrix structure.

Conglomerates with widely differing product groups may organise globally by product, with each operating division having its own geographic structure suited to its own needs: Figure 6.3.

BPP LEARNING MEDIA

Figure 6.3: Divisionalised structure

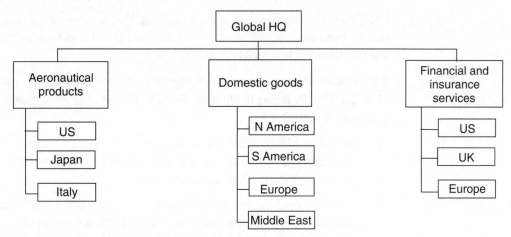

Companies with more integrated operations may prefer their top-level structure to be broken down geographically with product management conducted locally.

Very large and complex companies may be organised as a **heterarchy**. This is a rather organic structure with significant local control.

(a) **Some headquarters functions are diffused geographically**. For example, R&D might be in the UK, marketing in the US. Or again certain products will be made in one country, and others elsewhere. (Motor manufacturers do not make every model of car at each factory.) Some central functions might be split up: many firms are experimenting with having several centres for R&D.

(b) **Subsidiary managers have a strategic role for the corporation as a whole** (eg through bargaining and coalition forming).

(c) **Co-ordination is achieved through corporate culture and shared values** rather than a formal hierarchy. Employees with long experience might have worked in a number of different product divisions.

(d) **Alliances** can be formed with other company parts and other firms, perhaps in joint ventures or consortia.

5.3 Influences on structure and methods

A variety of factors influence management methods in the international setting; they pull in different directions and it may be that compromise is necessary. As always, a consideration of objectives is a good starting point. A company merely seeking to expand sales volume while concentrating on its home market will use very different methods from one seeking to operate in truly global markets such as energy and telecommunications.

Central control may be appropriate if the volume of international business or the company's experience in international operations is low. Centralisation is seen as promoting efficiency and prevents duplication of effort between regions. Even when operations are on a limited scale, when conformity with demanding technical standards is required, **functional representation** in international management may be necessary. Thus, a largely autonomous foreign subsidiary may have to accept supervision of its quality assurance or financial reporting functions.

If business is done globally, a form of **regional organisation** may be appropriate if there is some measure of social and economic integration within regions. The need for rapid response to local opportunities and threats may be served by a significant measure of **decentralisation**. National political and cultural sensitivities may reinforce this, but a shortage of local talent may limit it.

As far as **management processes and decision making** are concerned, typical problems include these.

(a)   **Poor information systems and communications**. However, the rapidly falling costs of telecommunications in real terms, the development of e-mail and video-conferencing facilities make this less excusable than before.

(b)   **Interpretation of information**. Culture filters information. It can also determine the priorities of the planners. By **failing to allow for diversity**, planners can make marketing on the ground more difficult.

   (i)   Managing a local market in a large country with a low population density and whose main source of earnings is natural resources would be different from marketing to a small country with a high population density.

   (ii)   High tech products may not be suitable to a country with a poorly developed educational and technological infrastructure as there might be no-one to service the equipment. So a high tech strategy at home would not work abroad.

   (iii)   Consumers in countries with very high rates of inflation will have different priorities to those who live in countries with low inflation. Managers' priorities will be to minimise any holdings of local currency, by converting it into a harder currency or into tangible assets. However, this makes financial reporting difficult.

5.4 Distance and implementation problems

The distance, as it were, between the corporate plan and its implementation on the ground is greater than it is for a company which only deals with one market.

(a)   **Physical**

   (i)   The degree of variation in environmental conditions is so much greater. Managers, in trying to get a global picture, may **aggregate data** from very dissimilar markets.

   (ii)   In order to compete effectively, local management must be able to respond to differing environmental conditions.

(b)   **Psychological.** Corporate planners may not share the same assumptions as local managers.

As a consequence of the greater variety of factors involved in planning, any attempt at central control is likely to be much less certain.

(a)   **Lack of experience.** The expertise and experience of head office planners might be limited by their careers in the 'head office' or by a gradual loss of a feel for their local roots.

(b)   **Time horizons.** Corporate planners will be seeking to satisfy the firm's **investors**, whose desire for a return might be dominated by their local considerations. This is typically a problem when a long term investment is required in an overseas market.

Action Programme 4

How can developments in ICT (a) help and (b) hinder international management?

5.5 Control systems

Meetings can become difficult and expensive when a company expands internationally. Air travel and hotel costs will be high and the stress on executives caused by extensive travel must be considered. Video-conferencing is emerging as an alternative to face-to-face meetings.

Culture can function as a control measure if resources are devoted to promoting shared values and principles. The importance of culture in operating a global heterarchy was discussed earlier.

In the specific area of **financial control**, international operations bring increased complexity.

(a) **Comparison** of national performance can be difficult because of widely different conditions. Only locally controllable cash flows should be considered and realistic expectations must be established.

(b) Different rates of interest may apply to **loan finance**; this will affect measures like return on investment, but may present an opportunity for reducing finance costs.

(c) **Financial** reporting rules vary across the world and considerable effort may be expended in converting financial statements.

(d) **Tax** is likely to be an issue, especially when remitting profits. **Transfer prices** are frequently examined by tax authorities as they can be used to move profits from one country to another.

(e) **Exchange rate risk** will have to be managed, which consumes time and money.

6 Human resource management

FAST FORWARD

Human resource management must accommodate the needs of both **indigenous** and **expatriate** staff.

The balance between local and expatriate staff must be managed. There are a number of influences.

- The availability of technical skills such as financial management
- The need for control
- The importance of product and company experience
- The need to provide promotion opportunities
- Costs associated with expatriates such as travel and higher salaries
- Cultural factors

6.1 Expatriates or locals?

For an international company, which has to think globally as well as act locally, there are a number of problems.

- Do you employ mainly expatriate staff to control local operations?
- Do you employ **local managers**, with the possible loss of central control?
- Is there such a thing as the **global manager**, equally at home in different cultures?

Expatriate staff are sometimes favoured over local staff.

(a) Poor **educational opportunities** in the market may require the import of skilled technicians and managers. For example, expatriates have been needed in many western firms' operations in Russia and Eastern Europe, simply because they understand the importance of profit.

(b) Some senior managers believe that a business run by expatriates is easier to **control** than one run by local staff.

(c)   If the firm is a macropyramid, expatriates might be better able than locals to **communicate** with the corporate centre.

(d)   The expatriate may **know more about the firm** overall, which is especially important if he or she is fronting a sales office.

The use of expatriates in overseas markets has certain disadvantages.

(a)   They **cost** more (eg subsidised housing, school fees).

(b)   **Culture shock**. The expatriate may fail to adjust to the culture (eg by associating only with other expatriates). This is likely to lead to poor management effectiveness, especially if the business requires personal contact.

(c)   A substantial training programme might be needed.

(i)   **Basic facts** about the country will be given with basic language training, and some briefings about cultural differences.

(ii)   **Immersion training** involves detailed language and cultural training and simulation of field social and business experiences. This is necessary to obtain an intellectual understanding and practical awareness of the culture.

Employing local managers raises the following issues.

(a)   A **glass ceiling** might exist in some companies. Talented local managers may not make it to board level if, as in many Japanese firms, most members of the board are drawn from one country.

(b)   In some cases, it may be hard for locals to assimilate into the corporate culture, and this might led to communication problems.

(c)   They will have greater local knowledge – the difficulty is to get them to understand the wider corporate picture, but this is true of most management at operational level.

Those firms which export sporadically might employ a home-based sales force. Their travel expenses will of course be high, and it might not always be easy to recruit people willing to cope with the pace.

6.1.1 Relevant issues to keep in mind

(a)   **Recruitment and training**. In countries with low levels of literacy, more effort might need to be spent on basic training.

(b)   **Career management**. Can overseas staff realistically expect promotion to the firm's highest levels if they do well?

(c)   **Appraisal schemes**. These can be a minefield at the best of times, and the possibilities for communications failure are endless. For example, in some cultures, an appraisal is a two way discussion whereas in others arguing back might be considered a sign of insubordination.

(d)   Problems associated with the status of women.

(e)   **Communications**. HRM tries to mobilise employees' commitment to the goals of the organisation. In far-flung global firms, the normal panoply of staff newsletters and team briefings may be hard to institute but are vital. Time differences also make communication difficult.

(i)   **E-mail** and satellite linkages between branch offices can be used for routine messages: e-mail is especially useful, as it allows swift access to a person's electronic mailbox.

(ii)   Major **conferences** are also necessary.

(iii)   Firms with many subsidiaries face additional problems of **language.** What language should be used for business communications? Some multinational firms have decreed English the language of official internal communications, even if they are not headquartered in the English speaking world.

Chapter Roundup

- The processes of **globalisation** have massively expanded international trade, but there are still areas of protection. In particular, regional trading groups have emerged that are to some extent opposed to one another.

- The social, legal, economic, political and technical **(SLEPT) business environment** differs widely across the globe. **Demographic differences** are particularly important for business.

- **Cultural factors** influence the ways of doing business, as well as management style and methods.

- In **high context** cultures, communication depends on far more than just the text of a message.

- **Management culture** drives management practice. The **Hofstede model** of national cultures indicates how far imported methods of management may be applicable in different countries.

- **Organisational structure** must suit both the global **need for control** and **local sensitivities**.

- **Human resource management** must accommodate the needs of both **indigenous** and **expatriate** staff.

Quick Quiz

1   What is the name of the body that regulates international trade?

2   What are the differences between a free trade area, a customs union and a common market?

3   What is demography?

4   Name two stereotypical aspects of business culture which differ between Japan and the USA.

5   What is the context of communication?

6   What are the four dimensions of the Hofstede model of management cultures?

7   **Wh**y is international financial control particularly complex?

8   What are the advantages of employing expatriates?

Answers to Quick Quiz

1   World Trade Organisation

2   The countries in a free trade area lower the barriers to trade amongst themselves. A customs union erects a common external tariff. A common market seeks economic unity, with free movement of the factors of production

3   The study of populations.

4   Here are some typically quoted differences

USA	Japan
Individualistic	Collectivist
High job mobility	Long service
Specialists valued	Generalist managers
Decisions made individually	Collective decision-making

5   The setting in which the message is passed: this includes the place and manner of the communication and the status of those involved

6   Power distance; uncertainty avoidance; individualism; masculinity

7   Different tax regimes, interest rates and exchange rates; conflicting financial reporting rules; widely different economic and market conditions

8   Their skills, their inside knowledge and experience and their familiarity with organisational communication methods, including the language used at base.

Action Programme Review

1   Some basic ideas:

- *Socio-cultural.* Language, values, behavioural norms and buying patterns may all vary, posing 'managing diversity' issues for both marketing plans and managers of international staff.

- *Technological.* Technology may facilitate international marketing and management (eg e-commerce, viral marketing, virtual teamworking), but may also pose challenges where technology infrastructure and adoption differs internationally.

- *Economic.* Disposable income and consumption are key issues for marketing, as are international trade agreements, exchange rates and other factors.

- *Environmental.* Infrastructure and values in regard to 'green' production and consumerism vary across nations (as indicated by arguments over the Kyoto Protocol, for example).

- *Political/legal.* Government policy, legislation (eg on worker health and safety, wages/conditions, equal opportunities and/or consumer protection, advertising standards, data protection and so on) and political stability (creating potential risk issues) vary.

- *Ethical.* Cultural attitudes shape ethical values, and business/marketing ethics may vary, eg in regard to labour conditions, the role of women and 'gifts'/bribes. This may be an issue for international operations, and also for management of outsourced and distribution channel activities (creating the risk of reputational damage).

2   The examples depend on your research and interests, but include up-to-date areas such as virtual retail outlets (and 'virtual fitting rooms'!); SMS mobile phone messaging promotion; GPS mobile phone store location; interactive kiosks; creative use of websites, blogs, YouTube-style user-generated content and so on.

Issues in overseas transfer include: infrastructure development; technology take-up; usage/consumption habits; age structure of the population; language barriers (costs of translation); data protection law (eg re export of mailing lists, different rules on unsolicited communication etc); the need to differentiate campaigns/messages for overseas audiences and so on.

3   (a)   A high-UA manager, expecting to find detailed and generally adhered-to rules for everything, may be horrified by the ad-hocracy of a low-UA organisation: if (s)he attempts to impose a high-UA culture, there may be resistance from employees and management.

BPP LEARNING MEDIA

(b)   A high-individuality manager may implement MbO on the basis of individual performance targets, results and rewards: this may fail to motivate collectivist workers, for whom group processes and performance is more important.

(c)   A low-masculinity manager may try to shelter the workforce from the effects of downsizing, taking time for consultation, retraining, voluntary measures and so on: this may seem unacceptably 'soft' to a high-masculinity parent firm.

4   ICT has been highly influential in facilitating international management by:

(a)   eliminating distance and time differences in communication (eg by automating query handling and message sending);

(b)   enabling 'virtual' collaboration (via web casts, data-sharing, virtual meetings software etc) so that the best people can be used for jobs, irrespective of location;

(c)   supporting remote performance monitoring and control (results reporting, file sharing etc);

(d)   offering language translation, currency conversion and other tools;

(e)   giving wide access to information on the cultural, legal, political and other factors relevant to other countries.

At the same time, there are challenges caused by (for example) over-reliance on the technology (ignoring human problems) and information overload.

Now try Question 6 at the end of the Study Text

Part B
Managing marketing projects

BPP
LEARNING MEDIA

7

Introducing project management

Syllabus content – knowledge and skill requirements

- The main stages of a project and the roles of people involved at each stage (2.1)
- The main characteristics of successful and less successful projects and the main reasons for success or failure (2.2)

Introduction

This chapter is the first of two on the important topic of project management. Project work forms a significant element of many aspects of marketing and marketing managers must be prepared to contribute to projects, often in a leadership role.

Section 1 explains the nature of projects and the scope of project management and outlines some of the management challenges inherent in project work. This leads naturally to a more detailed consideration of the work of the project manager in Section 2.

While it is common for individuals to work on a succession of self-contained projects that require minimal input from other people, the sort of projects we are dealing with here inevitably involve the contributions of a group of people. Section 3 is concerned with the project team members and how to manage them. An important aspect of this is assembling an appropriate mix of skills in the first place.

Section 4 considers the important topic of project stakeholders. Especially where larger projects are concerned, there are likely to be several identifiably distinct groups or individuals with an interest in its progress. To some extent it is part of the project manager's job to balance the demands and interests of these possibly disparate groups.

We conclude this chapter with two sections that examine the life cycle of the project. Section 5 introduces this concept and Section 6 looks at it in more detail.

1 The scope of project management

FAST FORWARD

A **project** is an undertaking that has a beginning and an end and is carried out to meet established goals within cost, schedule and quality objectives.

1.1 What is a project?

In general, the work which organisations undertake involves either **operations** or **projects**. Operations and projects are planned, controlled and executed. So how are projects distinguished from 'ordinary work'?

Projects	Operations
Have a defined beginning and end	On-going
Have resources allocated specifically to them, although often on a shared basis	Resources used 'full-time'
Are intended to be done only once (eg organising the 2005 London Marathon – the 2006 event is a separate project)	A mixture of many recurring tasks
Follow a plan towards a clear intended end-result	Goals and deadlines are more general
Often cut across organisational and functional lines	Usually follows the organisation or functional structure

An activity that meets the first four criteria above can be classified as a project, and therefore falls within the **scope of project management**. Whether an activity is classified as a project is important, as projects should be managed using **project management techniques**.

Give six examples of work you would consider suitable for a project management approach.

1.2 What is project management?

FAST FORWARD

A project will be deemed successful if it is completed at the specified level of **quality**, **on time** and within **budget**.

The objective of project management is a successful project. A project will be deemed successful if it is completed at the **specified level of quality**, **on time** and **within budget**.

Objective	Comment
Quality	The end result should conform to the project specification. In other words, the result should achieve what the project was supposed to do.
Budget	The project should be completed without exceeding authorised expenditure.
Timescale	The progress of the project must follow the planned process, so that the 'result' is ready for use at the agreed date. As time is money, proper time management can help contain costs.

Exam tip

So many types of task are now tackled on a project management basis, that you should be ready to apply PM concepts to a wide range of exam scenarios. In June 2006, the scenario concerned a multi-organisation project team put together to plan a trade conference: although one question explicitly addressed 'project management issues' (in the specific context of an international event), you had to remember throughout that the team was a *project* team (with different stakeholders) and the planning cycle was part of a project life span – and so on.

In December 2006, you were asked to outline different approaches to project management – and how this would apply in activities to project-manage a new outlet launch. Get to grips with the project lifecycle (stages) as a helpful framework – and then apply, apply, apply: give examples of each stage, checking for relevance to the scenario. Who are the stakeholders? What are the time, cost, quality objectives? What are the 'peculiarities' of the project team or logistical challenges of working on this context?

2 The project manager

FAST FORWARD

The person who takes ultimate responsibility for ensuring the desired result is achieved on time and within budget is the **project manager**.

Some project managers have the job title 'Project Manager'. These people usually have one major responsibility: the project. Most people in business will have 'normal work' responsibilities outside their project goals – which may lead to conflicting demands on their time. Anybody responsible for a project (large or small) is a project manager.

The role a project manager performs is in many ways similar to those performed by other managers. There are however some important differences, as shown in the table below.

Project manager	Operations manager
Are often 'generalists' with wide-ranging backgrounds and experience levels	Usually specialists in the areas managed
Oversee work in many functional areas	Relate closely to technical tasks in their area
Facilitate, rather than supervise team members	Have direct technical supervision responsibilities

A person should only take on the role of project manager if they have the time available to do the job effectively. Also, if somebody is to be held responsible for the project, they must be given the resources and authority required to complete project tasks.

FAST FORWARD

Duties of the project manager include: Planning, teambuilding, communication, co-ordinating project activities, monitoring and control, problem-resolution, quality control and risk management.

The duties of a project manager are summarised below.

Duty	Comment
Outline planning	Project planning (eg targets, sequencing) • Developing project targets such as overall costs or timescale needed (eg project should take 20 weeks). • Dividing the project into activities and placing these activities into the right sequence, often a complicated task if overlapping. • Developing a framework for the procedures and structures, manage the project (eg decide, in principle, to have weekly team meetings, performance reviews etc).
Detailed planning	Work breakdown structure, resource requirements, network analysis for scheduling.
Teambuilding	Build cohesion and team spirit.
Communication	The project manager must keep supervisors informed about progress as well as problems, and ensure that members of the project team are properly briefed.
Co-ordinating project activities	Between the project team and users, and other external parties (eg suppliers of hardware and software).
Monitoring and control	The project manager should estimate the causes for each departure from the standard, and take corrective measures.
Problem-resolution	Even with the best planning, unforeseen problems may arise.
Quality control	There is often a short-sighted trade-off between getting the project out on time and the project's quality.
Risk management	A key consideration is project failure and hence project risks and potential risk areas must be identified and monitored. Some academies suggest the use of management by exception as a tool for highlighting problems. However, this should not weaken the focus on other management objectives, approaches and activities.

Project management as a discipline developed because of a need to co-ordinate resources to obtain desired results within a set timeframe. Common project management tasks include establishing goals and objectives, developing a work-plan, scheduling, budgeting, co-ordinating a team and communicating.

The project management process helps project managers maintain control of projects and meet their responsibilities.

2.1 Project success factors

Projects, small or large, are prone to fail unless they are appropriately managed and some effort is applied to ensure that factors that might contribute to success are present. Here are some of the key factors.

- **Clearly defined mission and goals** effectively communicated to and understood by all participants.

- **Top management support** that is visible is important in sending out the right messages regarding the importance of the project

- **Competent project manager** with the necessary technical and inter-personal skills

- **Well designed operational process** to ensure that work proceeds efficiently

- **Competent team members** with the appropriate knowledge, skills and attitudes. A good team spirit helps to smooth the path to completion

- **Sufficient resources** in terms of finance, materials, people and processes

- **Excellent communication ethos** to ensure information is shared and there are no misunderstandings

- **Use of effective project management tools** such as charts, leading edge software and project progress meetings

- **Clear client focus** so that all work is done bearing in mind the needs of internal and external customers

Projects present some management challenges.

Project management ensures responsibilities are clearly defined and that resources are **focussed** on specific objectives. The **project management process** also provides a structure for communicating within and across organisational boundaries.

All projects share similar features and follow a similar process. This has led to the development of **project management tools and techniques** that can be applied to all projects, no matter how diverse. For example, with some limitations similar processes and techniques can be applied whether building a major structure (eg The new Wembley Football Stadium) or implementing a company-wide computer network.

All projects require a person who is ultimately responsible for delivering the required outcome. This person (whether officially given the title or not) is the **project manager**.

2.2 The responsibilities of a project manager

A project manager has responsibilities to both management and to the project team.

Responsibilities to management

- Ensure resources are used efficiently – strike a balance between cost, time and results

- Keep management informed with timely and accurate communications about achievements as well as problems

- Manage the project competently to the best of his or her ability

- Behave ethically, and adhere to the organisation's policies

- Maintain a customer orientation (whether the project is geared towards an internal or external customer) – customer satisfaction is a key indicator of project success

Responsibilities to the project and the project team

- Take action to keep the project on target for successful completion

- Ensure the project team has the resources required to perform tasks assigned

- Provide new team members with a proper briefing and help them integrate into the team

- Provide any support required when members leave the team either during the project or on completion

- Listen properly to team members so that potential problems are identified and can be dealt with as soon as possible

2.3 The skills required of a project manager

FAST FORWARD

Project managers require the following **skills**: Leadership and team building, organisational ability, communication skills (written, spoken, presentations, meetings), some technical knowledge of the project area and inter-personal skills.

To meet these responsibilities a project manager requires a wide successful range of skills. The skills required are similar to those required when managing a wider range of responsibilities. A project manager requires excellent technical and personal skills. Some of the skills required are described in the following table.

Type of skill	How the project manager should display the type of skill
Leadership and team building	<ul><li>Be **enthusiastic** about what the project will achieve.</li><li>Be **positive** (but realistic) about all aspects of the project.</li><li>Understand where the project fits into the **'big picture'**.</li><li>**Delegate** tasks appropriately – and not take on too much personally.</li><li>Build team spirit through encouraging **co-operation** and sharing of information.</li><li>Do not be restrained by organisational structures – a high tolerance for ambiguity (lack of clear-cut authority) will help the project manager.</li><li>Be prepared to motivate team members and give due praise and encouragement</li></ul>
Organisational	<ul><li>Ensure all project **documentation** is clear and distributed to all who require it.</li><li>Use project **management tools** to analyse and monitor project progress.</li></ul>
Communication	<ul><li>**Listen** to project team members. Exploit good ideas whatever the source.</li><li>Use **persuasion** to win over reluctant team members or stakeholders to support the project.</li><li>Ensure management is kept **informed** and is never surprised.</li><li>Encourage team members to share their knowledge and support each other</li></ul>
Technical	<ul><li>By providing (or at least providing access to) the **technical expertise** and experience needed to manage the project.</li></ul>

BPP LEARNING MEDIA

Type of skill	How the project manager should display the type of skill
Personal	• Be **flexible**. Circumstances may develop that require a change in plan. • Show resilience. Even successful projects will encounter difficulties that require repeated efforts to overcome. • Be **creative**. If one method of completing a task proves impractical a new approach may be required. • **Patience** is required even in the face of tight deadlines. The 'quick-fix' may eventually cost more time than a more thorough but initially more time-consuming solution. • **Keep in touch** with team members as their performance is key to the success of the project.

2.4 Project leadership styles

FAST FORWARD

The optimal **project leadership style** depends on a variety of factors.

As in other forms of management, different project managers have different styles of leadership. There is no 'best' leadership style, as individuals suit and react to different styles in different ways. The key is adopting a style that suits both the project leader and the project team.

Generally, leadership styles were covered in an earlier chapter. For the purposes of this chapter, we will use an adapted approach which draws on the *Tannenbaum and Schmidt* (1973) continuum of leadership styles, which seems appropriate to a project management environment: Figure 7.1.

Figure 7.1: A continuum of leadership styles

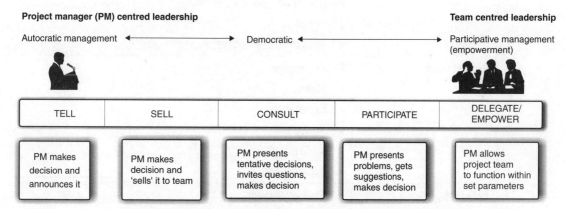

The leadership style adopted will affect the way decisions relating to the project are made. Although an autocratic style may prove successful in some situations (eg 'simple' or 'repetitive' projects), a more consultative style is likely to **build consensus** and allow project team members to feel that they have 'ownership' of the project. This should help to build greater **commitment** and maximise performance.

Not all decisions will be made in the same way. For example, decisions that do not have direct consequences for other project personnel may be made with no (or limited) consultation. A **balance** needs to be found between ensuring decisions can be made efficiently, and ensuring adequate consultation and participation in decision making.

A contingency approach is likely to be appropriate where the style adopted depends on the situation, eg if building project in progress is attacked by terrorists a strong 'tell' style might be required to sort out any problems arising. However, if a decision needs to be made regarding objects of art to go in the forecourt of a building, a 'consult' or 'participate' style might produce a more customer friendly outcome.

The various factors impacting on the optimal project management style that might be appropriate in any particular scenario can be shown diagrammatically: Figure 7.2.

Figure 7.2: Factors in choice of project management style

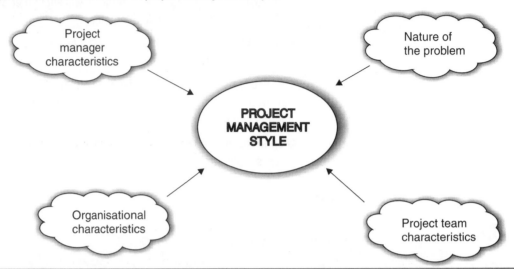

Factor	Characteristics
Project manager	<ul><li>Personal values and attitude</li><li>Knowledge</li><li>Skills</li><li>Experience</li></ul>
Organisation	<ul><li>Culture</li><li>Norms and values</li><li>Image</li><li>Mission and objective</li></ul>
Project team	<ul><li>Knowledge</li><li>Skills</li><li>Experience</li><li>Attitude</li><li>Motivation</li><li>Expectations</li></ul>
Problem	<ul><li>Task orientation</li><li>Creative content</li><li>Time available</li><li>Match to team experience</li><li>Impact of outcomes</li></ul>

3 The project team

3.1 Building a project team

A project team comprises people who report directly or indirectly to the project manager.

Project success depends to a large extent on the team members selected. The ideal project team achieves project completion on time, within budget and to the organisations quality standards – with the minimum amount of direct supervision from the project manager.

The team will comprise individuals with **differing skills and personalities**. The project manager should choose a balanced team that takes advantage of each team member's skills and compensates elsewhere for their weaknesses.

The project team will normally be drawn from existing staff, but highly recommended **outsiders with special skills** may be recruited. When building a team the project manager should ask the following questions.

(a)   **What skills** are required to complete each task of the project?

(b)   **Who** has the talent and skills to complete the required tasks, whether inside or outside the organisation?

(c)   Are the people identified **available**, **affordable**, and able to join the project team?

(d)   What level of **supervision** will be required?

This information should be **summarised in worksheet format**, as shown in the following example.

Project Skill Requirements		
Project Name: _____ **Date worksheet completed**: _____		
Project Manager: _____		
Task	**Skill needed**	**Responsibility**

The completed worksheet provides a document showing the skills required of the project team. Deciding who has the skills required for each task and if possible seconding those identified to the project team, should be done **as early as possible**. Team members should then be able to **participate** in the planning of schedules and budgets. This should encourage the acceptance of agreed deadlines, and a greater commitment to achieve project success.

Although the composition of the project team is critical, project managers often find it is not possible to assemble the ideal team, and have to do the best they can with the personnel available. If the project manager feels the best available team does not possess the skills and talent required, consideration must be given to deferring or even abandoning the project. Sometimes, depending on the nature of the project, it maybe possible to redefine a smaller and less ambitious project. In practice this is referred to going for the 'quick fix' solution, with the rest being put onto a 'wish list'.

Where possible, each member should be provided with a briefing which should cover:

- His/her role
- Technical and interpersonal skills required
- Management style

3.2 Managing the project team

Teamwork is an important factor for project success. The project manager should emphasise the importance of good communication, and solving problems by drawing on different resources and expertise.

The performance of the project team is likely to be enhanced by the following.

- Effective communication
- All members being aware of the team's purpose and the role of each team member
- Collaboration and creativity among team members
- Trusting, supportive atmosphere in group
- Willingness to share knowledge, information and experience
- A commitment to meeting the agreed schedule
- Innovative/creative behaviour
- Team members highly interdependent, interface effectively
- Capacity for conflict resolution
- Results orientation
- High energy levels and enthusiasm
- An acceptance of change
- Ability to recognise performance and celebrate success

Collaboration and interaction between team members will help ensure the skills of all team members are utilised, and should result in 'synergistic' solutions. Formal (eg meetings) and informal channels (eg e-mail links, a bulletin board) of **communication** should be set up to ensure this interaction takes place.

Team members should be responsible and accountable. The project manager should provide **regular updates** on project progress and timely **feedback** on team and individual performance.

Action Programme 2

From what you already know about team leadership (from Chapter 2), brainstorm some key abilities or activities of a project team leader.

3.3 Managing conflict within the project team

It may be that when people from wide-ranging backgrounds combine to form a project team that **conflict** will occasionally occur. Some conflicts may actually be **positive**, resulting in fresh ideas and energy being input to the project. Other conflicts can be **negative** and have the potential to bring the project to a standstill. Rumbling discontent can undermine morale, reduce motivation and diminish efficiency.

Most conflicts are capable of being resolved, but some might require more effort to achieve a resolution than is justified. In these instances it may be more efficient to use creativity to devise a method of working **around the problem**.

An open exchange of views between project personnel should be encouraged as this will help ensure all possible courses of action and their consequences are considered. The project manager should keep in touch with the relationships of team members and act as a conciliator if necessary.

Ideally, conflict should be harnessed for productive ends. Conflict can have **positive effects** such as those listed below.

- Results in better, well thought-out ideas
- Encourages people to search for new approaches

- Causes persistent problems to surface and be dealt with
- Forces people to clarify their views
- Causes tension which stimulates interest and creativity

Generally open corporate cultures are better at dealing with or obviating conflicts because grievances are less likely to brew for long periods. If there is an emphasis on interpersonal skills staff will be able to resolve differences more easily and attain solutions which respect individual standpoints and benefit the organisation.

3.3.1 Negotiation and resolution techniques

When conflict occurs the project manager should avoid displaying bias and adopt a logical, ordered approach towards achieving resolution. The following principles should be followed.

- Focus on the problem, not the personalities
- Define the problem carefully
- Try to develop options that would result in mutual gain
- Explore a wide variety of possible solutions
- Try to identify common ground and ways to increase this

Ideally the conflict will be resolved by the parties involved **agreeing** on a course of action. In cases where insufficient progress towards a resolution has occurred the project manager should attempt to bring about a resolution.

The project manager may need to use a variety of **techniques** in an attempt to resolve the conflict. Identify types of solutions possible – win/lose, compromise or win/win.

- Work through the problem using the **negotiation techniques** listed above.

- Ideally a win/win solution is preferable, but sometimes a half-way house compromise maybe necessary.

- Identify differences and decide on criteria for negotiation success. This is done by

  - exploring each party's differences and strength of feeling,
  - acknowledging the validity of each other's standpoint, and
  - encouraging mutual respect for each other's views.

- Emphasise areas of **agreement**.

- If the parties cannot reach agreement, the project manager will have to develop a **solution** that is **fair to both sides** and also in the **best interests of the business**. The project manager might wish to acknowledge both sides **commitment** to what is good for the business and how their contributions, though different, are well appreciated.

4 Project stakeholders

FAST FORWARD

Project stakeholders are the individuals and organisations who are involved in, or may be affected by, project activities.

In addition to the **Project Manager** and the **Project Team**, a number of other stakeholders is usually involved in a project.

- **Project sponsor** who is accountable for the resources invested into the project and responsible for the achievement of the project's business objectives. The sponsor may be an owner, financier, client etc., or their delegate.

- **Project support team** refers to the personnel working on a project who do not report to the project manager administratively.

- **Users** are the individual or group that will utilise the end product, process (system), or service produced by the project.

- **Risk manager.** For large projects it may be necessary to appoint someone to control the process of identifying, classifying and quantifying the risks associated with the project.

- **Quality manager.** For large projects it may be necessary to appoint someone to write the quality plan and develop quality assurance and control procedures.

Project stakeholders should all be **committed towards a common goal** – successful project completion. The Project Plan should be the common point of reference that states priorities and provides cohesion.

However, the individuals and groups that comprise the stakeholders all have different roles, therefore are likely to have different expectations. There is therefore the potential for stakeholder dissatisfaction. A wise project manager will therefore be careful in **identifying stakeholder expectations**, managing these as best possible and ensuring that the project is completed successfully, meeting all stakeholders expectations.

The individuals and groups that comprise the stakeholders all have different roles. A **stakeholder analysis** is a useful tool for identifying and clarifying the role of stakeholders. An example follows.

 Marketing at Work

STAKEHOLDER ANALYSIS - CALL CENTRE IMPLEMENTATION PROJECT

Stakeholder	Reason for Involvement	Importance2			Nature of Communic-ations	Current Attitude[1]				Detail of Attitude	Required Attitude[1]		Required Outcome	Knowledge	Previous Communications
		H	M	L		H	S	A	R		H	S			
Call Centre Team Managers	Will be significant user of system	✓			Awareness & Training	✓				Positive	✓		High commitment, understanding context and of need to upgrade	Awareness of the broad concept but low understanding of detail	Limited (some mention in team meetings), Internal newsletter article
User Group	Vehicle for communication of project details to other key stakeholders	✓			Awareness, consultation and work group	✓				Largely positive, not fully engaged, gap in understanding of role (lack of willingness to train own people)	✓		High knowledge of project, use of position to relay information to Users and Owners	High	Active involvement in process through user group meetings, Internal newsletter article
Group / Div Managers and Directors	Need to be aware of developments, impacts and potential for their area		✓		Awareness	✓	✓			Varying from ambivalence to positive / supportive		✓	Awareness of impact and potential	Low	Internal newsletter article
Users	Will be significant user of system	✓			Awareness & Training	✓		✓		Likely to be positive, maybe some resistance to need for greater structure	✓		Acceptance of system along with high technical knowledge and understanding of reasons for the change	Should be reasonably high (through user group reps)	Regular updates from UG reps, visits from IRT, informal discussion w/ CCC people as part of normal business, Internal newsletter article
Owners	Will be significant user of system and system output; increased accountability reliant on system use	✓			Awareness & Training, consultation through user group	✓				Likely to be positive (as they can see the benefits)	✓		Acceptance of system, high technical knowledge, impact on other areas	Should be reasonably high (through user group reps & direct dealings)	Regular updates from UG reps, visits from IRT, informal discussion w/ CCC people as part of normal business, Internal newsletter article
Wider Organisation	Support for direction / use of CCC; possible potential for use of system by others		✓		Awareness	✓	✓			Largely ambivalent, positive for those that see potential		✓	Awareness of the broad concept of integrated incident management	Very low	Internal newsletter article

Notes
1. H = High commitment, S = supportive, A = ambivalent, R = resistant
2. H = High commitment, M = medium, L = low

4.1 Managing stakeholder disputes

The first step is to establish a **framework** to predict the potential for disputes. This involves **risk management**, since an unforeseen event (a risk) has the potential to create conflict, and **dispute management**: the matching of dispute procedures with minimum impacts on costs, goodwill and progress.

The potential for disputes should be considered when managing all areas of a project. A skilled project manager should be able to organise working methods in such a way that minimises the likelihood of disputes.

Action Programme 3

What potential for conflict can you see in a project to introduce a customer care programme in an organisation?

FAST FORWARD

Most conflicts that arise during a project should be able to be resolved using **negotiation** and **resolution** techniques.

Resolution is the solution of a conflict. **Settlement** is an arrangement which brings an end to the conflict, but does not necessarily address the underlying causes.

Wherever there is a potential for conflict, a **process to resolve** it should be established before the conflict occurs.

We have already discussed negotiation and resolution techniques in the context of project team conflict in Section 3 of this chapter. Many of the principles discussed previously can be applied to stakeholder conflicts, although the relative positions of the stakeholders involved can complicate matters. Conflict between project stakeholders may be resolved by:

- **Negotiation** (perhaps with the assistance of others)
- **Mediation**
- **Partnering**
- A third party neutral may judge or intervene to **impose a solution**

Negotiation involves the parties discussing the problem. This may or may not settle or resolve the dispute, but it should certainly be the first step.

Mediation or 'assisted negotiation' may be necessary. This involves a third-party neutral (the mediator) intervening to reach a mutually agreeable outcome.

Partnering focuses on creating communication links between project participants with the intention of directing them to a common goal – the project outcome – ahead of their own self-interest.

On very large projects a **Disputes Review Board** (DRB) may be formed. This may comprise persons directly involved in the project engaged to maintain a 'watching brief' to identify and attend upon disputes as they arise. Usually there is a procedure in place which provides for the DRB to make an 'on the spot' decision before a formal dispute is notified so that the project work can proceed, and that may be followed by various rights of review at increasingly higher levels.

In practice, disputes are often resolved by the acceptance of the view of the party that has financial responsibility for the project. In such a situation mediation and negotiation may only deliver an outcome which is a reflection of the original power imbalance.

5 The project life cycle

A successful project relies on two activities – **planning** first, and then **doing**. These two activities form the basis of every project.

Projects can be divided into several phases to provide better management control. Collectively these phases comprise the **Project Life Cycle** (PLC).

Key concept

> **Project life cycle**. The major time periods through which any project passes. Each period may be identified as a phase and further broken down into stages.

Although the principles of the project life cycle apply to all projects, the number and name of the phases identified will vary depending on what the project aims to achieve, and the project model referred to.

When studying Project Management it is convenient to give generic names to the phases of the **Project Life Cycle**. Remember though, in **'real' situations** (or in examination questions!) the model can be modified to suit circumstances.

Figure 7.3 shows a generic model of the **five main phases of a project**.

Figure 7.3: The phases of a project (or project life cycle)

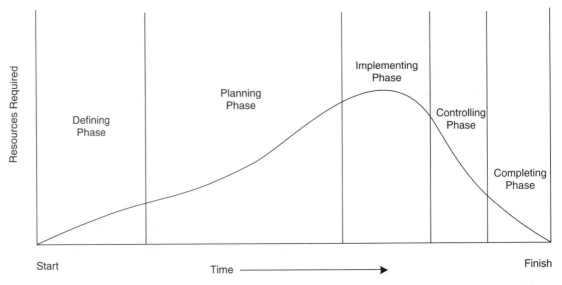

As shown on the diagram, resource use (such as funds and staff hours required) is low at the start of the project, higher towards the end and then drops rapidly as the project draws to a close.

Risk and uncertainty are highest at the start of the project. This is when the probability of successfully completing the project is lowest. The likelihood of successful completion increases the longer the project continues.

The cost of making changes to the project increases the further into the life cycle the project has progressed.

6 Project phases and stages

The phases of a project can be broken down into a number of **stages**. Again, the number of stages identified varies depending on type of project and the conventions of the organisation undertaking the project.

BPP LEARNING MEDIA

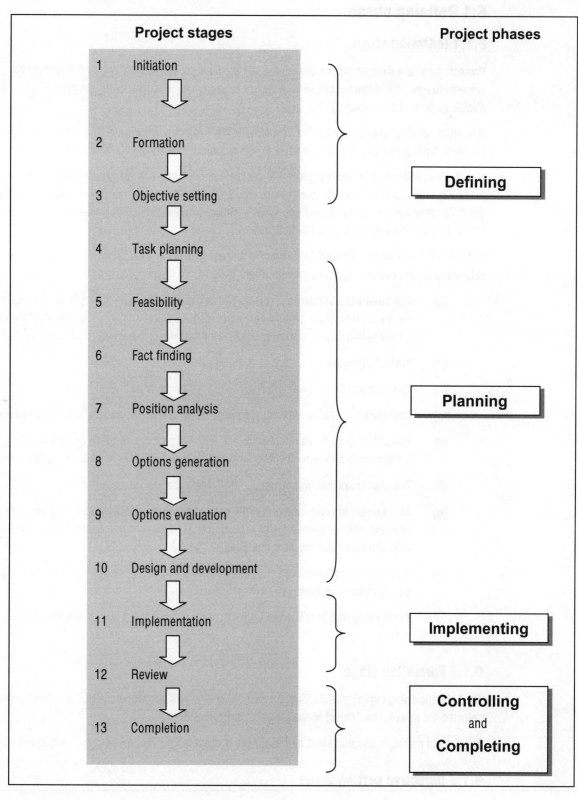

We now will look at each of these phases and stages.

6.1 Defining phase

6.1.1 Initiation stage

Projects originate from someone attempting to resolve a **problem**, or seeing an **opportunity** to do something new. The **defining phase** of a project is therefore concerned with deciding whether a project should begin and committing to do so.

It is often not clear precisely what the problem is. The project team should study, discuss and **analyse** the problem, from a number of different aspects (eg technical, financial).

Not all ideas will result in viable projects. A 'reality test' should be applied to all ideas. This is not a detailed feasibility study, and is intended to eliminate only concepts that are **obviously not viable**. For example, a small construction company should not waste resources investigating the possibility of submitting a tender to build the second channel tunnel.

At the start of a project, a **Project Initiation Document (PID)** may be drawn up, setting out the **terms of reference** for the project. Typical contents might include.

(a)   The **business objectives**. Projects should not be undertaken simply for their own sake: the business advantages should be clearly identified and be the first point of reference when progress is being reviewed, to make sure that the original aim is not lost sight of.

(b)   **Project objectives.**

(c)   The **scope** of the project: what it is intended to cover and what it is not.

(d)   **Constraints**, such as maximum amount to be spent and interim and final deadlines.

(e)   The **ultimate customer** of the project, who will resolve conflicts as they occur (for example between two different divisions who will both be using the new system) and finally accept it.

(f)   The **resources** that will be used – staff, technical resources, finance.

(g)   An **analysis of risks** inherent in the project and how they are to be avoided or reduced (for example, the consequences of replacing the old sales ledger system and only discovering after the event that the new one does not work).

(h)   A preliminary **project plan** (targets, activities and so on) and details of how the project is to be organised and managed.

(i)   **Purchasing and procurement policy**, perhaps specifying acceptable suppliers and delivery details.

6.1.2 Formation stage

The formation stage involves selecting the personnel who will be involved with the project. First to be selected are usually the **Project Manager** and the **Project Board**.

The project manager should **select and build the project team**. This process was explained earlier.

6.1.3 Objective setting stage

Before specific objectives can be set it is necessary to establish more general **project goals**. Clear goals and objectives give team members **quantifiable targets** to aim for. This should improve motivation and performance, as attempting to achieve a challenging goal is more inspiring than simply being told 'do your best.'

The **overall project goal** or project definition will be developed. On complex projects it is likely that the goal will be written in stages, with each definition being more detailed and refined than before. The project goal might be defined in a:

- Contract
- Product specification
- Customer's specification

Project objectives should be **SMART**:

- **S**pecific – so all involved are working towards well-defined ends
- **M**easurable – how will success be measured
- **A**greed upon – by all team members and stakeholders
- **R**ealistic – to motivate goals and objectives must be achievable
- **T**ime-bound – a date must be allocated to provide focus and aid priority setting

6.2 Planning phase

6.2.1 Task planning stage

The **planning phase** of a project aims to devise a workable scheme to accomplish the overall project goal. After the project team is in place and project goals and objectives have been set, the project should be broken down into **manageable tasks**. This process is often referred to as **Work Breakdown Structure (WBS)**.

By breaking the project down into a series of manageable tasks it is easier to determine the skills needed to complete the project. A **task list** should be produced showing what tasks need to be done and the work sequences necessary.

Building a task list for a complex project can be an involved and lengthy process. It can be difficult deciding what constitutes a task, and where one task ends and another begins.

Tasks should be:

(a) **Clear**. Eg 'Design the layout of the customer feedback questionnaire.'

(b) **Self-contained**. No gaps in time should be apparent on work-units grouped together to form a task. All work-units within a task should be related.

6.2.2 Feasibility and fact finding stage

Once all the tasks have been defined a basic **network diagram** can be developed, together with a **complete list of resources** required. Network diagrams are covered later in this chapter.

A more realistic judgement as to the **overall feasibility** of the project can now be made. Some large projects may involve a **pre-project feasibility study**, which establishes whether it is feasible to undertake the project at all. Feasibility and fact finding activities undertaken after the project has been initiated are more detailed.

For complex projects, a detailed **feasibility study** may be required to establish if the project can be achieved within acceptable **cost and time constraints**.

Key concept

> A **feasibility study** is a formal study to establish what type of solution could be implemented to meet the needs of the organisation. Practice will vary between different organisations.

Fact finding may be performed substantially during the feasibility study.

The activities carried out will differ depending on the nature of the project. For information systems projects the fact finding exercise would take the form of a systems investigation.

6.2.3 Position analysis, options generation and options evaluation stages

Once the current position has been clearly established options can be generated with the aim of utilising the internal strengths identified.

The process may involve options generation for a range of projects, only one of which can be chosen, eg should a new sales outlet be built in location C or should the limited finance available be spent on implementing a website that provides for on-line purchasing.

The general management technique of **SWOT analysis** can be applied to establish the current position, generate available options and evaluate those options.

Examples of projects where a wide-ranging SWOT analysis would be of value include:

- New product launches
- Proposed advertising campaign
- Move into a new market
- Change in selling method eg Launch of e-commerce
- Open a new factory
- Relocation of operations
- New brand launch
- Organisation re-structuring

The purpose of SWOT analysis (in the context of project management) is to ensure full consideration is given to possible approaches to the project and the effect the project will have on the organisation and its environment. The analysis should also ensure the project is compatible with the **overall strategy** of the organisation.

A **strengths and weaknesses analysis** should identify:

(a)   Strengths the organisation has that the project may be able to exploit.

(b)   Organisational weaknesses that may impact on the project. Strategies will be required to improve these areas or minimise their impact.

The **strengths** and **weaknesses** analysis has an **internal** focus. The identification of shortcomings in skills or resources could lead to a decision to purchase from outsiders or to train staff.

An **external appraisal** is required to identify **opportunities** which can be exploited by the company and also to anticipate environmental **threats** (a declining economy, competitors' actions, government legislation, industrial unrest etc) against which the company must protect itself.

For **opportunities**, it is necessary to decide the following.

- What opportunities exist in the business environment?
- What is their inherent profit-making potential?
- Whether the organisation can exploit the worthwhile opportunities.
- What is the comparative capability profile of competitors?
- What is the company's comparative performance potential in this field of opportunity?

For **threats**, it is necessary to decide the following.

- **What threats** might arise, to the company or its business environment?
- How market players will be **affected.**

Action Programme 4

What factors in the environment do you think might pose opportunities and/or threats for a marketing organisation?

The internal and external appraisals of SWOT analysis will be brought together.

- Major **strengths** and profitable opportunities can be **exploited** especially if strengths and opportunities are matched with each other.

- Major **weaknesses** and threats should be **countered**, or a contingency strategy or corrective strategy developed.

It is likely that **alternative strategies** will emerge from the identification of strengths, weaknesses, opportunities and threats.

Where a range of potential strategies have been identified, they each need to be **evaluated**.

Four steps are taken.

Step 1. The gap between the current position and the targeted position (project completion) is estimated.

Step 2. One or more courses of action are proposed.

Step 3. Each course is analysed in terms of how well it would meet the project aims. A weighted scoring or ranking system may be useful here.

Step 4. A course is chosen.

A variety of techniques are used to assess and value the options generated. Some will be assessed on financial criteria, such as **net present value**. Where this is not possible, or where the uncertainty in the environment is great, other models are used. **Scenario building** postulates a number of possible 'futures' (eg world-wide economic growth, interest rates, competitors).

Once a course of action has been chosen, it needs to be incorporated into the project plan.

6.3 Implementing phase

The **implementing phase** is concerned with co-ordinating people and other resources to carry out the project plan.

6.3.1 Design and development stage

The design and development stage is where the actual product, service or process that will be the end result of the project is worked on.

The activities carried out in this stage will vary greatly depending on the type of project. For example, in a software implementation this is when the programming of the software would take place; in a construction project, the building design would be finalised.

6.3.2 Implementation stage

After the process, service or product has been developed it will be **implemented or installed** so it is available to be used.

If the project involves a new system or process, a period of **parallel running** alongside the existing system or process may be carried out. This enables results to be checked, and any last-minute problems to be ironed out before the organisation is fully reliant on the new system or process.

6.4 Controlling phase

The **controlling phase** is concerned with ensuring project objectives are met by monitoring and measuring progress and taking corrective action when necessary.

6.4.1 Review stage

Actual performance should be reviewed against the objectives identified in the project plan. If performance is not as expected, control action will be necessary.

6.4.2 Completion stage

Completion involves formalising acceptance of the project and bringing it to an orderly end. Following installation and review there should be a meeting of the Project Board to:

- Check that all products are complete and delivered
- Check the status of any outstanding requests for change
- Check all project issues have been cleared
- Approve the project completion report (covered in section 5 of this chapter)
- Arrange for a post completion audit (also covered in section 5 of this chapter)

Action Programme 5

Outline the steps as given above as they apply to a project you undertook at work or at home. For example, a new advertising campaign or a programme of marketing research have the features of project management.

7 Project meetings

FAST FORWARD

Project meetings are important to keep in touch with progress and ensure problems are identified as soon as possible. Regular meetings are a key way of avoiding timetable slippages.

7.1 Rationale

Meetings are not always popular with people. However, they are an important management tool especially within a project management environment where problems and slippages can harm the successful completion of a project.

7.2 Types of project meeting

There are basically two types of meetings that are relevant to the management of projects.

Type of meeting	Purpose
Progress reporting meetings	It is important to hold these regularly at suitable intervals to monitor progress against schedule. If team members are required to report on a regular basis on how well they are doing is likely to keep them 'on their toes' and motivated.
	Otherwise complacency may emerge resulting in slippages in cost, quality and deadlines.
	In practice, meetings should be held at least on a monthly basis. Short weekly meetings may be helpful where there is a high risk of slippage.

BPP LEARNING MEDIA

Type of meeting	Purpose
Problem solving meetings	These should be held on a regular basis. It is important to identify and fix problems as soon as they arise.

Chapter Roundup

- A **project** is an undertaking that has a beginning and an end and is carried out to meet established goals within cost, schedule and quality objectives.

- A project will be deemed successful if it is completed at the specified level of **quality**, **on time** and within **budget**.

- The person who takes ultimate responsibility for ensuring the desired result is achieved on time and within budget is the **project manager**.

- **Duties** of the project manager include: Planning, teambuilding, communication, co-ordinating project activities, monitoring and control, problem-resolution, quality control and risk management.

- Project managers require the following **skills**: Leadership and team building, organisational ability, communication skills (written, spoken, presentations, meetings), some technical knowledge of the project area and inter-personal skills.

- The optimal **project leadership** style depends on a variety of factors.

- **Project stakeholders** are the individuals and organisations who are involved in, or may be affected by, project activities.

- Wherever there is a potential for conflict a **process to resolve** it should be established before the conflict occurs.

- Most conflicts that arise during a project should be able to be resolved using **negotiation** and **resolution** techniques.

- **Project meetings** are important to keep in touch with progress and ensure problems are identified as soon as possible. Regular meetings are a key way of avoiding timetable slippages.

Quick Quiz

1   What is a successful project?

2   List four areas a project manager should be skilled in.

    1   ....

    2   ....

    3   ....

    4   ....

3   Who is the project sponsor?

4   'Project management techniques encourage management by exception'.

True

False

5   List four ways a dispute between project stakeholders could be settled.

1   ....

2   ....

3   ....

4   ....

Answers to Quick Quiz

1   One that is completed on time, within budget and to specification

2   [Four of] Leadership, team building, organisational, communication, technical, personal

3   The project sponsor may be the owner, financier, client etc., or their delegate. The sponsor is accountable for the resources invested into the project and responsible for the achievement of the project's business objectives

4   True

5   Negotiation (perhaps with the assistance of others)
     Partnering
     Mediation
     A third party neutral may judge or intervene to impose a solution

Action Programme Review

1   Common examples of projects include:

- Building a new national football stadium
- Producing a new product, service or object
- Changing the structure of an organisation
- Implementing a new service style
- Streamlining the company's ordering service
- Reorganising the company car park to maximise parking
- Implementing a new business procedure or process

2   Most **effective project managers** display the ability to:

- Select the right people
- Connect them to the right cause
- Communicate regularly with team members
- Identify potential problems, not avoid them
- Solve problems that do arise
- Evaluate progress towards objectives
- Provide regular and fair feedback
- Be sensitive to the needs of team members
- Negotiate resolutions to conflicts
- Heal wounds inflicted by change
- Give praise for good work and targets met

3   You need to think through the key stakeholders, and what their interests/needs and concerns/fears are. For example, management will want to implement the scheme as cost-effectively as possible, while employees will be concerned to receive training and be paid fairly for their increased contribution. Management and programme drivers may want to be brutally honest in identifying current shortfalls in performance, while staff may wish to focus on maintaining morale and minimising change. Customers (a key stakeholder!) may have differing standards and expectations to the organisation. And so on.

4   Opportunities and threats might relate to any of the PEST factors, such as:

- **Political**: legislation may affect a company's (or an individual project's) prospects through the threats/ opportunities of pollution control or a ban on certain products, for example.

- **Economic**: a recession might imply poor sales.

- **Social attitudes**.

- **Technology**: new products or means of distribution may be developed.

- **Competitors** can threaten to increase their market-share with better and/or cheaper products or services.

Now try Question 7 at the end of the Study Text

Project management tools

Syllabus content – knowledge and skill requirements

- The importance of, and techniques for, establishing the project's scope, definition and goals (2.3)
- The main techniques available for planning, scheduling, resourcing and controlling activities on a project (2.4)
- The importance of preparing budgets and techniques for controlling progress throughout a project to ensure it is completed on time and within budget (2.5)
- The main techniques for evaluating the effectiveness of a project on its completion (2.6)

Introduction

You will generally be concerned during your career with projects related to the field of marketing. You should be aware, however, that all projects have things in common, whatever their objects. This means that it is possible to use much the same kit of tools and procedures to push a project forward, whatever its object.

We commence with an examination of the basic project management techniques that have been developed over decades. These tools include the **project budget**, the **Gantt chart**, **network analysis**, **PERT**, and the **resource histogram**. Network analysis and PERT are tools of immense potential to the extent that their use on complex projects is really a matter for specialists. We include them here so that you can become familiar with the ideas involved.

Section 2 discusses project management software. Since the aim of project management is to impose order on a potentially chaotic process, software can be very useful in keeping track of a large number of disparate developments.

Section 3 considers the important area of documentation and reports. These are essential for effective project planning and control.

Finally, Section 4 takes a brief look at the idea of risk management as applied to projects.

1 Management tools and techniques

FAST FORWARD

Various **tools and techniques** are available to plan and control projects.

1.1 The project budget

Building a project budget should be an orderly process that attempts to establish a realistic estimate of the cost of the project. There are two main methods for establishing the project budget; **top-down** and **bottom-up**.

Top-down budgeting describes the situation where the budget is imposed 'from above'. Project Managers are allocated a budget for the project based on an estimate made by senior management. The figure may prove realistic, especially if similar projects have been undertaken recently. However the technique is often used simply because it is quick, or because only a certain level of funding is available.

In **bottom-up budgeting** the project manager consults the project team, and others, to calculate a budget based on the tasks that make up the project. Work breakdown structure (WBS) is a useful tool in this process, as explained in the previous chapter.

It is useful to collate this information on a **Budgeting Worksheet**.

BPP LEARNING MEDIA

Budgeting Worksheet

Project Name: _____ Date worksheet completed: _____

Project Manager: _____

Task (code)	Responsible staff member or external supplier	Estimated material costs	Estimated labour costs	Total cost of task

Estimates (and therefore budgets) cannot be expected to be 100% accurate. Business **conditions may change**, the project plan may be amended or estimates may simply prove to be incorrect.

Any **estimate** must be accompanied by some **indication of expected accuracy**.

Action Programme 1

What actions could a project manager take to improve the accuracy of his or her budget estimates?

The overall level of cost estimates will be influenced by:

- **Project goals**. If a high level of quality is expected costs will be higher.

- **External vendors**. Some costs may need to be estimated by outside vendors. To be realistic, these people must understand exactly what would be expected of them.

- **Staff availability**. If staff are unavailable, potentially expensive contractors may be required.

- **Time schedules**. The quicker a task is required to be done the higher the cost is likely to be – particularly with external suppliers.

The budget may express all resources in monetary amounts, or may show money and other resources – such as staff hours.

During the project, actual expenditure is tracked against budget on either a separate **Budget Report,** or as part of a regular **Progress Report.** We will be looking at project documentation and reports later in this chapter.

Budgets should be presented for approval and **sign-off** to the stakeholder who has responsibility for the funds being used.

Before presenting a budget for approval it may have to be revised a number of times. The 'first draft' may be overly reliant on rough estimates, as insufficient time was available to obtain more accurate figures.

On presentation, the Project Manager may be asked to find ways to cut the budget. If he or she agrees that cuts can be made, the consequences of the cuts should be pointed out – eg a reduction in quality.

It may be decided that a project costs more than it is worth. If so, scrapping the project is a perfectly valid option. In such cases the budgeting process has highlighted the situation before too much time and effort has been spent on an unprofitable venture.

1.2 Gantt charts

A Gantt chart, named after the engineer Henry Gantt who pioneered the procedure in the early 1900s, is a horizontal bar chart used to plan the **time scale** for a project and to estimate the amount of **resources** required.

The Gantt chart displays the time relationships between tasks in a project. Two lines are usually used to show the time allocated for each task, and the actual time taken.

Figure 8.1 shows a simple Gantt chart, illustrating some of the activities involved in a machine installation project.

Figure 8.1: Gantt chart

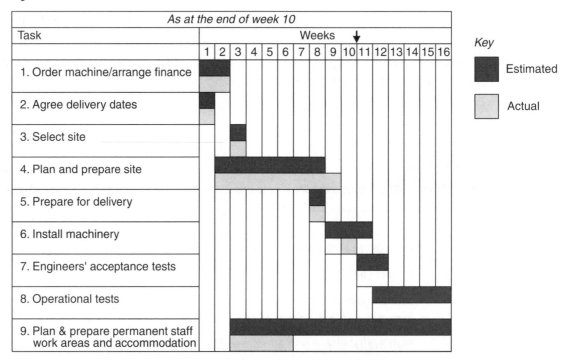

The chart shows that at the end of the tenth week Activity 9 is running behind schedule. More resources may have to be allocated to this activity if the staff accommodation is to be ready in time for the changeover to the new system.

Activity 4 had not been completed on time, and this has resulted in some disruption to the installation (Activity 6), which may mean further delays in the commencement of Activities 7 and 8.

A Gantt chart does not show the interrelationship between the various activities in the project as clearly as a **network diagram** (covered later in this chapter). A combination of Gantt charts and network analysis will often be used for project planning and resource allocation.

1.3 Network analysis

Network analysis, also known as **Critical Path Analysis** (CPA), is a useful technique to help with planning and controlling large projects, such as construction projects, research and development projects and the computerisation of systems.

BPP
LEARNING MEDIA

Key concept

> **Network analysis** requires breaking down the project into tasks, arranging them into a logical sequence and estimating the duration of each.
>
> This enables the series of tasks that determines the minimum possible duration of the project to be found.

CPA aims to ensure the progress of a project, so the project is completed in the **minimum amount of time**.

It pinpoints the tasks which are **on the critical path**, ie those parts which, if delayed beyond the allotted time, would **delay the completion** of the project as a whole.

The technique can also be used to assist in **allocating resources** such as labour and equipment.

The idea of critical path analysis is quite simple. The events and activities making up the whole project are represented in the form of a **diagram**.

Drawing the diagram or chart involves the following steps.

Step 1. Estimating the time needed to complete each individual activity or task that makes up a part of the project.

Step 2. Sorting out what activities must be done one after another, and which can be done at the same time, if required.

Step 3. Representing these in a network diagram.

Step 4. Estimating the critical path, which is the longest sequence of consecutive activities through the network.

The duration of the whole project will be fixed by the time taken to complete the largest path through the network. This path is called the **critical path** and activities on it are known as **critical activities**.

Activities on the critical path **must be started and completed on time**, otherwise the total project time will be extended. The method of finding the critical path is illustrated in the example below: Figure 8.2.

Network analysis shows the **sequence** of tasks and how long they are going to take. The diagrams are drawn from left to right.

Figure 8.2: A critical path network

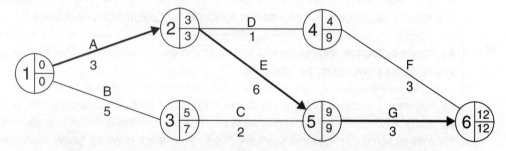

(a) **Events** (eg 1 and 2) are represented by circles. **Tasks** (eg A) connect events.

(b) The **critical path** is represented by drawing an extra line or a thicker line between the tasks on the path. It is the **minimum amount of time** that the project will take.

(c) It is the convention to note the earliest start date of any task in the *top* right hand corner of the circle.

(d) We can then work **backwards** identifying the **latest** dates when tasks have to start. These we insert in the bottom right quarter of the circle.

The **critical path** in the diagram above is AEG. Note the **float time** of five days for Activity F. Activity F can begin any time between days 4 and 9, thus giving the project manager a degree of flexibility.

(a)   **Total float** on a job is the time available (earliest start date to latest finish date) *less* time needed for the job. If, for example, job A's earliest start time was day 7 and its latest end time was day 17, and the job needed four days, total float would be:

$(17 - 7) - 4 = 6$ days

(b)   **Free float** is the delay possible in an activity on the assumption that all preceding jobs start as early as possible and all subsequent jobs also start at the earliest time.

(c)   **Independent float** is the delay possible if all preceding jobs have finished as late as possible, and all succeeding jobs have started as early as possible.

1.4 Project evaluation review technique (PERT)

Key concept

> **Project evaluation and review technique (PERT)** is a technique for allowing for uncertainty in determining project duration. Each task is assigned a best, worst, and most probable completion time estimate. These estimates are used to determine the average completion time. The average times are used to establish the critical path and the standard deviation of completion times for the entire project.

PERT is a modified form of network analysis designed to account for **uncertainty**. For each activity in the project, optimistic, most likely and pessimistic estimates of times are made, on the basis of past experience, or even guess-work. These estimates are converted into a mean time and also a standard deviation.

Once the mean time and standard deviation of the time have been calculated for each activity, it should be possible to do the following.

(a)   Estimate the **critical path** using expected (mean) activity times.

(b)   Estimate the standard deviation of the total project time.

1.5 Resource planning tools

A simple bar chart showing call centre time required on a telesales campaign is shown below: Figure 8.3 .

Another useful planning tool that shows the amount and timing of the requirement for a resource (or a range of resources) is the *resource histogram*. (You should have come across histograms – the diagrams of frequency distributions – in your studies for *Customer Communications* at Stage 1.

Key concept

> **A resource histogram** shows a view of project data in which resource requirements, usage, and availability are shown against a time scale.

An example of a resource histogram is shown in Figure 8.4 (Note the different widths of the bars, which are proportionate to the corresponding class intervals.) This example shows how you can indicate where there are resource surpluses and shortfalls: plans can be made to obtain further resources for peak times, or reschedule the work to flatten the peaks, or redeploy surplus resources.

Figure 8.3: Resource bar chart call centre time required

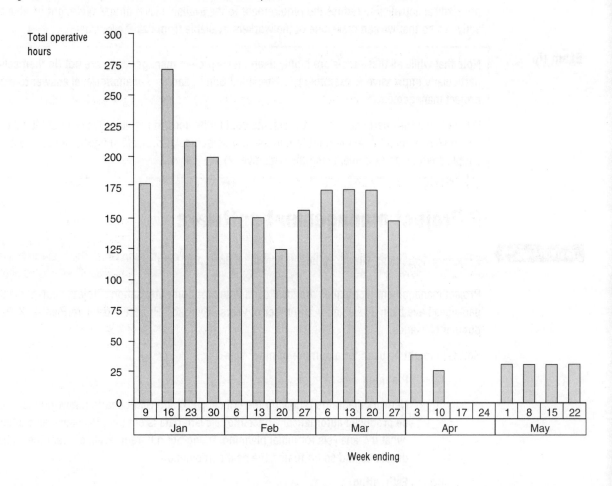

Figure 8.4: Resource histogram

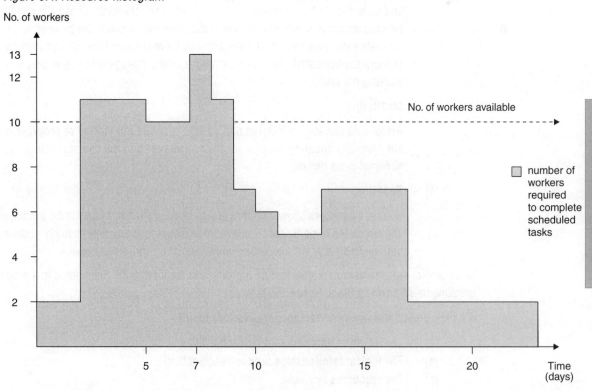

As shown in Figure 8.4, the number of workers required on the seventh day is 13. Can we reschedule the non-critical activities to reduce the requirement to the available level of 10? We might be able to rearrange activities so that we can make use of the workers available from day 9 onwards.

Exam tip

> Note that while all these tools are highly useful for a project manager, they are not (in themselves) particularly impressive to examiners... 'Prepare a Gantt chart' is *not* a pass-level answer to a question on project management!
>
> What should the chart show? What problems could it be used to highlight? How could it aid problem-solving? Why might it be the right tool to use in this particular project? (Might you even be able to *draw* a simple chart as an example, using the data given?)

2 Project management software

FAST FORWARD

> Project management can derive benefits from using appropriate **software**.

Project management techniques are ideal candidates for computerisation. Project management software packages have been available for a number of years. Microsoft Project and Micro Planner X-Pert are two popular packages.

Software might be used for a number of purposes.

(a) **Planning**

Network diagrams (showing the critical path) and Gantt charts (showing resource use) can be produced automatically once the relevant data is entered. Packages also allow a sort of 'what if?' analysis for initial planning, trying out different levels of resources, changing deadlines and so on to find the best combination.

(b) **Estimating**

As a project progresses, actual data will become known and can be entered into the package and collected for future reference. Since many projects involve basically similar tasks (interviewing users and so on), actual data from one project can be used to provide more accurate estimates for the next project. The software also facilitates and encourages the use of more sophisticated estimation techniques than managers might be prepared to use if working manually.

(c) **Monitoring**

Actual data can also be entered and used to facilitate monitoring of progress and automatically updating the plan for the critical path and the use of resources as circumstances dictate.

(d) **Reporting**

Software packages allow standard and tailored progress reports to be produced, printed out and circulated to participants and senior managers at any time, usually at the touch of a button. This helps with co-ordination of activities and project review.

Most project management packages feature a process of identifying the main steps in a project, and breaking these down further into specific tasks.

A typical project management package requires four **inputs**.

(a) The length of **time** required for each activity of the project.
(b) The **logical relationships** between each activity.
(c) The **resources** available.
(d) **When** the resources are available.

Action Programme 2

From your general knowledge of business software tools, what would you anticipate to be the advantages and disadvantages of using such tools for project management?

3 Documentation and reports

FAST FORWARD

Project **documentation** plays an important part in project control and communication.

We will now look at the main **documents and reports** used in project management. The name allocated to documents will vary across different organisations. What is constant is the need for clear and relevant documentation that helps monitor and control the project.

Remember that reports are not a substitute for **face-to-face communication**. Too many (or too lengthy) reports will result in **information overload**.

When outlining possible content of documents some duplication of items occurs. This does not mean that information should be repeated, but that the information may appear in one or other of the documents depending on the format adopted by the organisation.

3.1 Project charter

The Project Charter is presented at the **Project Initiation Meeting**. This meeting agrees the project organisation structure and the initial project plans, which may then be incorporated into the Project Charter. The aim of the meeting is to ensure:

- That everyone knows their role
- All agree on what job is to be done
- There are good business reasons for the project
- That any risks involved have been assessed

It is likely that the Charter will evolve as the project develops, until it is ultimately incorporated into the Project Management Plan.

The Project Charter defines the **terms of reference** for the project. The charter should contain the statements of project manager, team, stakeholders and sponsors about:

- The **scope** of the project – what it is intended to cover and what it is not
- The desirable attitudes and behaviours for the project
- The objectives for the team during the project, and for the completed project
- The processes the team commits to, to help it work efficiently and effectively

The charter is more 'abstract' than the project documentation that will follow it. The team must be involved in discussing the expectations that the charter raises for them about the behaviour of others. This will combat the cynicism of the 'yet another mission statement' attitude.

The charter is not likely to give many specifics about how the team and the project are to proceed. The Project Management Plan will do that.

3.2 Project management plan

The project manager should also develop a **Project Management Plan**.

The **project management plan** should include:

- Project objectives and how they will be achieved and verified
- How any **changes** to these procedures are to be **controlled**
- The **management and technical procedures**, and **standards**, to be used
- The **budget** and **time-scale**
- **Safety**, health and environmental policies
- Inherent **risks** and how they will be managed

The plan **evolves** over time. A high-level plan for the whole project and a detailed plan for the current and following stage is usually produced soon after project start-up. At each subsequent stage a detailed plan is produced for the following stage and, if required, the overall project plan is revised. An important feature of the plan is likely to be arrangements for ensuring quality.

- Standards to be used throughout the project
- Controls that aim to ensure quality
- Checks to ensure quality

3.3 Progress reports

The frequency and contents of progress reports will vary depending on the length of, and the progress being made on, a project.

The progress report is a **control tool** intended to show the discrepancies between where the project is, and where the plan says it should be. A common form of progress reports uses two columns – one for **planned** time and expenditure and one for **actual**. Any additional content will depend on the format adopted. Some organisations include only the 'raw facts' in the report, and use these as a basis for discussion regarding reasons for variances and action to be taken, at a project review meeting.

The report should monitor progress towards key **milestones.**

Key concept

A **milestone** is a significant event in the project, usually completion of a major aspect of the project.

On project completion the project manager will produce the **Completion Report.** The main purpose of the completion report is to document the end of the project. The report should include a **summary** of the project outcome and include the details shown below.

(a)   Project objectives and the outcomes achieved.

(b)   The final project budget report showing expected and actual expenditure (If an external client is involved this information may be sensitive – the report may exclude or amend the budget report).

(c)   A brief outline of time taken compared with the original schedule.

The completion report will also include provision for any **on-going issues** that will need to be addressed after completion. Such issues would be related to the project, but not part of the project. (If they are part of the project the project is not yet complete!) Responsibilities and procedures relating to any such issues should be laid down in the report.

The manager may find it useful to distribute a provisional report and request **feedback**. This should ensure the version presented for client sign-off at the completion meeting is acceptable to all parties.

A more detailed review of the project follows a few months after completion: this is the **post-completion audit**.

3.4 The post-completion audit

Key concept

> The **post-completion audit** is a formal review of the project that examines the lessons that may be learned and used for the benefit of future projects.

The audit looks at all aspects of the project with regard to two questions.

(a) Did the end result of the project meet the **client's expectations**?

- The actual **design** and **construction** of the end product
- Was the project achieved **on time**?
- Was the project **completed within budget**?

(b) Was the **management of the project** as successful as it might have been, or were there bottlenecks or problems? This review covers:

- Problems that might occur on future projects with similar characteristics.
- The performance of the team individually and as a group.

In other words, any project is an opportunity to learn how to manage future projects more effectively.

The post-completion audit should involve **input from the project team**. A simple questionnaire could be developed for all team members to complete, and a reasonably informal meeting held to obtain feedback, on what went well (and why), and what didn't (and why).

This information should be formalised in a report. The **post-completion audit report** should contain the following.

(a) A **summary** should be provided, emphasising any areas where the structures and tools used to manage the project have been found to be **unsatisfactory**.

(b) A **review** of the end result of the project should be provided, and compared against the results expected. Reasons for any significant **discrepancies** between the two should be provided, preferably with suggestions of how any future projects could **prevent these problems recurring**.

(c) A **cost-benefit review** should be included, comparing the forecast costs and benefits identified at the time of the feasibility study with actual costs and benefits.

(d) **Recommendations** should be made as to any steps which should be taken to **improve** the project management procedures used.

Lessons learnt that relate to the way the **project was managed** should contribute to the smooth running of future projects.

A starting point for any new project should be a **review** of the documentation of any **similar projects** undertaken in the past.

Action Programme 3

You are a project manager, and milestone reports indicate that your project is beginning to fall behind schedule.

Brainstorm some of your options for dealing with this slippage.

[Key skill for marketers: Problem solving]

3.4.1 Project change procedure

Some of the reactions to slippage discussed above would involve changes that would significantly affect the overall project. Other possible causes of changes to the original project plan include:

- The availability of new technology
- Changes in personnel
- A realisation that user requirements were misunderstood
- Changes in the business environment
- New legislation

The **earlier** a change is made the **less expensive** it should prove. However, changes will cost time and money and should not be undertaken lightly.

When considering a change **an investigation** should be conducted to discover:

- The consequences of **not** implementing the proposed change.
- The impact of the change on **time, cost** and quality.
- The expected costs and benefits of the change.
- The risks associated with the change, and with the status-quo.

The process of ensuring that proper consideration is given to the impact of proposed changes is known as **change control.**

Changes will need to be implemented into the project plan and communicated to all stakeholders.

4 Risk management

FAST FORWARD

Risk management is a key aspect of project management.

The identification of risks involves an overview of the project to establish what could go wrong, and the consequences.

- What are the sources of risk?
- What is the likelihood of the risk presenting itself?
- To what extent can the risk be controlled?
- What are the consequences of that risk presenting itself?
- To what extent can those consequences be controlled?

The likelihood and consequences of risks can be plotted on a matrix: Figure 8.5.

Figure 8.5: Risk assessment matrix

	Low	Med	High
High	M	H	VH
Med	L	M	H
Low	VL	L	M

Potential impact (vertical axis) / Threat Likelihood (horizontal axis)

Developing a **contingency plan** that contains strategies for risks that fall into the VH quadrant should have priority, followed by risks falling into the two H quadrants. Following the principle of **management by exception**, the most efficient way of dealing with risks outside these quadrants may be to do nothing unless the risk presents itself.

There are four main strategies that could be employed when managing risk:

(a) **Avoidance**: the factors which give rise to the risk are removed.

(b) **Reduction**: the potential for the risk cannot be removed but analysis has enabled the identification of ways to reduce the incidence and / or the consequences.

(c) **Transference**: the risk is passed on to someone else – or is perhaps financed by an insurer.

(d) **Absorption**: the potential risk is accepted in the hope or expectation that the incidence and consequences can be coped with if necessary.

Chapter Roundup

- Various **tools and techniques** are available to plan and control projects.

- Project management can derive benefits from using appropriate **software**.

- Project **documentation** plays an important part in project control and communication.

- **Risk management** is a key aspect of project management.

Quick Quiz

1   List five typical stages of a project.

    1   ....

    2   ....

    3   ....

    4   ....

    5   ....

2   What would you expect a Project Initiation Document to contain?

3   What is Work Breakdown Structure?

4   What is the purpose of a Gantt chart?

5   What is the Project Quality Plan used for?

6   Why do many project managers prefer to use project management software?

7   Briefly outline the relationship between quality, cost and time in the context of a marketing project.

8   What should the risk management process achieve?

Answers to Quick Quiz

1   Defining, Planning, Implementing, Controlling, Completing.

2   Contents could include: Project objectives, the scope of the project, overall budget, final deadlines, the ultimate customer, resources, risks inherent in the project, a preliminary project plan (targets, activities and so on) and details of how the project is to be organised and managed.

3   Work Breakdown Structure (WBS) is the process of breaking down the project into manageable tasks.

4   A Gantt chart displays the time relationships between tasks in a project. It is a horizontal bar chart used to estimate the amount and timing of resources required.

5   The Project Quality Plan is used to guide both project execution and project control. It outlines how the project will be planned, monitored and implemented.

6   A project management software package saves time and produces high quality output. As with all software, it is dependant on the quality of the data fed into the package – the length of time required for each activity of the project, the logical relationships between each activity, the resources available and when the resources are available.

7   The quality of work produced is dependant upon (among other things) the time available and the resources (ie cost) available to the project. Insufficient time and / or resources will have an adverse effect on the quality of work produced.

8   The risk management process should identify and quantify the risks associated with the project, and decide on how the risks should be managed.

Action Programme Review

1   Estimates can be **improved** by:

- **Learning** from past mistakes and using past (adjusted/real) figures
- Ensuring sufficient design **information** to cost all project/product elements
- Ensuring as **detailed a specification as possible** from the customer
- Properly **analysing the job** into its constituent units (using a work breakdown structure)
- Using accurate labour budgets and costs (eg realistic time requirements, pay rates etc)

2   The advantages of using project management software are summarised on the following table.

Advantage	Comment
Enables quick re-planning	Estimates can be changed many times and a new schedule produced almost instantly. Changes to the plan can be reflected immediately.
Document quality	Well-presented plans give a professional impression and are easier to understand.
Encourages constant progress tracking	The project manager is able to compare actual progress against planned progress and investigate problem areas promptly.
What if? analysis	Software enables the effect of various scenarios to be calculated quickly and easily. Many project managers conduct this type of analysis using copies of the plan in separate computer files – leaving the actual plan untouched.

BPP)))
LEARNING MEDIA

Two **disadvantages** of project management software are:

(a) Some packages are difficult to use.

(b) Some project managers become so interested in producing perfect plans that they spend too much time producing documents and not enough time managing the project.

3

Action	Comment
Do nothing	After considering all options it may be decided that things should be allowed to continue as they are.
Add resources	If capable staff are available and it is practicable to add more people to certain tasks it may be possible to recover some lost ground. Could some work be subcontracted?
Work smarter	Consider whether the methods currently being used are the most suitable – for example could prototyping be used.
Replan	If the assumptions the original plan was based on have been proved invalid a more realistic plan should be devised.
Reschedule	A complete replan may not be necessary – it may be possible to recover some time by changing the phasing of certain deliverables.
Introduce incentives	If the main problem is team performance, incentives such as bonus payments could be linked to work deadlines and quality.
Change the specification	If the original objectives of the project are unrealistic given the time and money available it may be necessary to negotiate a change in the specification.

Now try Question 8 at the end of the Study Text

Part C
Brainworks: Case study

BPP
LEARNING MEDIA

Brainworks plc

1 Using the case study

Brainworks plc is not an exam question, in style or standard, but a learning aid designed to help you achieve the learning outcomes for *Marketing Management in Practice*. This examination is intended to integrate the whole of Stage 2, so the syllabus is written in very demanding terms. Acquisition of knowledge will not be enough to pass this exam; you must be able to apply your knowledge in a realistic setting. We think the best way we can help you to do this is to present the syllabus content **in the context of a wide-ranging case study**.

Parts A and B of this book deal with Elements 1 and 2 of the knowledge and skills requirements of the syllabus for *Marketing Management in Practice*. These Elements deal with new technical material that has not been covered before in the other syllabus modules. Therefore, these two parts use the kind of approach you have seen in the other BPP Stage 2 Study Texts.

Brainworks comes into its own in the rest of the Study Text. Elements 3,4 and 5 of the syllabus deal with matters that are covered in depth in the other three modules of Stage 2. However, there is a difference, in that in this module you are required to do much more with the basic material.

For example, Element 3 of the *Marketing Communications* syllabus requires you to do such things as these:

- 'Identify the causes of conflict in trade channels'

- 'Explain the role of trust, commitment and satisfaction … in the marketing channel and business-to-business contexts'

- 'Explain how the marketing mix can be suitably configured for use in a range of marketing channels and business-to-business situations'

This is pretty detailed stuff. Element 5 of the *Marketing Management in Practice* syllabus simply says:

- 'Use marketing communications techniques to provide support for members of a marketing channel'

The emphasis has shifted from detail to the big picture, from discussing ideas to managing real situations.

In this part of this Study Text we will use Brainworks plc to pose realistic problems of the type envisaged by the syllabus for your consideration. We will then show you how appropriate techniques might be used and possible solutions developed.

Brainworks plc is a **fictitious** company facing a number of issues relating to its products and markets. The market and environmental data have been developed for the case study and does not purport to factual accuracy.

Exam tip

> Use the Brainwork's cash study as an example of methodology: don't get stuck on the details. Remember: your focus will be the specific context set in the exam. Is it a product or service context? Consumer or B2B or G2C: government-to-citizen)? Well established, start-up or temporary/project (in which case, as in June 2006, the examiner does not consider long-term strategic direction models such as The Ansoff Matrix relevant)? Private sector or public? FMCG, fashion, construction, business services? Local or international? Learn to identify all these aspects of context…

2 Brainworks plc

2.1 History

Brainworks Holdings plc (BW) is one of the world's largest private employment agencies. Every day, it is responsible for sending over 1.5 million people to work. To put it in context, this is twice as many as are employed by General Motors, one of the world's largest car companies, and exceeds the population of some of the world's smaller countries.

Although BW is based in the UK, in 1995 it acquired **PeoplePower** of the US, for £500m.

BW enjoyed rapid and spectacular growth in the UK before taking over **PeoplePower**.

(a) BW began in the 1960s supplying programmers and systems analysts to the IT industry. The rapid growth of the IT industry and the growth of the micro-computers and networking have created an almost inexhaustible demand for computer-literate personnel. Some of BW's employees end up training client staff as well as doing the jobs they were originally expected to do.

(b) Economic changes in the UK and the US in recent years have shaken out the labour markets in those countries, and introduced long-term changes.

  (i) In the UK and many other advanced economies, employment in manufacturing is falling, whereas service sector employment is rising.

  (ii) Many of the new service sector jobs are temporary or part-time positions. Many firms are employing a core full-time permanent workforce supplemented by a periphery of part-time workers, freelances or workers on temporary contracts.

(c) The US also has seen a decline in the manufacturing employment and a huge growth in the service sector. PeoplePower's main market was the provision of secretarial and other business services, although it had expanded aggressively into health care and nursing.

By 1999, despite one or two anxious moments in the early 1990s recession, BW was the world's largest agency, with revenues of £4.5bn per year of which £3bn come from PeoplePower. Obviously, margins are more important than any statement of gross revenues. Typically, 85% of the revenue BW earns is accounted for by the salaries it pays its hire-workforce and by other salary-related deductions such as payroll taxes and National Insurance.

2.2 Organisation structure

BW is organised into a variety of divisions and subsidiaries, outlined in the diagram below. BW (UK) manages the firm's operations in the UK: Figure 9.1.

Figure 9.1: Organisation chart for BW Holdings Plc

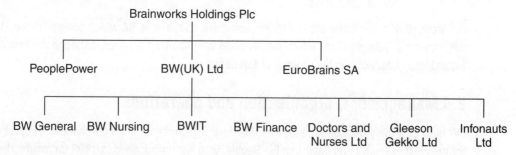

2.3 Supplying workers

2.3.1 Agency work

The market for temporary workers is very fragmented. There are hundreds of agencies. BW accounts for 8% of the world market. BW's nearest two competitors are two European companies: Diad, based in Switzerland, and Colec, based in France. These have recently announced a merger. Together, their combined revenues will amount to £4bn per year. Both have announced their intention to expand into the UK. They are starting to recruit for consultants.

The third largest European agency, Strand, is based in the Netherlands, and is making efforts to expand into Germany.

Another element of competition comes not from other agencies but from business service firms, which supply catering and cleaning services to firms. Agencies such as BW had previously supplied such workers.

However, to put the matter in context, in the USA, by the late 1990s workers from agencies such as BW amounted to 2% of the US workforce, up from 1% in 1989. In the UK, this is slightly higher at 2.5%. In continental Europe, on average, whilst temporary work has been increasing, it currently accounts for only 1% of the workforce. This average conceals wide variations, however: in the Netherlands, 3% of all workers are employed by agencies.

The potential is probably much greater for agencies such as BW to expand. In France, for example, up to 20% of the workforce is employed on a temporary basis, but works directly for the companies concerned.

For temporary workers, BW (UK) has these divisions.

- **BW Nursing** for health care staff
- **BW IT** for information technology staff
- **BW Finance** for temporary accounting and banking staff
- **BW General** deals with everyone else, such as secretaries and cleaners.

2.3.2 Recruitment for permanent positions

As well as providing temporary workers on specific assignments, BW acts as a recruitment agency to secure full time employees. Here, BW's activities are concentrated in the UK. BW(UK) operates through three subsidiaries.

(a) **Doctors and Nurses Ltd** – supplying health care professionals to NHS and private hospitals. This was acquired in 1983.

(b) **Gleeson Gekko Ltd** – supplying accounting and banking staff to the UK financial services sector.

(c) **Infonauts Ltd** – for IT specialists. In recent years, there has been a great demand from firms who wish to advertise on the Internet, and there has been a surge in demand for staff who are capable of designing and, as importantly, maintaining Internet websites which internet users can access.

In Europe, BW's operations are run by its subsidiary, **Eurobrains SA** which covers France, Germany, the Netherlands and Belgium and which mainly deals with financial services, although the firm intends to expand into IT services, in the manner of **Infonauts**.

2.4 Management, organisation and operations

BW has had a fairly turbulent management history. The architect of its purchase of **PeoplePower** was former chief executive and chairman Bill Begbie, who was imprisoned in 1999 for insider dealing. Announcing the takeover of PeoplePower, he said: 'My vision is to build BW into the biggest and best human resources agency in the world'.

The current chief executive is Willard Mann, from the US. Previously chief executive at PeoplePower, he was re-hired by BW's shareholders and bankers after Begbie's downfall. Willard Mann had fought BW's acquisition of PeoplePower, and has made no secret of his intention to split up the business: 'I am not convinced by the value of economies of scale in a business such as ours at an international level. If you grow too big, diseconomies set in. The whole thing is a distraction.'

BPP LEARNING MEDIA

The Board of Directors includes Willard Mann, Chris Bicknell, the finance director, Steve Reynolds, the marketing director, and Peter Richardson, the human resources director, who deals with BW's own staff (or consultants as they are called).

Each BW subsidiary and division has its own board of directors. BW(UK) has the same team as the main board plus the chairman of each subsidiary. This arrangement has been set up to exercise central control to ensure that performance targets are met or exceeded.

Each of BW(UK)'s **subsidiaries** for permanent staff has its *own* network of offices dotted around its main markets. Doctors & Nurses, Gleeson Gekko and Infonauts each have a network of offices in the UK, although Gleeson Gekko is concentrated in London.

For the **temporary staff divisions** (Nursing, IT, Finance and General), BW(UK) has four hundred offices in the UK, and aims to be the natural choice for a variety of assignments. All of BW's temporary markets are dealt with from these offices. The average number of consultants in each office is eight. Bill Begbie made it a management policy that every office must have at least one representative from each 'temporary staff' division (Nursing, IT, Finance General).

2.4.1 Managing each office

BW(UK). In the UK, BW employs consultants in each office, who are responsible for placing applicants with jobs. Each consultant keeps his or her own file of temporary workers which he or she matches to the demands made by business clients.

PeoplePower has a similar set-up, except that it is not organised on an area basis: 'Americans don't mind moving around'. Instead, PeoplePower maintains separate offices for each main type of **business customer**. New York is central for financial staff, California for IT staff. PeoplePower invested very heavily in computer linkups. Willard Mann wants to install video-conferencing systems to interview potential contract workers, so that an IT specialist in Texas could be interviewed over the conferencing system by someone in, say, the San Francisco office.

2.5 Human resources

BW and its subsidiaries are obviously concerned for the human resources needs of their clients, but they have their own human resources to look after as well.

In the UK, BW's consultants are paid a low basic salary, but get a substantial commission and a flat fee of £100 every time an employee is placed. Consultants have a six month probation period. They are given some initial training by sitting in on interviews. At each office, the practice is for existing consultants to pass on one of their business clients to the new recruit. Each office has a manager who determines what these clients will be. Appraisals take place when convenient. Non performers are booted out fairly quickly.

PeoplePower on the other hand does not pay commission on each placement. Rather, each office has a profit target. Consultants get a bonus based on the total profit made by the office and PeoplePower as a whole. Appraisals take place every year. Each PeoplePower consultant is supposed to build up a 'personal competence' of unique knowledge, for example a type of employee or a market, for the firm as a whole.

Begbie had wanted to dismantle the US system, and replace it with something on the lines of the UK but the resistance was too high.

Each PeoplePower consultant is supposed to build up a good personal relationship with the companies he or she deals with, and is expected to phone regularly even in the absence of any particular request to see if there are any unmet needs which PeoplePower could satisfy.

2.6 Management

Begbie liked to think of himself as a charismatic leader. He had himself photographed with leading politicians, and sought mentions in the business press.

'I see the firm has having essentially a family atmosphere,' he said, 'After all we are a people business. Everybody's contribution is valued. And I have an open door policy'. He regularly visited the local offices in the UK.

Willard Mann, on the other hand, is rather more serious. He pays few site visits, although he speaks regularly to senior managers. He does, however, take a great interest in the profit targets of each of the main businesses, and takes cashflow especially seriously.

2.7 Mission and strategy

Begbie's vision was to build BW to the biggest and best temporary employment agency in the world, hence the purchase of PeoplePower. In line with his thinking, Begbie devised a mission statement for BW, which appears framed in every office of the company.

'BW's mission is simply this: to provide our clients with the right workers at the right time; to offer the right work to the temporary staff we hire out; to offer profits to our shareholders; and to satisfy our employees and the community'.

Willard Mann cannot be bothered with mission statements: 'especially with a firm as diverse as ours. Our staff need to be taken seriously, not preached at; anyhow, mission statements give too many hostages to fortune'.

He states 'Our current corporate objective is to increase shareholder value, in whatever way, operational or organisational. The strategy? By increasing revenues through existing businesses, and by shaving costs where possible'. As Willard says, 'Employment law in most of Europe is a nightmare, and I've got enough trouble on my hands without expanding overseas'.

2.8 Marketing

Recent financial results have been disappointing. PeoplePower has been successful, but the BW(UK) and EuroBrains have not increased their profits significantly.

Indeed, confidential market research suggests that the adverse publicity regarding Begbie's fall dented the trust placed in the business. More worrying, the research revealed that while business clients are fairly satisfied with BW's services, they are not loyal; and that jobseekers rate BW fairly low in comparison with other agencies. One competitor, for example, is known to send handwritten thank you notes to contract staff who do particularly well for its clients. Other agencies offer the agency staff sickness benefits and even paid holidays.

The marketing director of BW has a number of worries about the UK market.

'Some of our bigger business clients are getting fed up having to deal with local offices all the time. Sometimes they have to deal with several offices just to get a reasonable pool of applicants. Another problem is that some of the ''temporary'' work is becoming long-term for six months or so, to cope with changes in demand. It is also embarrassing and irritating that the consultants obviously compete with one another. I am also concerned that our market share may be slipping.'

Action Programme 1

As a first step and to consolidate your understanding of this case material, produce a PESTEL and SWOT analysis for BW. You should draw upon any knowledge that you may have of the employment agency sector.

Action Programme Review

Here are some basic points. You may have thought of others.

PESTEL

Political	Different political environments in US, UK and Europe, with widely different labour laws.
Economic	Tax rates; pressures on companies to cut costs eg 'freezes' on recruitment.
Social	Work patterns, ageing populations, attitudes to temporary workers.
Technological	Use of computer systems to control operations – knowledge management to cut duplication of effort.
Environmental	Expectation that all 21st century companies be environmentally aware – PR benefits?
Legal	Employment legislation (eg minimum wage), Data Protection, working hours regulations.

SWOT

Strengths	Weaknesses
Strong leadership Size/revenues IT expertise	Consultants competing, no knowledge sharing
	Reputation tarnished
	Dependence on People Power revenues
	Lack of useful mission statement
Opportunities	**Threats**
Diverse activities	Increase competition from Diad Colec
Potential to expand	Fragmented market

BPP
LEARNING MEDIA

Managing knowledge and market research

10

Syllabus content – knowledge and skill requirements

- The concept, and examples, of the application of information and knowledge management, highlighting the role of marketing and employees within the organisation (3.1)

- Designing a research project aimed at providing information as part of a marketing audit or for marketing and business decisions (3.2)

- Managing a marketing research project by gathering relevant information on time and within the agreed budget (3.3)

- Arrangements to record, store and, if appropriate, update information in the MkIS, a database created for the purpose or another system (3.4)

- Analysis and interpretation of information and presentation, as a written or oral presentation, appropriate conclusions or recommendations that inform the marketing and business decisions for which the research was undertaken (3.5)

- Review and evaluation of the effectiveness of the activities and the role of the individual and team in this process (3.6)

1 Managing knowledge

FAST FORWARD

Many organisations have a great deal of **knowledge** that they cannot easily access because it lies in the records maintained by individuals for their own work

Steve Reynolds, the marketing director, has been talking to his next-door-neighbour, who is a Chartered Management Accountant. Steve has been talking about his concerns that service to his key accounts in the UK is hindered by BW's structure.

Steve explained some of his problems in terms of the banking industry. Banks deal with Gleeson Gekko for permanent professional recruiting; with BW Finance for temporary professional staff and with BW General for support staff of all kinds. This causes considerable frustration, both in the client HR departments that have to deal with this fragmentation and among the staff themselves. As people become more capable and learn new skills and as they become more mobile between jobs, the divisions between permanents and temporaries and between expert and less qualified staff are becoming blurred. It is often difficult for both recruiters and workpeople to know which agency to approach; naturally, the eventual tendency is to approach them all. BW thus finds itself involved in costly **duplication of effort**.

In addition to this, it is becoming more common for client companies to want to try out new professional staff on a temporary contract and only make an offer of permanent employment after due consideration. If this happens, BW will not only lose a good temporary off their books, they will also lose the commission they might have earned by providing a permanent staff member in the first place.

Steve's neighbour, a very experienced manager of both people and systems suggested that Steve was making a rather good case for a **major reorganisation** at BW. Steve explained that this wasn't really a starter, but something had to be done. The neighbour then suggested that it might be possible to do something with information technology: some kind of **database system** might be set up to cover all the people the various arms of BW had on their books for placements, of whatever kind.

Steve was immediately taken with this idea and thought very hard about it over the next few days.

1.1 Example problem

Explain how knowledge management techniques could be used in BW(UK) to assist in the marketing of its services.

1.2 Knowledge management techniques

FAST FORWARD

Knowledge management aims to exploit existing knowledge and to create new knowledge so that it may be exploited in turn. Knowledge management is most effective when IT systems are used.

Knowledge management is founded on the idea that knowledge is a major source of competitive advantage in business. Its aim is to exploit existing knowledge and to create new knowledge so that it may be exploited in turn. This is not easy. All organisations possess a great deal of data, but it tends to be unorganised and inaccessible. It is often locked up inside the memories of people who do not realise the value of what they know. Even when it is recorded in some way it may be difficult and time consuming to get at, as is the case with most paper archives.

In the case of BW(UK), the situation is compounded, from an organisational point of view by being in the interest of consultants to keep the details of the good quality temporary staff they deal with very much to themselves, since their income depends on the placings they personally make

Studies have indicated that 20 to 30 percent of company resources are wasted because organisations are not aware of what knowledge they already possess. Lew Platt, Chief Executive of Hewlett Packard, has articulated this in the phrase 'If only HP knew what HP knows, we would be three times as profitable'.

BPP LEARNING MEDIA

1.3 Data, information and knowledge

FAST FORWARD

Data consists of individual facts; **information** is data that is organised or analysed in some way. **Knowledge** is created from information when **patterns** or **trends** are discovered that are of significance outside the original **context** in which the information was set.

There is an important conceptual hierarchy underpinning knowledge management. This distinguishes between **data**, **information** and **knowledge**. The distinctions are not clear-cut and, to some extent, are differences of degree rather than kind. An understanding of the terms is best approached by considering the relationships between them.

Data typically consists of **individual facts**, but in a business context may include more complex items such as opinions, reactions and beliefs. It is important to realise that a quantity of data, no matter how large, does not constitute information.

Information is data that is **organised** in some useful way. For instance, an individual credit sale will produce a single invoice identifying the goods, the price, the customer, the date of the sale and so on. These things are data: their usefulness does not extend beyond the purpose of the invoice, which is to collect the sum due. Even if we possess a copy of every invoice raised during a financial year, we still only have data. However, if we process that data we start to create information. For instance, a simple combination of analysis and arithmetic enables us to state total sales for the year, to break that down into sales for each product and to each customer, to identify major customers and so on. These are pieces of information: they are useful for the management of the business, rather than just inputs into its administrative systems.

Here is a table that summarises the **progression from data to knowledge**. It introduces some other distinguishing factors.

	Data	Information	Knowledge
Nature	Facts	Relationships between processed facts	Patterns discerned in information
Importance of context	Total	Some	Context independent
Importance to business	Mundane	Probably useful for management	May be strategically useful

There is one final important point to note here and that is that the progression from data to knowledge is not the same in all circumstances. The difference will often be associated with the scale of operations. Take the example of a customer going into insolvent liquidation with £200,000 outstanding on its account. For a small supplier with an annual turnover of, say, £10 million, a bad debt of this size would be of strategic importance and might constitute a threat to its continued existence. Advance notice of the possibility would be valuable knowledge. However, for a company operating on a global scale, the bad debt write-off would be annoying but still only one item in a list of bad debts – data, in other words.

Within BW(UK), the details of temporary workers held by the consultants represent valuable knowledge to those individuals, because, as we pointed out earlier, they make the difference between success and failure as a placement consultant. However, from the point of view of the organisation, they are little more than unorganised data, since they cannot be used in a strategic way, to provide a quantum improvement in service to either client organisations or to the temporary workers themselves. This was identified as a weakness in our SWOT analysis in the previous chapter.

1.4 Knowledge management systems

FAST FORWARD ⟫ IT systems used for handling data, information and knowledge include simple office automation applications such as **spreadsheets** that can organise and analyse data into information; **Groupware** and **expert systems** for handling information; and **data warehousing** and **datamining** software that can be used to generate knowledge from both information and from simple data.

Recognition of the value of information and knowledge and understanding of the need to organise data and make it accessible have provoked the development of sophisticated IT systems.

Office automation systems are IT applications that improve productivity in an office. These include word processing and voice messaging systems.

Groupware, such as Lotus Notes provides functions for collaborative work groups. In a sales context, for instance, it would provide a facility for recording and retrieving all the information relevant to individual customers, including notes of visits, notes of telephone calls and basic data like address, credit terms and contact name. These items could be updated by anyone who had contact with a customer and would then be available to all sales people.

Groupware also provides such facilities as messaging, appointment scheduling, to-do lists and jotters.

An **intranet** is an internal network used to share information using Internet technology and protocols. The firewall surrounding an intranet fends off unauthorised access from outside the organisation. Each employee has a browser, used to access a server computer that holds corporate information on a wide variety of topics, and in some cases also offers access to the Internet. Applications include company newspapers, induction material, procedure and policy manuals and internal databases.

(a)   Savings accrue from the elimination of storage, printing and distribution of documents that can be made available to employees on-line.

(b)   Documents on-line are often more widely used than those that are kept filed away, especially if the document is bulky (eg manuals) and needs to be searched. This means that there are improvements in productivity and efficiency.

(c)   It is much easier to update information in electronic form.

IT systems can be used to store vast amounts of data in accessible form. A **data warehouse** receives data from operational systems, such as a sales order processing system, and stores it in its most fundamental form, without any summarisation of transactions. Analytical and query software is provided so that reports can be produced at any level of summarisation and incorporating any comparisons or relationships desired.

The value of a data warehouse is enhanced when **datamining** software is used. True datamining software discovers previously unknown relationships and provides insights that can not be obtained through ordinary summary reports. These hidden patterns and relationships constitute knowledge, as defined above, and can be used to guide decision making and to predict future behaviour. Datamining is thus a contribution to organisational learning.

   Marketing at Work

The American retailer Wal-Mart discovered an unexpected relationship between the sale of nappies and beer! Wal-Mart found that both tended to sell at the same time, just after working hours, and concluded that men with small children stopped off to buy nappies on their way home, and bought beer at the same time. Logically therefore, if the two items were put in the same shopping aisle, sales of both should increase. Wal-Mart tried this and it worked.

BPP ⟫⟫⟫
LEARNING MEDIA

Here is an amended version of our earlier table. This one includes the relevant IT systems.

	Data	Information	Knowledge
Nature	Facts	Relationships between processed facts	Patterns discerned in information
Importance of context	Total	Some	Context independent
Importance to business	Mundane	Probably useful for management	May be strategically useful
Relevant IT systems	Office automation Data warehouse	Groupware Expert systems Report writing software	Datamining

1.5 Knowledge management at BW(UK)

On the face of it, the staff of BW(UK) ought to be able to offer a much **better service to their client organisations** if they managed their knowledge better. A system such as Lotus Notes could hold all the details of all their registered temporary workers and make it available to all staff in all offices via an intranet. This ought to mean that vacancies could be matched with available staff very rapidly. The database could be searched very rapidly for people with suitable qualifications and experience who were available in the right geographical areas. It would also be possible to establish the profile of the existing pool of people; this information could be used to identify areas of shortage and surplus, for instance. Such information would be very useful when advising clients on reward packages.

An immediate problem would be that this would represent a significant **change to the current way of working**. At the moment, consultants have their own, unique lists of workers; they would have to surrender this private resource in return for access to a wider database. Some, who felt their lists were large and valuable, would be unwilling to do this. It would be necessary to adjust the reward plan for the consultants so that was based on success in providing good service to clients. The human resources director could advise here.

It would probably be inappropriate, for the same reason, to attempt a similar exercise with the details of clients. Such things are easy to do and are frequently done in the world of telesales. A single, intranet-accessible database would be of great value in analysing the client population. It could be used for detecting trends in requirements, establishing just who are the high value clients and so on. It would also facilitate the handover of clients between consultants, as happens when a new consultant joins. However, so long as there is a premium of consultants' retaining and servicing their own clients, BW(UK) will need to tread warily here. A client database and contact logging system will, however, almost certainly be a medium term target.

A change of the magnitude proposed would also be an opportunity to make formal recognition of the fact that the temporary workers themselves are a valuable stakeholder group. We already know that they do not rate BW(UK) very highly; this is a major problem that needs to be addressed sooner rather than later. These workpeople are, after all, the essence of the company's business. The most effective way of improving the company's standing in their eyes (and thus their willingness to remain on its books) would be to offer an improved service to them, which an IT-based system ought to be able to do.

1.6 File conversion

FAST FORWARD

File conversion is needed when IT systems are introduced to replace paper systems for handling data and information. It normally starts with the creation of standardised paper files. The emphasis is on checking **accuracy** at all stages of the data entry process.

File conversion is the process of converting existing records into a format suitable for use with a new system. In the case of BW(UK)'s IT-based system, this will undoubtedly involve an extensive effort in keyboard data entry.

Assuming that Steve Reynolds and his colleagues in the HR department succeed in convincing BW(UK)'s consultants to surrender control over their data, the process of converting it from its current state into a digital database could then be undertaken.

This process would be complicated by the doubtless varied and probably idiosyncratic recording styles of the individual consultants. Significant effort would have to go into checking for accuracy and completeness.

The first stage of the data conversion process would probably be the design of an appropriate paper form that would mimic the appropriate data entry screen in the chosen IT application. Existing records could then be manually transcribed into the standardised format and subsequently entered via keyboard into the new system.

It might be possible to work direct from the existing records, but, as mentioned above, this might be very challenging for the keyboard operators.

The process of transcribing records to a standardised format would present an opportunity to check the data: inaccurate and out of date material should be discarded at this stage. Further validation and verification should take place at subsequent stages. One obvious check that could be made would be to have consultants check each of their own record once entered on the new system.

2 Designing and managing research

FAST FORWARD

A market research project requires clear **objectives** and careful **planning**. Secondary sources may be researched in-house; most smaller organisations will require the services of market research professionals if they wish to do primary research.

Some time has passed since Steve Reynolds discussed his data management problem with his next-door-neighbour. A suitable IT system has been installed and the data entered in an appropriate form. A new term has been coined – the workpeople BW(UK) manage and promote are now known as '**external staff**'. This emphasises their crucial contribution to the success of the company, while distinguishing them from the people that the company actually employs.

Steve has also made progress with his more ambitious project to centralise information on client organisations. The general feeling among consultants was hostile at first, but Steve managed the necessary change rather well, using a combination of consultation and low-key persuasion. His internal marketing campaign focussed on convincing a small number of influential, long-serving consultants that they would find the new system useful.

Existing data about clients is now largely available on-line using the new system, which is called RG762. Steve is keen to **expand the usefulness** of the system by researching and then entering basic data about potential client organisations so that informed approaches can be made to them

2.1 Example problem

Explain how a research project to meet Steve Reynolds' requirements should be designed and managed. What further questions might Steve consider beyond this (rather basic) project?

2.2 Problem definition and research objectives

The first stage of any marketing research programme is **problem definition** and the setting of **research objectives**. It is important to be very clear as to just what the objectives of any research exercise actually are before the data-gathering process begins. This implies a process of project definition and the asking of outcome-determining questions designed to elicit a proper definition of the required information.

Steve appears to want simple data that is probably easily available already from published **secondary sources** such as companies' annual reports, trade publications and commercial directories. However, it may be that on reflection, he will decide a more far-reaching programme is needed.

His aim seems to be couched very much in terms of using the new system in the context of basic **market development**; that is, expanding the market for the services BW(UK) currently offers. It would be worth asking if he had considered the possibility of parallel **product development**, that is, the development of new products for offer to both existing clients and potential new ones.

Steve should ask more probing questions to enable more analysis of the market from the in-depth RG 762 database. By asking such questions, **gaps in knowledge** can be identified and filled. For example:

- What new services could we offer in our various markets?

- Are we up-to-date in our knowledge of changing legislation and regulations?

- What do our clients and external staff think of us?

- Are we pricing our services at market rates?

- How should we advertise? Have our campaigns to date been effective?

- Should we expand overseas?

- What impact is the Internet having on the market for temporary and permanent staff – should we have a website?

If Steve were receptive to the idea of product development, this would have significant implications for the research project. As he has indicated, his original idea was to collect and systematise information about non-client companies that would be of the same type as information already held about existing clients. This might indicate new opportunities for the kind of services BW(UK) already provides.

However, if BW(UK) is to be able to develop successful new products, the research project must also gather information that will enable the company to discern the existence of currently **unmet needs**. This may not be so easily available from secondary sources and may therefore require the undertaking of **primary research**.

Assuming that Steve decides to undertake the more ambitious project, we might expect to see research objectives established along the lines given below.

(a) **Identify potential new clients** and determine for each:

- Nature of business, turnover and ROI
- Contact details, including name of HR director or manager
- Geographical location
- Size of workforce and total staff cost
- Whether independent or part of a group and if the latter, which one

(b) For **existing clients** determine:

- Current usage of our services, analysed by type of external staff, month, whether temporary or permanent and duration

- Degree of satisfaction with our services, nature of any problems encountered and decision maker's attitude to the type of service we offer

- Extent of unsatisfied needs within client organisations

Note that these are merely suggestions; the managers responsible for any marketing project will have very specific ideas for what they want to establish.

2.3 Planning the research

The research objectives we have sketched above break into two neat parts that illustrate the next stage in the market research process.

Objective (a) is fairly complete and specific and lends itself to **internal desk research** using published sources. It could almost be handed over to one of the BW(UK) staff with an indication of when a report was required and in what form. The time scale envisaged would constitute and effective budget, since the only resource being used would be one person's time. (Note that this assumes the Marketing Department is already in possession of the necessary secondary sources).

Objective (b) is much less simple. Establishing the answers to these questions will almost certainly require the use of techniques such as interviews, questionnaires and statistical analysis. As such it is likely that the services of a **market research bureau** will be required.

2.4 Briefing the bureau

It will be necessary to reach a contractual understanding with the chosen market research bureau. The basis of this understanding will be the agreed research plan. This is likely to contain the elements shown below.

Background information on the project, including orientation information on the client, its markets and products

- A specification of agreed research objectives
- A memorandum of the research methods to be employed
- Time and financial budgets
- Specification as to who shall own the resulting data
- A note of reporting requirements

2.5 Managing the research

Whether research is conducted in-house or contracted out, the research project requires management.

In the case of in-house research, represented here by the first of our suggested objectives above, the person carrying out the desk research should know to whom to report. It would be appropriate with a project of this importance for daily reports to be made on progress achieved, difficulties encountered and so on. The work could be carried out by an experienced marketing assistant, perhaps reporting to a marketing manager.

The work contracted-out to a bureau will also require some continuing management effort. While the bureau should be quite capable of supervising its own work and maintaining its own quality standards, it will need a **point of contact** at an appropriate level of authority within BW(UK). There will probably be interim progress reports to be made and there is always the possibility that early research may reveal things that call for a reconsideration of the objectives and methods of the overall research programme. There must be a named person with whom the bureau can take such matters up.

BPP)))
LEARNING MEDIA

Exam tip

One of the most basic (and popular) types of question in this exam is: 'what are the information requirements …? (for a given project or initiative) and 'How can this information be obtained?' Get used to asking these two questions for any plan you encounter. (Market segmentation? Customer care programme? Brand development?) What information will you need, from whom and how best obtained.

The June 2006 exam asked three questions in relation to (a) developing a conference programme and (b) planning *next* year's programme on the basis of feedback from delegates. The December 2006 exam asked the questions in relation to the selection of locations for new hair salons. Note that in neither case (given that they were 'start up' projects) could you use a Standard Marketing Information System or MkIS model. Nor, in the second case, could you rely on 'market research' (other than to establish demand): you had to look for *area* attributes, which matched the salon chain's *positioning* aspirations.

Think in context – and think beyond the obvious. (Not all information can be gathered by a single questionnaire…).

3 Interpreting and presenting information

FAST FORWARD

The principles distinguishing data, information and knowledge may be applied to the output from a **market research project**. This will help decide what to include in reports to senior management.

Steve Reynolds' chosen market research bureau, Joplin Katzenbach Limited, has carried out its work and submitted its report. Steve is now pondering the best use to make of this information. He was particularly interested in the potential for developing BW(UK)'s business in the West of England as, historically, the company had not been well represented there. He had therefore called for a separate report on that region

The bureau provided a great deal of tabulated data, which is rather indigestible, but they also summarised much of it. The weakness of their report was that they did not attempt to draw conclusions from their work and Steve is now facing this task himself. He wants to highlight facts that seem important to the future development of BW(UK)'s business in the West of England.

3.1 Example problem

Using the information given below, prepare an outline for a briefing for the board of BW(UK). Your report should emphasise matters that are of strategic marketing importance. You will find that the process of preparing your brief will prompt you to ask a number of questions to which the data gives little or no answer. Say what extra data you would need to obtain from the body of the report.

3.2 Extracts from the executive summary prepared by the market research bureau

Numbers of staff given below are not precise and anyway should be expected to fluctuate. Generally, we believe that are accurate to **plus or minus** 5%. Numbers and categories of organisations are accurate as at 7 days before the submission of this report.

There are 48,247 private sector organisations within BW(UK)'s stated geographical area of interest, employing 335,000 staff. Of these, 1,213 are manufacturing companies employing 100 staff or more, 2,474 are service companies employing 100 staff or more and the remainder are employ fewer than 100 staff.

Independent research indicates that within the manufacturing sector, 7% of staff may be described as managers of one kind or another, 14% are clerical staff, 18% are technicians in fields related to the manufacturing process and the remainder are process workers of all grades.

The **public sector** organisations in the area include 27 NHS regional hospitals and 987 other medical facilities ranging in size from GP health centres to private hospitals employing up to 300 medical staff. The total number of doctors employed is in excess of 18,000. There are 27,500 nursing staff and 15,600 administrative staff employed in these establishments. The administrative staff figure includes 2,800 financial support staff.

Of the **service companies**, 17 are major providers of services to local authorities. Their services include street cleansing and rubbish collection; buildings maintenance; building design and construction; catering; premises cleaning and janitorial services; and security services. These 17 companies employ 19,400 staff between them. This group is dominated by three very large companies that employ over 60% of those staff. These are Butribol plc, ANHT plc and Button Brothers.

There are 1825 **bank branches** in the area, including the head offices of two of the UK clearing banks. Total employment in banking is 43,900, of whom 5,700 are employed in head offices. Regional banking headquarters, of which there are 9 in the area employ a further 2,170 staff. The remainder of the banking staff are employed in smaller branches. The average number employed in a branch is 63.

Also in the financial services sector are 423 **accountancy practices**. The great majority of these (309) are small firms with total staff of less than 50 in all categories. The remainder are the regional headquarters of international and national firms and the head offices of important regional players. There are over 6,400 qualified accountants working in the region, 13,400 part-qualifieds and 4,800 support staff.

3.3 Information from BW(UK)'s own marketing information system

BW(UK) currently has active accounts for the organisations shown below.

- 13 regional hospitals and 423 other medical sites for all types of staff and a further 5 regional hospitals and 115 other medical sites for clerical, administrative and cleaning staff.

- Both bank head offices, 6 regional offices and 1276 branches for all types of staff, 143 branches for cleaning staff only and 349 branches for banking operations staff only, of all grades.

- 19847 private sector companies of which 812 are known to be manufacturing companies. Staff provision for these companies has largely been in the finance and retail sales areas.

- 71 catering organisations, of which 4 are major players, providing catering services on a very large scale. The others are hotels, restaurants and in-house catering operations in large companies and public sector bodies.

- 247 cleaning companies, including the cleaning division of Butribol plc.

- 119 accountancy practices, 108 of whom only ever require professional staff. The largest area of demand is for senior unqualified staff.

3.4 Board briefing notes – marketing opportunities

Based on Joplin Katzenbach Limited results and our MkIS.

3.4.1 Health care

We have a strong position in the hospitals and health service providers sector with about a 50% market share for all types of staff. We have an opportunity in a further 12% of the sector where we supply all grades of staff other than medical professionals.

Query. We need to know why these sites do not come to us for medical staff so that we can pitch for the business.

BPP
LEARNING MEDIA

3.4.2 Banking

We are even better placed in the banking sector, with both national head offices and two thirds of other banking sites as our clients for all grades of staff. However, as in the health care sector, a significant number of sites do not come to us for all their staff

Query. As for hospitals.

3.4.3 Accountancy

We deal with roughly a quarter of the accountancy practices in the region, largely in the provision of senior unqualified staff.

Query. What is the breakdown of our client base by numbers employed? Are they representative of the overall structure of the profession in the region or is our business biased towards a particular point on the size scale.

3.4.4 Private sector companies

We have contracts with roughly two fifths of the private sector companies in the region, which is a respectable total, but appear to be heavily under represented in the manufacturing sector. Assuming that the number of companies and of their staff is split between the manufacturing and service sectors in the proportion of roughly one third to two thirds, we would expect to have far more manufacturing companies as our clients.

$(48,247 \times 1/3 \times 2/5 = 6,433)$

Queries Is this a valid assumption? Do we have companies on our books that are manufacturers but we are unaware of it? Is there a market dynamic that makes manufacturing companies less prone to need our services?

Penetration has been greatest in finance and retail sales. This seems an unbalanced performance.

Query. Are there good reasons why we should accept this bias?

3.4.5 Cleaning

Our penetration of the cleaning sector is uncertain.

Queries. How many cleaning staff are there in total? Is it possible to establish the split of cleaning staff between cleaning contractors and in-house staff? What proportion of companies that provide cleaning service use agencies like ours to find staff?

4 Role of good attitude

The success of knowledge management depends greatly on the attitudes of management and staff to the gathering and sharing of information internally and externally.

Information and knowledge are big sources of competitive advantage and hence major factors in the creation of corporate value and shareholder wealth. Hence, there must be proper systems and work practices to ensure that these are captured and accessible to the business rather than being hoarded by individual employees in their heads.

In modern business, knowledge if an important asset and should be subject to proper stewardship approaches.

Chapter Roundup

- Many organisations have a great deal of **knowledge** that they cannot easily access because it lies in the records maintained by individuals for their own work.

- **Knowledge management** aims to exploit existing knowledge and to create new knowledge so that it may be exploited in turn. Knowledge management is most effective when IT systems are used.

- **Data** consists of individual facts; **information** is data that is organised or analysed in some way. **Knowledge** is created from information when **patterns** or **trends** are discovered that are of significance outside the original **context** in which the information was set.

- IT systems used for handling data, information and knowledge include simple office automation applications such as **spreadsheets** that can organise and analyse data into information; **Groupware** and **expert systems** for handling information; and **data warehousing** and **datamining** software that can be used to generate knowledge from both information and from simple data.

- **File conversion** is needed when IT systems are introduced to replace paper systems for handling data and information. It normally starts with the creation of standardised paper files. The emphasis is on checking **accuracy** at all stages of the data entry process.

- A market research project requires clear **objectives** and careful **planning**. Secondary sources may be researched in-house; most smaller organisations will require the services of market research professionals if they wish to do primary research.

- The principles distinguishing data, information and knowledge may be applied to the output from a **market research project**. This will help decide what to include in reports to senior management.

BPP
LEARNING MEDIA

Developing and implementing marketing plans

11

Syllabus content – knowledge and skill requirements

- Development of an operational marketing plan, selecting an appropriate marketing mix for an organisation operating in any context (4.1)
- Use of the main techniques available for planning, scheduling and resourcing activities within the plan (4.2)
- Appropriate measures for evaluating and controlling the marketing plan (4.3)
- Review and evaluation of the effectiveness of planning activities and the role of the individual and team in this process (4.4)

1 A marketing plan for Brainworks

FAST FORWARD
A **marketing plan** for an organisation Like BW(UK) is complicated by the disparate nature of its component parts. No single course of action would be appropriate for all the subsidiaries involved. The marketing plan must make allowances for this.

Having put the BW(UK) knowledge management system and MkIS on a sound footing, Steve Reynolds is now turning his attention to the overall shape of the marketing operation in the UK. It is apparent that, just as BW itself grew by opportunistic acquisition, so there is **little co-ordination of marketing effort** in the company. For example, each of the divisions and subsidiary companies still runs its own promotion; Gleeson Gekko is particularly jealous of its autonomy, emphasising its role in the head hunting market and asserting that its status there would be compromised by any association with temporary staff supply.

Similarly, Infonauts Ltd, whose consultants have considerable experience in the IT field, promotes an image of laid-back, cool, California-inspired eccentricity in its business dealings. This has not prevented them from surviving the collapse of the Dot.com boom by shifting rapidly into other IT-related fields such as games development, control engineering and third generation mobile phone development.

As Steve considers the need for greater cohesiveness in marketing within BW(UK), he assembles some basic facts, figures and ideas.

The turnover and marketing expenses of each of the individual companies and divisions ('subsidiaries') of BW(UK) are given below in millions of pounds sterling.

	Turnover	Marketing expenses
BW Nursing	147	1.2
BW IT	37	0.6
BW Finance	84	1.7
BW General	101	0.9
Doctors and Nurses Ltd	27	0.2
Gleeson Gekko Ltd	159	2.7
Infonauts Ltd	98	1.4

The marketing organisation within the subsidiaries is rather complex and might almost be described as random.

Gleeson Gekko has its own Marketing Director on a salary almost as large as Steve Reynolds'; this person was taken on to the staff some four years ago and his efforts appear to have had a marked effect on the company's turnover. He has developed a close relationship with Beagle Trumper Codrington, a relatively newly formed advertising agency and together they have organised a very successful campaign of rather quirky, sardonic promotion that seems to appeal to the frustrated anarchists in the finance sector.

Infonauts has a single marketing assistant who has considerable experience of the media used to promote the company. This has included the successful use of posters on public transport in London and other major conurbations, a medium not used at all by other subsidiaries.

Doctor and Nurses Ltd relies almost entirely on personal selling to place its candidates, though it does a little corporate advertising as a reminder of its presence and services. The company was founded by Margaret Staines, a hospital physician who was disappointed with the bureaucracy she found in the NHS and wanted to be more independent. She has a major personal commitment to the ideals of the NHS and goes to great lengths to place candidates sympathetically. Dr Staines has developed very good relationships with senior doctors in the NHS region in which she started her company, and expects her staff of consultants to do the same in the areas they handle. She anticipates significant business opportunities in the future in line with the government's intention to increase spending on the NHS. She estimates that there will be continuing shortages of medical staff because of the very long training lead times.

BPP
LEARNING MEDIA

BW Nursing has recently collaborated with BW General and BW IT to spend £12.7 million on establishing a state-of-the-art **call centre** to handle enquiries for short-term temporaries. (The cost of this venture is not included in the marketing expense figures given above). The operators in this call-centre have also undertaken a programme of telesales activities, which has proven moderately successful. However, the cost of setting up the operation has forced an element of **retrenchment** into the three subsidiaries' budgets which has in turn led to a severe fall in their marketing spend. Between them, these subsidiaries have only two marketing staff: one has only recently taken on this role, the other has two years' experience. The less experienced person, Gillian Curtis, was formerly the secretary to the Sales Director of BW General and demonstrated considerable interest in the promotional arts, successfully organising two golf days and three business breakfasts.

The threatened entry of the combined Diad-Colec operation has now come to pass. They have opened offices in 9 major UK cities and have started supplying temporaries in the financial, clerical, administrative and catering sectors. There is little information available about their current progress, but BW Finance's divisional Marketing Director, Tom French, has compiled a record of their promotional activity. They appear to be spending heavily on corporate advertising and promotional events, having taken regular spreads in *Banking Times, Accountancy Journal* and *City*, and having hosted 450 guests from the finance sector at the recent Winterbourne Abbey arts festival and golf championship.

Tom French, whose judgement Steve Reynolds is inclined to trust, is sure that Diad-Colec will be a major challenge to BW(UK)'s revenues within three years. He takes this view partly because he has also established that they will enter the health care permanent and temporary recruiting market within six months. Dr Staines agrees with this assessment, based on her own industry soundings.

1.1 Example problem

Prepare a draft marketing plan for BW(UK).

Note Fairly obviously, there is no single correct response to this requirement. BW(UK) is a large and rather disparate organisation and its marketing planning might well be done by division. We have written a marketing plan that seems to us to take into account the available information, including that in the original setting, the ideas developed in the previous chapter and the new information given above.

You may feel you have some much better ideas and may even disagree with our plan. That is fine, so long as you have reasons to back your views.

Exam tip

The Senior Examiner's report to the June 2006 exam helpfully suggested the kind of structure expected for an *outline marketing plan*. You aren't required to put excessive detail into the structure (in the form of contents lists, executive summaries and so on).

Instead, focus on:

- Environmental analysis (eg using PESTLE or Porter's Five Forces model)

- Appreciation of context (eg international, product/service, B2C/B2B issues)

- SMART marketing objectives

- Outline tactics across the marketing mix (4Ps) – or extended marketing mix (7Ps) in a service context

- Feedback/control mechanisms and measures

1.2 BW(UK) marketing plan

FAST FORWARD A marketing plan should have an effective **layout**.

1   Executive summary

1.1   We expect to achieve substantial growth from the government's stated intention to expand the budget of the NHS. However, we cannot be complacent as a major new competitor, Diad-Colec, has entered the financial and catering markets and is expected to expand into other markets as well.

1.2   Our image with both clients and external staff is no more than adequate. This is affecting our performance.

1.3   We aim to improve our overall turnover by 8.5% and to enhance our corporate and brand image.

1.4   We aim to achieve these objectives by spending £1.1 million on a promotional campaign in addition to normal advertising; by making better use of our new RG762 computer system and our new call centre; and by enlisting the support of both internal and external staff in improving the quality of our service to customers.

2   Situation analysis

2.1   **The environment.** There are two important environmental developments affecting BW(UK). These are

- The entry of Diad-Colec into the UK
- The UK government's commitment to spend a great deal more of GNP on health care

2.2   **NHS**. The growth in NHS spending is unlikely to be matched by growth in permanent employment because of the long lead times involved in training medical staff: to the extent that the slack will be taken up at all, it is likely to be by employing more mature mothers with grown families and by importing doctors and nurses from other countries. Many of the first category are likely to wish to work part-time, at first at least, while many of the second category are likely to learn rapidly that agency work pays well. In both cases, there are good opportunities for us.

2.2.1   We are also likely to see increased demand for NHS administrative and support staff in all grades.

2.2.2   The NHS expansion therefore should provide an expanding market for us. We must as a minimum maintain our market share

2.3   **Diad-Colec**. Diad-Colec is something of an unknown quantity, but they are here in strength and are already making an impact in the financial and catering markets. We must expect that sheer novelty and, possibly, penetration pricing will lead to the loss of some clients; however, we must be ready to counter Diad-Colec's advance with our own aggressive tactics.

2.4   **Market dynamics**. In both the health care and banking markets for temporary staff our penetration differs between professional staff and cleaning and administrative staff. It would be a very natural improvement to our position to base expansion in both markets on product development and to attempt to achieve a single integrated client base in each. Cross-selling may be our course here and there are clear opportunities for greater co-operation between divisions.

2.5   **Further problems within our markets**

2.5.1   Recent well-publicised change at the top of BW has adversely affected the way we are seen by some clients. In addition, while we seem to provide reasonable satisfaction to our clients, we find they are not at all loyal to us. Some of them are irritated by the fragmentation of our divisional structure (which may explain some of the differential penetration outlined above). Similarly, there is a tradition of competitiveness within some of our offices that is having a counter-productive effect: clients find it strange that we do not speak with one voice.

BPP LEARNING MEDIA

2.5.2 Our long term external workers find that other agencies offer more desirable reward packages, including staff sickness benefits and even holidays.

2.5.3 Temporary contracts that become longer term and even permanent are becoming more common and depriving us of revenue.

3 Marketing strategy

3.1 Marketing objectives

3.1.1 Revenue growth. Objectives for percentage revenue growth are given below for the 12 months commencing January 20XX. They are given net of inflation: that is, they are additional to any increase caused by rising prices. These figures have been agreed with subsidiary boards.

BW Nursing and Doctors and Nurses Ltd – plus 10%
BW General   – plus 4%
BW Finance – plus 4%
BW IT – plus 6%
Gleeson Gekko – plus 14%
Infonauts Ltd – plus 7%

3.1.2 Brand values. We aim for an unquantified but significant improvement in our brand image. We wish to be recognised as the market leader and as having a reputation for high quality in our services.

3.2 Target market. Our target market is all employers who need contract, temporary or replacement staff in the sectors we are equipped to serve. We do not recognise any employer as being too small for our service, thought the extent to which we target employers for business development purposes will depend to some extent on their capacity to generate larger volumes of work for us.

3.3 Product positioning. We face severe competition, not least from Diad-Colec, who are entering the catering and financial markets in force. Currently, there is little to differentiate our services from those of our competitors, who meet us head-on in the marketplace. We must attempt to rectify this in two ways: by the excellence of our service to both clients and external staff and by a suitable campaign of promotion.

3.4 Marketing mix

We propose to develop our marketing mix in the ways outlined below.

3.4.1 Product. The BW General/BW Nursing/BW IT combined call centre is now up and running and, in tandem with our new RG762 knowledge management system, offers us an opportunity to improve the quality of our service. We will institute a study to investigate the feasibility of extending the use of this facility to other divisions within BW(UK). At the same time, we propose to enhance the satisfaction of our external staff with our operation in two ways.

- The provision of a scheme of short-term sickness insurance cover

- The introduction of a system of career management for external staff: this can be implemented without further development on the RG762 system.

These two benefits will, we hope, enhance the motivation and satisfaction of our external staff, enhancing the positive image they project of us by association with our services.

3.4.2 Price. We propose no change to our current system of setting prices. However, we urge divisions to be aware of the significant price-consciousness of employers seeking temporary staff.

3.4.3 Promotion. Our need to respond to increased competition and to improve our brand image means that we must undertake a major new promotional campaign. We shall be inviting agencies to pitch for this in the immediate future.

3.4.4 People. We are a people business and we cannot overstate the importance to our commercial success of having well-trained and motivated people, both internally and externally. A programme of internal marketing designed to enhance our quality performance will be designed in consultation with divisional HR and marketing staff. This will be rolled out within six months.

3.4.5 Processes. We have already improved our internal processes with the installation of the RG762 system. We must now build upon this with particular reference to our personal selling campaign so that more accurately targeted approaches can be made.

4   Numerical forecasts

4.1   Turnover increase. The targets laid out above for individual operating divisions amount to a total increase in turnover of £55.3 million, or 8.5%, all after any increase due to changing prices.

4.2   Promotional expense. Current total promotional expense amounts to £8.7 million: we budget £10.2 million for the next 12 months, an increase of 17%. Of this increase, £1.1 million will be spent centrally on corporate promotion; the remainder will be spent by subsidiaries.

5   Controls

5.1   Organisation. The current organisation will continue in that subsidiaries will maintain responsibility for the marketing efforts directly related to their own operations. It is clear that BW Nursing, BW IT and BW General need extra marketing expertise at a senior level and their budgets include provision for the recruitment of a Marketing Director and Marketing Manager to be shared, part-time between them.

5.2   Corporate promotion. The corporate brand promotion will be managed from the head office of BW(UK). Appropriate communication targets will be agreed with the chosen agency.

5.3   Routine management accounting information will be used to assess the degree of success achieved in increasing turnover.

Marketing at Work

As in interesting example of how **digital technology** affects a wide range of mix decisions, *Ad News* in Australia reported in June 2007 on the issues faced by the global music industry.

- CD sales have plummeted, in the face of digital music downloads and peer-to-peer file-sharing applications such as Limewire

- Legal download growth (through iTunes and other legal digital music providers) is slowing

- The cash cows of mobile music and ringtones are facing increasing competition from other mobile content forms, such as video and games.

The crisis has forced many music labels such as *Sony BMG* to reassess their business models and look for new (digital) revenue streams and communication avenues, including:

- Selling advertising on their web sites

- Tying up deals with portals (eg MSN and Yahoo!) for the provision of music and videos

- Running sponsorships and competitions (eg Sony BMG's campaigns with Kellogg's and Ferrero's and plans for an on-line *Idol*-style band competition to be sponsored by a well-known Australian beer brand, Lion Nathan's Toohey's Extra Dry).

New competition, new products new channels, new media .....

2 Controlling and evaluating

FAST FORWARD

Marketing operations must be carefully controlled. **Project management techniques** are applicable to much marketing work .

It is not sufficient, of course, simply to write a marketing plan, no matter how creative and apposite it may be. The proof of the pudding is in the eating and the proof of the marketing plan is in the execution. What is planned must be made to come to pass and this requires management of a high order.

Earlier in this Study Text we discussed some of the important theories that lie behind skilful management and we concerned ourselves in particular with the special techniques of **project management**. Now, while the implementation of a marketing plan ought to be a fairly routine undertaking for marketing management, it may be that some of these techniques could be usefully applied. This might be particularly the case where a new promotional campaign, such as that envisaged by Steve Reynolds, is concerned, since there is no doubt that time is of the essence in launching such a campaign if the assumptions and data upon which it is based are not to be overtaken by events.

In this context, we might expect Steve to set a series of **milestones** towards the launch of the new promotional campaign, with target dates set for milestones such as those below.

- All agency proposals received
- Agency selection complete
- Presentation of finished promotional material
- Campaign starts in media

Whatever methods he chooses to make use of, Steve now has the vital task of putting the BW(UK) marketing plan into action.

We also know that Steve Reynolds intends to improve the use of the RG762 computerised data handling system and to maximise the commercial advantage provided by the new call centre. Doing this will almost certainly require a large element of project management, including the aspects listed below.

- Appointment of a project manager
- Creation of a cross-disciplinary project team
- Establishment of project objectives
- Establishment of time constraints
- Planning and control of the use of staff resources in all three companies concerned
- Design and testing of new systems and techniques
- Implementation, including training and technical installation

2.1 Example problem

Explain the techniques Steve might use to manage the effective implementation of the BW(UK) marketing plan.

Solution

2.1.1 Internal marketing

The first requirement is to ensure that all the people concerned know and understand what part they have to play. Steve will already have discussed his major proposals with the senior people in each subsidiary and should have achieved a measure of consensus among them to support the plan. As details become clearer and requirements firm up, further face to face communication at senior level will be required.

This process will probably be supplemented by campaign of **internal marketing**. BW(UK) is a service business and its success depends very much on the people element of the extended marketing mix. We already know that Steve intends that there should be a suitable programme of internal marketing.

Such a programme must be organised carefully: Steve must decide several things.

- The exact messages he wants to put across

- The means of communication he will adopt

- Whether the programme can be mounted from internal resources or whether external assistance must be bought in

- How he will tie his message into the organisation's incentive and review systems.

2.1.2 Monitoring

> **Internal reporting systems** are essential for monitoring the progress of marketing activities and their degree of success. Numerical measures may be devised to quantify progress and success.

Each of the BW subsidiaries needs its own system of **internal management reporting**. Such systems should be designed to provide senior managers with the information they need to monitor and control progress. Typically, periodic reports will be produced each month, though there is a case for restricting detailed reports to a quarterly cycle, with supplementary monthly reports confined to leading indicators such as turnover, profit, stock value and headcount.

Reports will normally be initiated by accounting staff since they are largely based on transaction data. However, raw data needs **interpretation**, so many organisations include some element of interpretation in their reports; this should be provided by those qualified to comment. Thus, in a manufacturing organisation, when costs have risen it would make sense for the production and purchasing managers to comment, while a fall in turnover is probably best discussed by a sales or marketing person. The danger of such interpretation is the natural human tendency to seek praise and reject blame: it is difficult to be totally objective about the performance of your own department.

It is likely that BW(UK)'s subsidiaries will find it appropriate to make use of some **performance measures** that are tailored to their business as well as common measure such as those mentioned above. Here are some examples of information that might be of interest to the temporary staff divisions.

- Number of temporary contracts achieved

- Number of staff placed

- Number of contract person-days lost because of unavailability of staff

- Average duration of temporary contract achieved

- Average value of temporary contract achieved

- Proportion of registered temporary staff employed throughout the period in full time person equivalents

- Number of new temporary staff taken on to the books

It is normal for each parameter reported to include figures for the current period and the year to date, together with comparative figures. These may be the corresponding figures from the previous year, but where there is a mature system of budgetary control, the budget figures are more satisfactory for control purposes, since they represent the approved plan: they focus on the future rather than the past.

The BW(UK) subsidiaries seem to have a range of **organisational structures**; however, it is likely that in each the routine reports would go to a small strategic apex group of managers. It seems that not in every case would these include a mainstream marketing person. This will be quite normal in the real world.

BPP
LEARNING MEDIA

Organisation structures are rarely logical and consistent, especially in dynamic organisations. We will look at the marketing organisation Steve Reynolds is faced with next.

2.1.3 Organisation structure

FAST FORWARD

Organisation structure can be a form of control; alternatively it can hamper control.

Steve Reynolds is in a rather difficult position in that he is responsible for the marketing activities within a rather disparate group. There is **no standardisation** of organisation within the subsidiaries: this reflects their differing status as operating division or operating company and the variety of conditions within their markets. Steve cannot exercise control by dealing with all the subsidiaries in a common fashion. Instead, he must tailor his input to each according to the local conditions.

For example, Gleeson Gekko has an experienced and senior marketing person operating at board level. Such a person is likely to be able to take full responsibility for creating and managing the marketing plan for the company within the framework of the overall BW(UK) marketing plan. This person is unlikely to respond well to an autocratic approach and probably should be dealt with as an equal. A very light hand is needed.

Doctors and Nurses Ltd, by contrast does not appear to have any specialist marketing staff at all. However, Dr Staines seems to have an **almost instinctive grasp** of what works within her own specialised market. It may be appropriate for Steve Reynolds to offer specialist advice and expertise in technical marketing areas, such as the co-ordination of the proposed brand development promotion, but this is another case in which a light touch is needed.

The third subsidiary operating company, Infonauts Limited, falls somewhere between the other two in the extent of the formal marketing expertise available to it, but probably requires the greatest input from Steve Reynolds. The Infonauts marketing person has had some success as a media buyer and may have a good grasp of other aspects of marketing. However, Steve will probably have to provide **a degree of close supervision** to ensure that corporate priorities are pursued. It may be necessary to recruit extra staff to provide skills to complement those the exiting person possesses.

BW Finance has a Divisional marketing director, Tom French, and presumably some marketing staff as well. It may be that this operating division represents the most typical style of organisation as far as marketing is concerned. We know that Steve is inclined to trust Tom French's judgement: the challenge will be to avoid a false sense of security and maintain an appropriate degree of supervision. This can probably be achieved by scrutiny of BW Finance's routine management reports.

BW General, BW IT and BW Nursing have only two marketing staff between them and neither is particularly highly qualified or experienced. Steve plans to recruit two rather higher-powered marketing staff to give these three subsidiaries the expertise they need.

The idea of sharing staff between the companies seems a little odd at first glance. We may surmise that Steve is using this idea as part of a plan to push these three subsidiaries together. There may well be a number of synergies to be obtained by increasing co-operation between them: staffs, premises and lists of external workers could probably be rationalised with beneficial effects on service and costs.

Chapter roundup

- A **marketing plan** for an organisation Like BW(UK) is complicated by the disparate nature of its component parts. No single course of action would be appropriate for all the subsidiaries involved. The marketing plan must make allowances for this.

- A marketing plan should have an effective **layout**.

- Marketing operations must be carefully controlled. **Project management techniques** are applicable to much marketing work .

- **Internal reporting systems** are essential for monitoring the progress of marketing activities and their degree of success. Numerical measures may be devised to quantify progress and success.

- **Organisation structure** can be a form of control; alternatively it can hamper control.

BPP
LEARNING MEDIA

Delivering communications and customer service programmes

Syllabus content – knowledge and skill requirements

- Design, development, execution and evaluation of communications campaigns by a team of marketers, including external agencies and suppliers (5.1)
- Use of appropriate marketing communications to develop relationships or communicate with a range of stakeholders (5.2)
- Managing and monitoring the provision of effective customer service (5.3)
- Use of marketing communications to provide support for members of a marketing channel (5.4)
- Use of marketing communications techniques for an internal marketing plan to support management of change within an organisation (5.5)
- Review and evaluation of the effectiveness of communications activities and the role of the individual and team in this process (5.6)

1 A communications campaign for Brainworks

1.1 Background information

FAST FORWARD

> Any promotional campaign, whether internal or external, must have **clear objectives**. Only then can the design of the promotion be effective.

BW(UK) is committed to spending £1.1 million on a corporate promotional campaign and intends to use the service of an agency to do this in the most effective way. As is common, the company intends to request bids from a range of agencies before selecting one to do the work. In fact, BW(UK) already makes use of the services of one agency for work in relation to its four operating divisions, BW Nursing, BW IT, BW General and BW Finance. However, Gleeson Gekko maintains its independence in this field, using the services of Beagle Trumper Codrington; Doctors and Nurses relies almost entirely on personal selling and Infonauts organises its own advertising. This is typical of the organisation's heterogeneous approach to marketing.

As has already been mentioned, the process of moving from intention to execution will require tight management if resources are to be used efficiently. This management process will incorporate some of the characteristics and techniques of project management.

1.2 Communication objectives

FAST FORWARD

> Objectives must be clearly stated in terms of what the promotion is intended to achieve: analysis into **cognitive**, **affective** and **behavioural** objectives is useful.

It will be necessary to brief the chosen agency in detail so that there is a clear understanding of what is to be done. Advertising is still as much an art as a science and there is plenty of scope for missing the point.

A good starting point would be a **statement of objectives**; indeed, without clear objectives it is highly likely that money spent on promotion will be wasted, achieving nothing to the point or, in the worst case, being counterproductive. Indeed, it is only if clear objectives exist that any attempt can be made to measure the effectiveness of the eventual promotional campaign.

It is clear that Steve has a number of themes in mind for his campaign.

- Improve the company's general standing in the market place
- Enhance the image of the business in the eyes of its external staff
- Promote the BW(UK) brand values of high quality and market leading service
- Meet the threat from Diad-Colec head-on
- Support the internal marketing campaign (to enhance motivation and promote acceptance of the changes that are taking place)
- Contribute to the achievement of the numerical targets in the marketing plan
- Overcome some of the price-consciousness among employers seeking temporary staff

The first three objectives arise from a realisation that both **client companies** and **external staff** do not have a particularly high opinion of BW(UK). Steps are being taken to make practical improvements in the quality of the service offered to both these groups of stakeholders. It will be for the campaign to make the maximum impact in presenting them to the audience.

Exam tip

> In his report on the December 2003 sitting, the examiner noted the importance of identifying the relevant stakeholders: "It is not possible to evaluate the effectiveness of the communications activities unless the communications **targets** (are) identified."

The means by which the other objectives can be met are less clear, but it may be that if the first three objectives are met, success with the others will follow.

1.3 Example problem

Discuss the marketing and management processes that Steve Reynolds will have to undertake in order to meet BW(UK)'s objectives for its corporate promotion campaign.

1.3.1 Objectives

The objectives as they currently exist are rather vague and would benefit from further thought.

Communication objectives are commonly analysed into three types which we summarise below.

- **Cognitive**: the target audience is aware of the product and its capabilities and realises that it can meet some of its needs.

- **Affective**: the target audience experiences an emotional response such as approval, desire or sympathy towards the product.

- **Behavioural**: the target audience takes some suggested action such as requesting further details, taking up a trial offer or even purchasing the product.

Note that we have talked about 'the product': these ideas apply equally to services and, indeed, the organisation.

To what extent is the proposed campaign about **informing** the target public?

We might suggest that BW(UK) is already extremely well-known in the marketplace: it is, after all, the brand leader in many of its markets. However, there are certainly some new developments that it might be worthwhile to inform the public about.

- The plan for **sickness insurance** and **career management** for external staff and their potential for increasing their motivation

- The new **joint call centre**

- BW(UK)'s **wide range of external staff** – this might be of particular significance in the banking and health care market, given Steve Reynolds interest in clients in these industries that do not source all their staff from the company.

Secondly, to what extent are the objectives **affective**, that is, aimed at influencing emotional reaction?

Steve Reynolds is certainly interested in promoting loyalty among both clients and external staff, and this general area of objective might be seen as particularly important.

Finally, to what extent are there **action** objectives? Ultimately, of course, the aim is for clients to choose BW(UK) when they require staff recruitment services, but are there specific objectives of the classical 'phone this number for a free estimate' type? Probably not, is our conclusion here.

Looking at our list of themes in the light of this analysis, and bearing in mind the problems we have discerned, it would be fair to say that all three types of objective are intertwined here, but all are not necessarily present to the same extent. It may be that they cannot all be addressed by the campaign Steve has in mind. We may suppose that the experienced staff of the chosen agency would enter into detailed discussions on this topic with Steve and, probably, Willard Mann.

1.3.2 Brand management

At the moment a **BW brand** can hardly be said to exist. The organisation is fragmented in its markets, its methods and its promotional methods. We know that Steve has reluctantly accepted that a major programme of reorganisation would be unacceptable at the moment and, effectively, is trying to paper over some of the cracks with the proposed campaign. It is likely that the subsidiary divisions can be dealt with more or less unitarily, but Steve has accepted that Gleeson Gekko and Doctors and Nurses at least will not be affected by the need for a consistent corporate image.

This may not always be the case in the future, but it makes sense to proceed with caution: the more independent parts of the BW(UK) empire have already established their own brand images and values and much thought would be required before making any attempt to make serious modifications to them.

Exam tip

You should have a detailed grasp of branding theory (what a brand is; brand identity; brand families and brand extension; and so on) from your other studies at Stage 2 – and you may be required to bring them to bear on a question for this exam (as with any other specific marketing planning or marketing communications approach). A December 2006 question, for example, asked you to identify the branding issues for an expanding chain of hair salons, given data about its intended positioning and clientele. The examiner expected you to underpin your answer with demonstrated theoretical knowledge, taking into account the *fashion* context of the would-be-brand.

1.3.3 Promotion planning

FAST FORWARD

The **promotional mix** must be carefully related to the nature of the target audiences. Similarly, **communications media** must be chosen that are appropriate.

It will be necessary for the chosen agency to agree with the company the promotional methods to be used. The promotion mix offers a wide range of methods of putting a promotional message across to the target audience. Traditionally, these are normally grouped into the categories given below.

- **Advertising**
- **Public relations**
- **Sales promotion**
- **Personal selling**

To these we might add **direct marketing** as a distinct form of promotion, since its importance has soared with the development of Internet commerce and other forms of telemarketing.

It seems likely that all of these forms of promotion will have their part to play in the forthcoming campaign.

1.3.4 Advertising

Advertising is likely to play a major role in the selected promotional mix. BW(UK) wants a campaign that will enhance its standing with both clients and external staff. The numbers involved with the second category alone mean that some form of **mass communication** method must be used. The numbers of existing and potential clients may well be almost as large, particularly considering that there will be several people within each client organisation that the company would like to reach. These will include all the decision-makers and potential decision-makers in the HR function, plus all those executives who may find it appropriate to hold an opinion on the subjects of temporary staff and recruitment to permanent positions.

1.3.5 Public relations

The campaign is likely to need significant PR support. PR is an important tool in the promotional kit for enhancing and maintaining corporate image and that is, of course, a major part of the aim of the campaign. Experienced PR people will be needed to obtain appropriate press coverage at the launch of the campaign, to deal with subsequent enquiries and to shape the development of subsequent press and community relations activities.

Also under this heading, we might also consider **sponsorship**. Sponsorship can be useful in promoting a desired image, but the choice of client is of vital importance. For example, sponsoring the arts seems to work for banks while sponsoring the playing of ball games seems to work for more laddish enterprises. Probably neither of these is appropriate for BW(UK), but there may be a cause that is: one might perhaps suggest a foundation for the relief of distressed office workers or something similar.

1.3.6 Sales promotion

Sales promotion as a promotional technique is often associated with **retail sales** and such devices as coupons and twofers. It might therefore be imagined that it would have little part to play in BW(UK)'s campaign. This is not necessarily the case, since a little subtle discounting might be very useful in encouraging new clients to try the improved BW service. This would have to be handled with taste and discretion: a direct mail campaign targeting senior HR people might be a useful technique to introduce such discounts.

1.3.7 Personal selling

Large parts of the BW(UK) empire depend heavily on personal selling, albeit principally via the telephone. We know that there is some concern about the way that consultants seem to compete with one another and the effect that this has on clients. It will be very important for BW(UK)'s continuing personal selling effort to be fully integrated into the overall campaign. Sales staff must be fully briefed on the details of the campaign.

They must know when it starts, what their role is within it, how to respond to enquiries and how to incorporate it into their daily routine.

1.3.8 Direct marketing

The staff of the new BW call-centre have undertaken some telemarketing work recently and, no doubt, the consultant staff generally have been in the habit of doing a little telephone prospecting from time to time. However, it is likely that the new campaign will have a place for highly targeted direct marketing operations.

Thanks to Steve Reynolds' vision, the company's RG762 information system can be used to identify senior people in target companies. These would be decision makers at the strategic apex and in the HR function. Such people are usually very busy and unlikely to respond well to bland direct mail or telemarketing, but they may be prepared to countenance visits from consultants. Indeed, we can assume that these already happen to some extent with major clients. This leads us back to personal selling. A programme of visits co-ordinated with other aspects of the campaign might be used.

While the ultimate aim might be that clients should as a matter of policy make use of BW(UK)'s services, a perhaps more attainable goal would be to create an acceptance of BW(UK)'s claims to market leadership and a belief in the quality of its service. The HR managers who have operational responsibility for choosing which agency to use would then be inclined to use BW(UK) and their seniors would be inclined to accept that this was a rational decision.

xam tip

> Try to think through a wide range of traditional – and non-traditional – communication methods and media. The examiner has emphasised that 'mass TV, press and radio with celebrity sponsorship' is *not* the only or best) solution in all direct marketing situations!
>
> BW hasn't gone particularly hi-tech or creative (as befits its market) – but in youth, entertainment, fashion and FMCG markets, you may want to be more adventurous! Don't neglect Internet, mobile phone, interactive, viral/grassroots and other options... (The June 2006 exam made 25 marks available for recommending 'e-based' methods of conference promotion, as part of an integrated campaign).

1.3.9 Communications media

Another important part of the campaign planning process will be the selection of appropriate media.

A very important point to bear in mind here is that BW(UK) is not marketing a consumer product, so the usual mass market media re not appropriate. However, part of the campaign is aimed at current and potential external staff, who are much more numerous than the decision makers referred to above.

It is likely that fairly specialised print media will be the main channel of communications for the new campaign.

(a)   **External staff.** Several categories of external staff can be reached though their professional journals, such as *Nursing Times* and *Accountancy Age*. Local newspapers may be appropriate for other categories. This will be particularly the case in London, where both the Underground free sheet *Metro* and the *Evening Standard* are widely read by commuters. Low paid external staff, such as those working in unskilled cleaning and catering positions may possibly be contacted through local Job Centres.

(b)   **Clients**. The decision makers fall into two categories, as discussed above: HR professionals and senior general managers. The HR professionals can be contacted *via* their own professional magazines, such as *People Management*, while the more senior figures may be targeted through publications such as the *Financial Times* and other broad sheet newspapers and possibly through magazines such as *Fortune, Management Today* and the *Harvard Business Review*.

Another medium that might be useful is the **advertising hoarding**. Their large size grabs the attention and suitable sites might be found to target different categories of external staff.

 Marketing at Work

Technical press

There are just under 5000 magazines and newspapers in the trade and technical press sector, with a combined advertising revenue in excess of £1 billion. Advertising in such publications is an essential part of much business-to-business promotion, since they are seen as essential reading by a very large proportion of their target audience.

Exam tip

Note that a 'marketing communications plan' (as requested in the December 2006 exam) is *not* the same as a 'marketing plan' (as requested in June 2006). It requires:

- Communication environment analysis
- *Target publics*
- SMART objects
- Outline tactics for each element of the *communications* mix
- Feedback/control mechanisms and measures

2 Internal marketing and customer service

2.1 Enhancing customer service

FAST FORWARD

All service businesses are extremely dependant on the ability of their **people** to provide service that satisfies their customers. This has implications for recruitment, training, management methods and reward policy.

BW(UK) is a service business. Its product is the provision of people to do work. It is thus subject to the perennial problem of the service business: **the quality of what it provides depends on the day-to-day performance of its people**. In the eyes of any given client, the company is only as good as the most recent example of performance by its people.

Indeed, the company is subject to this constraint **twice**: once when it supplies staff and again when those staff themselves do work. Both occasions are opportunities for failure of service. The consultants can be speedy, friendly and efficient in dealing with requests for staff but BW(UK)'s image will suffer if the staff supplied are not of a high standard. Similarly, even if high quality staff are eventually supplied, inefficiency or inappropriate behaviour on the part of the consultants will rapidly destroy the company's prospects.

BW(UK) must commit itself to an unceasing search for the highest quality of service at all levels and in all contexts. This has a number of implications, mostly for HR management policy and action.

(a)   **Recruitment** must be as careful as possible so that people with an appropriate attitude are hired.

(b)   **Training** must be careful and centred on the need for service of a high standard.

(c)   **Motivation** must be maintained by skilful management and the use of appropriate recognition devices, such as 'Employee of the Month'.

(d)   **Reward policy** must focus on service to customers, so that staff know that mere length of service or attention to no-service element of the work will not be rewarded as highly as will satisfying customers.

2.2 Monitoring customer service

FAST FORWARD

Quality of service must be **monitored** in an objective and effective fashion. Devices that can be used include customer satisfaction surveys, mystery shoppers and the recording and analysis of customer complaints.

There must also be a system for the constant **monitoring of customer satisfaction**. This can be done in a number of ways.

(a)   **Customer satisfaction surveys**. It is normal for sales people to maintain contact with established customers and to field complaints. However, in the absence of a formal system of recording and sharing such information, it is largely unavailable for management purposes. BW(UK)'s RG762 knowledge management system should be used for this purpose. However, this will not be sufficient. There should be a scheme of **customer satisfaction surveys** operated outside the sales consultant loop by specially trained staff. Enquiries should be standardised so that data are obtained that are comparable over time and from client to client. This work can be done by postal enquiry, but this is likely to produce incomplete and even skewed information since the respondees have to opt into the system. Telephone interviews are more effective, though clearly more costly.

(b)   **Mystery shoppers**. Mystery shoppers are widely used in retailing to obtain objective, statistically valid feedback on the quality of service provided in stores. A similar programme could be undertaken by BW(UK), possibly using the services of consultants. The mystery shoppers could make enquiries and place requests for particular staff. The quality of service provided could then be assessed objectively.

(c) **Analysis and reporting of complaints**. Customer complaints are a vital resource for any service business and should be treated **positively**. They represent opportunities for improving service and thus enhancing the company's competitive edge. All complaints should be logged and analysed for importance and implications. This information should be reported in summary form in the management reports prepared by each subsidiary.

Exam tip

> Relationship marketing and service marketing are important parts of modern marketing theory. In his report on the December 2003 sitting, the examiner indicated that candidates will be expected to demonstrate knowledge of these areas in future sittings.

2.3 Internal marketing

FAST FORWARD

> Good customer service may be promoted through **internal marketing**.

The draft marketing plan for BW(UK) included a promise that an internal marketing programme would focus on the promotion of a high standard of customer service. In fact, internal marketing has come to be almost synonymous with the requirement for improvements in service standards. It is very important that the internal marketing campaign is supported at the highest level, as indeed must the whole drive to improve service.

The extended marketing mix offers a useful model for the design of a suitable campaign.

(a) **Product**. The product must be designed carefully. Mere exhortation to be better is not enough. Thought must be given to just what constitutes good service before it can be marketed. Typical examples of parameters are answering phones in a given number of rings and responding to correspondence within a given number of days. These are simple examples: the senior management of BW(UK) will have to produce **specific attributes** that **define good service** in their various business operations.

(b) **Promotion**. The major part of the programme will consist of communication. This must be effective and not unreasonably costly. The interest of the staff concerned must be maintained, so, once again, meetings that degenerate into exhortation must be avoided. Interactive, participatory training will be required, using skilled communicators working with small groups. This can be backed up with reminders *via* e mail and posters. The internal promotional campaign should be integrated with the external campaign, so the ability to do this will be one of the criteria used in the selection of the successful agency.

(c) **Place**. Place is obviously the workplace, but attention must be given to the ambience of the rooms where the training takes place. Properly qualified and experienced training staff will attempt to do this anyway, but they will need proper support: there may be budgetary implications.

(d) **Physical evidence**. Services are intangible, as we know, so it is common to give something material to the customer as a symbol of the service that has been provided. In the case of training, there are often notes and handouts of various kinds. These will be filed away at best and thrown away at worst. There is a need for some attractive article, integrated into the overall internal and external campaigns that people will be happy to keep in their pockets or on their desks. Suppose there was a theme in the external campaign that BW(UK) external staff were as busy as bees: a stuffed cuddly bee would be ideal physical evidence.

Chapter roundup

- Any promotional campaign, whether internal or external, must have **clear objectives**. Only then can the design of the promotion be effective.

- Objectives must be clearly stated in terms of what the promotion is intended to achieve: analysis into **cognitive**, **affective** and **behavioural** objectives is useful.

- The **promotional mix** must be carefully related to the nature of the target audiences. Similarly, **communications media** must be chosen that are appropriate.

- All service businesses are extremely dependant on the ability of their **people** to provide service that satisfies their customers. This has implications for recruitment, training, management methods and reward policy.

- Quality of service must be **monitored** in an objective and effective fashion. Devices that can be used include customer satisfaction surveys, mystery shoppers and the recording and analysis of customer complaints.

- Good customer service may be promoted through **internal marketing**.

Question and Answer bank

BPP
LEARNING MEDIA

1 Change managers   40 mins

As a member of a Business Consultancy Team, you are working with a traditionally run, product orientated manufacturing firm. Faced with increased competition and declining profitability, the senior management team has broadly accepted the need for organisational and cultural change.

You have been asked to make notes that will form the basis of a report to managers to explain the benefits of a shift to a marketing orientation and to outline the process of doing so.

(25 marks)

2 Managing teams   40 mins

(a)   What are the characteristics of an effective work team? Describe briefly one training method by which an effective team can be developed.   **(13 marks)**

(b)   What are the disadvantages of a participative style of management? How can these be minimised?

(12 marks)

(25 marks)

3 Recruitment issues   40 mins

John Chen is a friend of yours. He runs a medium sized marketing consultancy business. In conversation you discover he has a very high staff turnover - much higher than average for the area.

Closer questions reveals that the bulk of the turnover is among young trainees recruited locally by John himself. 60% tend to leave in the first month of employment.

He recruits on the basis of ten minute interview because he believes you can sum anyone up in that time. He blames the turnover on local schools who fill kids' heads with ideas above their station.

He is interested in your advice. What selection methods would you introduce to John Chen to help him to improve his selection? What would you suggest in terms of his attitude to local schools?

(25 marks)

4 Staff appraisal schemes   40 mins

As assistant to the marketing director, you have been asked to help with the implementation of staff appraisals in the marketing department.

(a)   Describe the benefits of a well run appraisal scheme to individuals, managers and the organisation as a whole.   **(15 marks)**

(b)   Outline the procedures necessary to put such a scheme into practice.   **(10 marks)**

(25 marks)

5 Change agent   40 mins

Joyti Patel became a supervisor three months ago at the age of 24. She is very able and well qualified (BA(Hons)). She was spotted very quickly as potential management material and this is her first managerial appointment. She wants to succeed and she believes that the best way to do so is to encourage performance by supporting her staff in every possible way. The staff are all older than she is and have all worked in the department for at least three years. Their previous supervisor has recently retired after managing the section for fifteen years.

On her own initiative Joyti has already made two innovations.

(a)   She has rearranged the office to give a better workflow, at the same time having it redecorated and getting new office furniture.

(b)   She arranged that the annual section outing should go to a different seaside resort and she planned a full programme of exciting events.

Much to Joyti's surprise each of these innovations has met considerable resistance and resentment.

Required

(a)   Describe the cause(s) of the difficulties that Joyti has encountered.   **(12 marks)**

(b)   How would you help Joyti to plan her innovations and learn to manage her department more effectively?   **(13 marks)**

(25 marks)

6 Organisation structures   40 mins

What organisation structures can a multi-national enterprise (MNE) use? Examine the usefulness of two different structures.

(25 marks)

7 ABC   40 mins

Project management in the ABC company

Dave is the project manager leading a project team installing new marketing database software at the ABC Company. The installation is currently three weeks behind schedule, with only seven weeks left before the installation should be complete. Due to the time constraints, Dave has cancelled all project meetings to try and focus his team on meeting the project deadlines. While this action has had some slight improvement in the amount of work being carried out, members of the team have been complaining that they cannot discuss problems easily. Most of the team are professional staff.

Over the last week, the two systems analysts working on the project have both moved onto other assignments due to double bookings by the project management company. The project manager has asked two other team members with a small amount of systems analysis experience to take over these now vacant roles. To try and impress upon them the seriousness of the situation, Dave has also made the two replacements responsible for any mistakes in the analysis documentation.

In the last few days, the working situation in the team has become significantly worse, with many minor quarrels and disagreements breaking out. Dave has reacted by asking the team to ensure they focus on completing the project.

Required

(a)   Identify and explain where the ABC Company project is being poorly managed.   **(12 marks)**

(b)   Explain how the project manager can help resolve these difficulties.   **(13 marks)**

(25 marks)

Guidance note

You may find it easier to structure your answer with headings for each problem you identify, and then in two separate paragraphs, answer the two parts of the question. This should ensure that actions to resolve the problem are included in your answer.

8 Project management   40 mins

(a)   Give examples why a marketing manager would need project management skills   **(12 marks)**

(b)   Discuss the types of project planning tools a marketing manager might have to use.   **(13 marks)**

                                                                     (25 marks)

1 Change managers

Objectives

1   To encourage the management team to recognise the changing environment and need for cultural change.

2   To encourage them to recognise the difference between product and customer oriented approaches.

3   To help them identify the essential steps needed to implement change.

Reasons and Tasks

1   **Why the need to change?**

The environment is constantly changing:

(a)   new technology
(b)   increased competition.

This has been evidenced by declining profits.

2   **What has happened?**

Fundamentally, a change in the levels of demand and supply has changed the balance of power making it a buyer's market. Buyers have a choice and will go to the supplier most precisely matching their needs.

To survive in such an environment, that firm has to be you. So before committing resources to production, customers' needs should be found out in advance.

It might be faster delivery, special services or advice, rather than lower prices, which entice a buyer.

3   **What will a shift do for you?**

A change towards a marketing culture will focus the business on the needs of its customers and will:

(a)   ensure flexible, responsive operations.
(b)   avoid wasting resources by producing goods no one wants.
(c)   help you identify ways of adding value and improving profitability.

4   **What has to be done?**

Change is not an easy process. It takes time and requires commitment and resources from senior management.

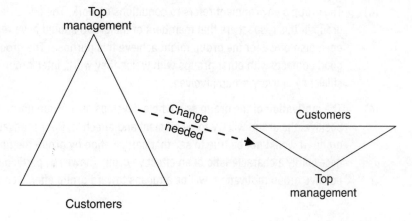

The change needed will transform the company by bringing senior managers closer to the customers and placing the customers at the top, not the bottom, of business decision-making.

The change is essentially a change of attitude - but the old attitude is ingrained in the very structure of the business. Objectives set in terms of products rather than customers and managers organised in specialist chimneys - very limited horizontal communication.

Reorganisation and training as well as motivation and team building will be critical to any change. Management will need to develop both communication and information systems as well as a marketing function.

2 Managing teams

Tutorial note. This answer makes use of Handy's Model. You could also have used Belbin's typology as a basis for your answer to the first part of the question.

Part (a)

C B Handy in his book 'Understanding Organisations' describes a contingency approach to analysing group effectiveness. The factors involved are the 'givens', which are the group, the group's task and the group's environment, the 'intervening variables', which are group motivation, the style of leadership and processes and procedures, and the 'outcomes', which are the group's productivity and the satisfaction of group members.

Characteristics of an effective work team

Characteristics of an effective work team can be identified in each of the variables.

(a) The group itself should contain a suitable **blend** of the individual skills and abilities of its members, so that the group not only has enough personnel to do its job, and people with sufficient experience and skill, but also it should blend the individual members in an effective way. A project team, for example, probably needs a man of ideas, a man of drive and energy, a logical evaluator of suggestions, a man who can do the detailed, routine work and a 'conciliator' who can bring individuals to negotiate and settle their differences.

(b) The group's task must be **clearly defined**, otherwise it cannot be effective in carrying it out. The group should also be given the resources to do its job properly and if necessary, it should have the authority to carry out certain actions which it considers necessary as part of its task.

(c) If the task is a temporary one, the work group should be a temporary project team which will be disbanded when its job is done. If the task is a continuing one, the work group should be given a defined place and role in the formal organisation structure.

(d) The group's environment refers to conditions of work. The characteristics of an effective work group in this respect are that members of the group should have **ready contact** with each other. An open plan office for the group might achieve this purpose. The group must also have easy and good contacts with other groups with which they work; inter-group conflicts will reduce the efficiency of every group involved.

(e) The **motivation** of the group as a whole develops as a group norm. If motivation is good and positive, the group will try to be efficient and effective. Poor motivation will result in an ineffective group. It would not be true to say that participation by group members in decision-making is necessarily a characteristic of an effective group; however, participation, when it promotes a positive group motivation, will be a means toward group effectiveness.

BPP
LEARNING MEDIA

(f)   The style of a group's leader also plays an influential role in determining group effectiveness. This style might be autocratic, democratic or laissez-faire. Likert distinguished between exploitive authoritative, benevolent authoritative, consultative authoritative and participative group management, and suggested that the latter type will promote a more effective group.

(g)   An effective work group will use well-designed processes and procedures. Characteristics of these might be a formally designed management information system, or the use of modelling and operational research techniques, a management by objectives system, up-to-date technology, or scientific management techniques etc. A formal group structure should not necessarily be rigid, but each member of the group should be aware of his own individual responsibilities and tasks.

The characteristics so far described should create outcomes which prove the group's effectiveness. The effective group will be efficient in its work, if the work is continuous, or it will achieve its task, as defined in its terms of reference. At the same time, it should be expected that in a group which works well and accomplishes its tasks, the individual members will show a marked amount of job satisfaction.

Training method

Training can help to create an effective work group both by building up a group identity and also by showing other members how each individual thinks and reacts in various situation. Although group learning is not common in industry, it is used by various non-industrial organisations. 'T groups' is one name given to group training, in which a series of exercises are carried out. Each exercise will involve certain members of the group, and at the end of the exercise, other group members will be asked to comment on how the exercise was performed. These exercises and discussions enable individuals to understand how they react in a given situation and how these reactions appear to other people. This helps to develop an understanding of how members of a group inter-act and to suggest ways in which these interactions can be made to work more constructively.

Part (b)

Disadvantages of participative style

There are a number of potential disadvantages of a participative style.

(a)   The degree of participation can vary. A consultative style of leadership allows some participation, and so too does a democratic style. A potential disadvantage of the participative style is that a manager might intend to allow participation to a limited extent, whereas subordinates expect to have an increasingly greater say in decisions that are taken.

(b)   A long time might be required to reach decisions, and the decision reached might be an unsuitable compromise.

(c)   Employees might be motivated to consider the interests of their own group, without having any loyalty for the organisation as a whole. A junior employee in one small section might participate in the decisions of his section, but will have little influence over decisions by his department or division.

(d)   The superior might be able to adopt a participative style, but be unable to reward subordinates for their work. If there is no progress from more effort to more rewards, subordinates might quickly lose interest and motivation.

(e)   Some work does not lend itself to a participative style. Highly programmed, routine work is a case in point. Unless subordinates are allowed to re-structure the jobs in their section so as to remove the monotony from jobs, participation in decision-making will be futile because decisions will be programmed or automatic.

(f)   Not all employees necessarily want to participate in decision-making. Some might be content to accept orders.

(g) There might be disagreements between subordinates so that some decisions cannot be reached by common agreement. In such cases, the people losing the argument might resent the decision which is taken against them and might try to sabotage subsequent activities in order to prove themselves right.

Minimisation of disadvantages

The disadvantages of a participative style of management might be overcome as follows.

(a) The extent of participation should be established clearly for everyone to understand. In other words, the leadership style should be consistent.

(b) Authority should be delegated sufficiently to enable small groups to take decisions about matters which are of some interest to them. One way of doing this in a large organisation might be to split the organisation up into many semi-independent divisions, and to encourage decentralisation within each division.

(c) Jobs should be re-structured so as to provide challenging work for work groups.

(d) The participative style should be promoted by senior management and implemented throughout the organisation, provided that the circumstances allow this to be one without adverse consequences.

(e) Managers should be given powers to reward or punish subordinates, so that subordinates will believe that by making more contributions to group discussions they will eventually receive fair reward.

(f) Senior managers must pay careful attention to co-ordination of the goals and activities of sub-units within the organisation.

    (i) The goals of the organisation should be made clear to all employees. Decisions by groups should be taken after giving full consideration to the needs of the organisation.

    (ii) A procedure for resolving inter-group differences should be provided. Likert suggested the idea of a linking pin in which the leader of one group is a participating member of a more senior gap, so that there is a continual overlap throughout organisation. The ultimate task of co-ordination would be carried out at board level.

3 Recruitment issues

> **Tutorial note.** In answering this question, it is not enough just to list selection procedures. The solutions have to be relevant to the given circumstances, and you also need to consider *why* problems have arisen. The second part of the question demands imaginative solutions.

Background. High staff turnover is a problem. It should not be accepted as normal and John needs to see the cost and waste that constantly re-interviewing for staff involves. The impact on staff morale and motivation must also be a problem.

Selection methods

(a) There should be a labour turnover target within the framework of a personnel plan (eg reducing turnover from the current level to 30% within 12 months?)

(b) Job descriptions, but more importantly personnel specifications, should be prepared and studied by the interviewer (Mr Chen).

BPP LEARNING MEDIA

(c)   The jobs should be advertised in such a way that the short-term as well as long-term career prospects of employees should be explained, together with the nature of the work recruits will be expected to do.

(d)   Applicants for a job should be asked to fill in an application form. The questions asked should:

(i)   help the selector to decide whether the applicant is possibly suitable for the job

(ii)   provide the interviewer with a basis for asking questions at the interview.

(e)   The interviews should be planned, and should last longer than 10 minutes. They should enable not only the interviewer to assess the candidate, but the candidate to find out more about the job and assess the organisation. Candidates should be encouraged to talk at interviews and to answer questions.

(f)   Candidates need to be judged against the requirements for the job and the personnel specification.

Before going on to consider Mr. Chen's relations with local schools, it is worth considering his failure to recruit applicants who stay in the job. New recruits tend to leave quickly which suggests that the job they have taken is nothing like what they were led to expect. Clearly, the problem could be due to a combination of two factors.

Failure of applicants to understand what the job entails

Failure of Mr Chen to select the right sort of applicant

Misunderstanding by applicants can be put right in the following ways.

(a)   Provide more information about jobs and career prospects in advertisements and brochures.

(b)   Asking applicants to explain why they are seeking a career in marketing when they fill in an application form. Obvious misunderstandings can be identified from what the applicant writes.

(c)   Making sure that the job is explained again at the interview.

(d)   Inviting candidates at interviews to put questions about the job, career prospects and the company as an employer.

(e)   Better liaison with schools.

Failure of the interviewer to do his job properly can be put right in the following ways.

(a)   Mr Chen should show willingness to adopt the selection methods recommended above. If his judgement of people is suspect (which is quite possible) it might be suggested in particular that he gives candidates a score or rating out of a maximum number of points for each quality in the personnel specification. A scoring or rating system might help to clarify the interviewer's judgement by putting figures to opinions.

(b)   If he considers himself unable to change his methods or opinions, he should be advised to delegate the job of interviewing and selection to a subordinate.

(c)   He should try to find out more about potential applicants, by having a better liaison with local schools.

His **attitude to local schools** might be partially justified, but mere criticism is not constructive, and he should do something about the problem. Better careers literature about jobs in marketing should be made available to schools careers offices and other people enquiring about jobs, and he should discuss his recruitment problems with these schools. However, he could promote a better liaison and communication with school teachers and school children by implementing a number of possible schemes, eg:

(a)   Inviting teachers and children to open days at the company

(b)   Sending staff (or going himself) to talk to schools

Mr Chen should be set a target of reducing the rate of staff turnover to 30%, comparable with those of other firms in the area.

Conclusion

The aim of recruitment and selection is to provide the quantity and quality of human resources needed to fulfil the organisation's objectives.

(a)   Recruitment is concerned with finding applicants.

(b)   Selection is concerned with choosing between applicants.

Getting the wrong people, or people who do not stay long, is a waste of money and effort - John should be advised that the situation can be changed with some careful planning and a more serious approach to the process.

4 Staff appraisal schemes

(a)   There are several benefits both to staff and their employers of well run appraisal schemes, which is why they are now a normal part of management in many established and successful businesses. It is widely recognised that the training and development of staff should be a priority for any organisation.

(i)   Benefits to the individual

An individual taking part in an effective appraisal scheme gains an opportunity to discuss his or her work objectively. Performance can be evaluated and constructive criticism and encouragement can be offered. Future career progression, including training and development needs, can be considered.

The employees should feel able to contribute in a structured way to company policy by offering insights based on their own experience. There may not be time to discuss matters of a possibly personal nature under normal circumstances, and the chance to do so in an organised way will lead to improved relations with the individual's manager.

(ii)   Benefits to the manager

Appraisal schemes provide the manager with objective guidelines for staff assessment. The actual process of the appraisal allows the manager to gain a better understanding of staff needs. The formal opportunity for discussion and a commitment to agreed action on both sides will lead to improved relationships.

(iii)   Benefits to the organisation

The use of an appraisal scheme offers an organisation standardised information about its employees. Individual performance can then be improved, encouraged and developed, based on the information provided. The organisation will be able to plan its use of human resources more accurately.

(iv)   Implications for marketing

Appraisal schemes are designed to maximise individual performance, and improve communications. This is an advantage for any department but is particularly important for marketing. As marketing is the interface between the company and its customers, disgruntled and/or ineffective employees can have an immediate impact on revenue. Also, there is usually considerable competition for capable marketers and sales people. A company which fails to offer adequate understanding of career opportunities is likely to lose its most successful people. Continuous staff development is essential for successful implementation of Total Quality Management or other such schemes.

BPP
LEARNING MEDIA

(b) **Implementation**

To implement the scheme successfully would involve the following.

(i) The concerns of all those involved must be identified and any objections overcome. Staff may see the appraisal as threatening and as a form of disciplinary action. The developmental aspects of the scheme and benefits to the individual must be stressed. The scheme has a better chance of acceptance if the atmosphere is generally open, and if the company is seen to be reasonably profitable. This will reassure staff that funds are available for the promised training, and that candidates are not being selected for redundancy.

(ii) **Management skills**

Managers who are to appraise people need to be briefed on the skills required. They particularly need to understand the need for two-way discussion, an ultimate agreement on action necessary, and the objectivity required on the part of the appraiser.

(iii) **Adequate resources**

Resources of time and money must exist to support training and development. Without this, staff commitment will be short lived and they will be unlikely to 'buy' any future schemes.

(iv) **Preparation**

Actual appraisals themselves should take place within a planned time scale - say three months. The interviews should cover a predetermined range of questions, dealing with a range of topics. Some of these will be standard to all interviews and others will be job specific. Interviews should be conducted in private and be free from interruptions. Wherever possible, management should distance pay increases from appraisal interviews and thereby concentrate on the developmental aspects of the exercise. Management must be prepared to act positively and quickly to any problems or opportunities which come to light as a result of the appraisal process.

(v) **Review the process**

After appraisals have been done and results communicated, managers should review the process. Refinements can then be made to improve future appraisal rounds. In order to be successful and achieve the stated aims, appraisals need to be repeated on a regular basis. A year is the most common period, as this gives all parties the opportunity to undertake the agreed action. Results can then be reviewed in respect of goals set at the first appraisal.

(vi) **Organisational growth**

Appraisals are more likely to succeed as mechanisms for staff development and career planning in organisations committed to sustained growth. Only if this is the case are the necessary openings for promotion and career progression available.

5 Change agent

(a) The causes of Joyti's difficulties

(i) She is a newcomer to the group. Newcomers often experience hostility at first because existing group members fear that they will not accept group norms. This is particularly the case when the newcomer arrives as the head of the group, because a group leader will have the authority to impose new, possibly unwelcome, group norms.

(ii) All the other group members are older than Joyti and have been in the department for three years or more. There may be resentment that a younger person has been brought in over the heads of more experienced staff.

(iii) Joyti's educational qualifications have contributed towards her rapid advancement in the organisation. Staff with less academic backgrounds may feel too much, while too little attention is paid to experience.

(iv) Resistance to Joyti's innovations could also be caused by a feeling of frustrated ambition amongst some of her subordinates. During the long tenure of her predecessor one or more of the group members may have aspired to the position of department head after his retirement.

(v) The innovations themselves may be the cause of the resentment. Re-arranging and re-decorating the office may have disrupted familiar work arrangements. Resistance is a common problem, perhaps arising from people's fears that they will be unable to cope with new techniques or from their fear of redundancies.

(vi) Joyti seems to have brought in changes on her own initiative. Her subordinates may resent the fact that they have not been consulted.

(b) Suggestions for improvement

(i) Joyti needs to discuss with each of the group what objectives she is setting herself in running the department. She should emphasise that she is anxious not to disrupt established procedures unnecessarily. She should explain how her philosophy for the department differs from that of her predecessor and how it fits in with the overall goals of the organisation. This may help her staff to understand her actions better and to co-operate in achieving her aims.

(ii) Her subordinates will be anxious about how they themselves fit into her plans for the department. She should reassure them that she wishes to work co-operatively with them. She should explain the benefits she intended by her innovations and in particular put to rest any fears they may have about the effects of the new technology on their jobs.

(iii) In general, she should try to understand the adverse effects on her staff of changes in their patterns of working. Where innovation is necessary to should be preceded by an effective programme of communication and consultation so that employees understand the reasons for it and the effects of it. Co-operative participation in new ideas will be more likely if subordinates are themselves encouraged to think about work procedures and suggest improvements.

(iv) Joyti has risen quickly to a managerial position and may be short of experience in handling subordinates. The initial difficulties might be reduced by appropriate counselling from her own superiors and perhaps formal training in management techniques.

(v) She needs to win the *respect* of her subordinates, to overcome resistance they might have to her ideas for change.

6 Organisation structures

No universally accepted definition of a multinational enterprise exists but for this purpose we may assume that it sells a range of products in a significant number of different countries.

A multinational enterprise (MNE) can use a wide variety of organisational structures. Classification of them tends to suggest that there are a predefined number of alternatives, of which the MNE can choose one. In fact, there is an infinite spectrum of alternatives and each MNE adopts the structure which its senior management believe will best serve its corporate objectives.

The following, or variations of them, tend to be the most common organisational structures for MNE's.

(a)   **By function**

Employees in each subsidiary or branch report to their superior in the same function (such as marketing, finance, production and so forth). The senior manager in each function for each subsidiary then reports to the MNE's head office.

(b)   **By area**

All functions for each geographic area of the MNE's activities report to a manager who is in overall charge for his or her own area. He in turn is likely to report to a head office manager responsible for a number of different areas.

(c)   **By product line**

The MNE's structure in this case puts managers in charge of particular products, or groups of related products. The responsibilities of such managers may transcend both geographic area and function.

(d)   **Matrix structure**

Managers report along more than one line of authority. If, for example, they are marketing specialists, they may report along function lines to other marketing specialist, but they may also report to managers of other disciplines along, say, geographical or product lines.

(e)   **By project team**

Personnel are grouped together to meet the particular needs of a specific project. The project teams are assembled and disbanded whenever projects start and finish.

The usefulness of organisation by geographic and matrix structures

Organisations along geographic lines has been popular among MNEs for most of the twentieth century. There are two principal business situations in which this type of structure is preferred. Firstly, it tends to be used by MNEs with closely related product lines sold in similar end user markets around the world. For example oil companies and car manufacturers often use this type of structure. Secondly, at the opposite end of the spectrum, it is used when geographic units are the best way of meeting the needs of local markets. For products that are very culturally sensitive, such as foods or clothes, it can be an effective organisational structure.

A disadvantage of the geographic structure is that it does not cope well with the needs of true multinational conglomerates with very diverse product lines, since there is then little rationale for treating particular geographic areas as separate markets. The matrix structure was developed to handle the needs of very complex business operations. Neither national organisations nor product groups are treated as the single most important factor in organising the business. In theory it is a highly effective organisational structure since it brings to bear all the skills of the MNE around the world in any location where they are needed. In practice, however, it can result in organisational paralysis as managers report to two or more superiors and try to meet the sometimes conflicting demands of each. Potential for management conflict is inherent in the matrix structure. It can be minimised and harnessed in very well run companies that invest heavily in control systems. Otherwise it can create more problems than it solves by turning managers attention inwards to resolve intra-organisational problems rather than outwards to identify and meet the needs of customers.

7 ABC

Areas where the ABC Company project is being poorly managed [see paragraphs marked (a)] and suggestions as to how the project manager could improve the situation [see paragraphs marked (b)] are outlined below.

1   Leadership style

(a)   The leadership style of the manager is fairly autocratic; that is team members are being told what to do without the opportunity to discuss the decisions being made. This leadership style tends to be appropriate for staff who need a lot of guidance through a project.

(b)   In this situation, most of the staff have professional qualifications, indicating that they are able to think though problems for themselves and monitor their own work effectively. A more appropriate management style would be participative. Dave could discuss the work to be done and then let staff carry out this work. This approach would benefit staff by providing them with more responsibility and benefit Dave by freeing up more time to monitor the overall progress of the project.

2   Lack of communication

(a)   The cancelling of project meetings can have an adverse effect on morale, as well as making communication between the team members more difficult. While it appears that more work will be carried out on the project, if staff feel that they are not being communicated to, or that they cannot discuss problems, then overall work efficiently is likely to suffer.

(b)   This problem is easy to resolve; Dave should re-introduce the team meetings and apologise for making the mistake of cancelling them in the first place. This will provide an appropriate channel of communication and help team members realise it was not their fault that the meetings were cancelled.

3   Lack of project updates

(a)   The other problem with cancelling team meetings is that project team members will not be aware of how the project is progressing overall. Team members may not feel motivated to work harder if they perceive that other members are not "pulling their weight". The possibility of conflicts within the team suggest that morale and trust may be low, and so motivation may be an issue.

(b)   Re-introducing the team meetings will assist communication and help all team members to see how the project is progressing. When all team members can see that everyone is working hard, then this will have a positive impact on morale and the overall amount of work being done.

4   Accountability for errors

(a)   Making team members accountable for errors is acceptable, where those members made mistakes in the first place. However, in this situation, the "trainee" systems analysts were not responsible for a large percentage of the analysis work as this was carried out by the previous analysts.

(b)   Dave should really be grateful that these two team members are attempting to continue this important work, and not place hindrances in their way. An appropriate way of maintaining motivation would be to simply ask for explanation of any errors found; accountability for those errors can be decided later, if necessary.

5   Conflicts within the team

(a)   The number of small disputes within the team indicate that working relationships are not good. These problems will tend to affect overall communication and working efficiently within the team, as members will not feel that they can discuss problems with each other.

(b)   In this situation, Dave is wrong to ignore the problem; his team is already behind schedule and trying to hide the problem is more likely to make it worse. Dave must attempt to resolve the conflicts in some way, preferably by meeting and discussing with the team members why the conflicts are arising.

If the problems cannot be resolved, the project will continue to fall behind schedule. The conflicts and the lack of trained analysts may indicate that the project deadlines need to be moved, or the project cancelled until a full working team with good relationships can be established.

8 Project management

Part (a)

It is the dream of many managers to turn their departments into smoothly running machines; to have reduced all problems to routine; and to have the organisation cruise along like a sophisticated motor car. Unfortunately, the demands made by stakeholders change so rapidly that they are forced to modify and even to rebuild their organisational cars while they are in motion. Any head of department is likely to have to introduce and manage changes; the marketing manager is not immune to this.

A typical example is the introduction of a new IT system. IT develops so rapidly that, even allowing for sales hype, it is wasteful of effort not to update every few years. A new system is certain to bring new ways of working; may have serious implications for employment headcount; and will inevitably have implications for the availability and use of management information. The installation of such a system, with its requirements for file transfer, data capture and hardware installation will be a major project. There are also significant HRM implications, including probable requirements for recruitment, selection, training and redevelopment.

This simple example illustrates the characteristics of projects. It would have a specific start and end point and a well defined objective; it is unique and is not repetitious; and there would be involvement across functional lines. The standard objectives of **quality**, **budget** and **timescale** would apply.

These features and objectives would require the deployment of particular managerial skills. There is a premium on handling the unexpected and achieving non-routine objectives in project management. Some of the management skills required are particularly important, more so than in routine operations. These include teambuilding within the project team, liaising with contractors and assessing progress.

Part (b)

The fundamental project planning tool is **work breakdown structure**. This is the process of analysing the project content into distinct elements of work. This allows the order in which work must be done to be established and the resource requirements to be determined. The breakdown of work is probably best performed on an iterative, top-down basis. Thus, the project would first be broken down into major phases. These might be separated in time, place or nature of work, for example. Each phase could then be analysed into its principal elements and an overall time estimate made for each. The process of refinement would be continued until a detailed breakdown was complete, with the work reduced to distinct elements and the sequence of operations fully specified.

The **Gantt chart** is a frequently used aid to project planning. Elements of the project are listed vertically in the left hand margin. The x axis shows time and the planned duration of each activity is shown as a horizontal bar on the appropriate line. Actual durations may also be shown; this allows an instant visual check on progress.

The establishment of resources required is part of the work breakdown process and may be detailed on a **resource histogram**. This shows the resource requirement on the y axis against time on the x axis. A more sophisticated planning technique is **network analysis**. This requires skill to use effectively. It is particularly useful for identifying the **critical path**, that is, the sequence of activities that determines the overall length of the project. Clearly, managing these activities is a high priority and may require the diversion of resources if a project deadline is to be met. Network analysis, though taught in most professional syllabi, is not a technique to be embarked on lightly.

Pilot paper and answer plans

BPP
LEARNING MEDIA

BPP
LEARNING MEDIA

The Chartered
Institute of Marketing

CIM Professional Series Stage 2

Marketing Management in Practice

Marketing Management in Practice

Time:

Date:

3 Hours Duration

This examination is in two sections.

PART A – Is compulsory and worth 50% of total marks.

PART B – Has **FOUR** questions; select **TWO**. Each answer will be worth 25% of the total marks.

DO NOT repeat the question in your answer, but show clearly the number of the question attempted on the appropriate pages of the answer book.

Rough workings should be included in the answer book and ruled through after use.

© The Chartered Institute of Marketing

CIM Professional Series
Stage 2

Marketing Management in Practice – Specimen Paper

PART A

International Sonatas Hotel

The International Sonatas Group has been developing over the last ten years. By a series of new developments and acquisitions the group now owns over 50 hotels in capital cities and international business centres around the world.

The Central Marketing and Business Development Department are responsible for strategy, policy (e.g. house style for advertisements) and international marketing communications. This includes an excellent interactive web site, which gives full details of the hotels around the world and provides online booking facilities.

'City Sonata'

A spirit of revival had spread over the new development area. Twenty years ago this was a wasteland of industrial decay, now there were modern office buildings housing major international organisations, with more major projects under construction. With good road and rail links and easy access to the international airport the area is perfect for international business operations.

'City Sonata' is nearing its final phase, with completion only a few months away. A totally modern hotel with full conference facilities, it had been built to the highest standards of comfort, with every facility for the business traveller. For leisure activities, the hotel is located a few minutes from the romantic waterside. The city centre arts area (which has a full range of attractions: theatres, concert halls, museums, art galleries, etc.) is only a short rail or taxi ride away.

'City Sonata' is the group's first development in this country, but it is intended to be a 'flagship' venture, with plans for several other hotels located at other major commercial centres around the country.

Your Role

You are Sam Smith and you have just been appointed as Marketing Manager for 'City Sonata'. You are to be responsible for the development of a small marketing team to market 'City Sonata' within the framework set by the corporate marketing function.

The opening date is in six months time.

Note: in the above context 'City Sonata' can be considered to be located in any international commercial city of your choice.

Appendix One

Overview of the Hotel

- 450 executive double rooms and an additional 40 luxury penthouse suites. All rooms have Internet access.

- 10 multi-function business meeting rooms for 10 to 200 delegates. The ballroom can accommodate larger events with up to 500 delegates.

- Business centre with computer, photocopying and secretarial facilities.

- Perfumery counter, news stand, car rental and other travel services.

- Three restaurants serving traditional local dishes, an international/French restaurant and a 'Pizza House' Italian restaurant. In addition there are two bars. One traditional and the other a disco nightclub.

- There is a gymnasium and small swimming pool.

Appendix Two

Excerpt from Job Description for Sonata Hotel Marketing Manager

Reports to Hotel Manager

Role

To co-ordinate local and national marketing activities within international strategies and plans.

Scope of the Role

To be responsible for the day-to-day marketing communications activities for the hotel on a regional basis, and in consultation with the international Central Marketing Department on a national basis.

To be responsible for the planning and implementation of local promotional activities.

To liaise and co-ordinate local marketing activities within the international strategies and programmes developed by the international Central Marketing and Business Development Department.

To assist management in the development of a marketing customer care orientation for all staff in the hotel.

To be responsible for the management of the Business Centre.

To be responsible for the profitable development of the Conference/Banqueting activities.

To contribute to the profitable development of the hotel with appropriate marketing and promotional initiatives to meet local trading needs.

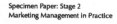

Memo from International Marketing Director, International Sonata Hotels

To: Sam Smith, City Sonata

From: John Jones, Central Corporate Marketing, Hong Kong

Date: May 30th 2003

Marketing Role City Sonata

Welcome to the group.

As the International Group Marketing Conference is late in the year, after your opening, here are just a few key issues regarding the hotel launch. We will welcome your ideas for discussion at the conference at the end of the year for the longer-term development of the hotel.

Internet Marketing

This will be done centrally through our international web site. However, when you appoint your local agency, please ensure that they can work with us on the development of your specific pages (we will need appropriate images etc.).

International Marketing and National Business Marketing

This will be done centrally for you within our overall corporate activities. However, we anticipate that as with many of our other business hotels, without appropriate local marketing activities there will be very low occupancy at weekends when business activity is low. You are expected to develop local promotional activities to profitably fill as many of these rooms as possible at the weekend.

Marketing Information

As you know the hotel has in-house standard software for tracking bookings etc. However, you will need to develop some local approaches for your weekend promotions. Our experience is that global strategies work well for the global executive business, but for the weekend leisure business, regional strategies are needed to exploit the local environment and opportunities.

Conference Business

We will forward international conference enquiries to you. It is your team's responsibility to convert these into profitable business. National conference business requires local knowledge, and so you are required to develop a local communications strategy to develop national conference business.

257

PART A

Question 1.

a.   You have to recruit and build your own small marketing team with the assistance of the local Personnel Manager. How would you go about selecting, training, building and motivating your marketing team?

(25 marks)

b.   Outline a marketing plan to develop profitable weekend business for the hotel. Lengthy environmental and SWOT analyses are NOT required.

(25 marks)
(50 marks in total)

PART B – Answer TWO Questions Only

Question 2.

a. What marketing research would be required prior to the implementation of your weekend business plan and how would you collect this information?

(15 marks)

b. What MkIS system would you implement to monitor, control and develop this weekend business?

(10 marks)
(25 marks in total)

Question 3.

Outline the marketing communications activities you would undertake to gain national conference enquiries and convert national and international enquiries into successful events for your clients and profitable business for the hotel.

(25 marks)

Question 4.

Part of the role is 'to assist management in the development of a marketing customer care orientation for all staff in the hotel.'

a. What internal marketing activities would you consider appropriate to developing a customer care culture for all the hotel staff?

(15 marks)

b. How would you monitor the level of client-perceived service quality?

(10 marks)
(25 marks in total)

Question 5.

Your first 'conference' booking is for an international software company, with its national office located close to the hotel, producing products for the financial services sector. The software has been developed in India, and the software development team from India will be presenting this new product to 100 potential clients. A conference is a 'project'. You have decided to use this conference to write a 'Project Guide to Conferences' for your conference staff, which is also to be made available to your conference clients as part of the service. Write in outline a project guide to planning actions before, during and after a sales launch conference.

(25 marks)

Question 1

(a)   **General considerations**

International hotel context – relevant experience useful

Time scale – hotel opens in 6 months

Budget – how many staff at what cost each? See personnel manager

Selecting

Clear idea of roles to be filled needed – own role includes marketing communications, promotion, customer care orientation, management of business centre – probably need section administrator, plus someone with experience of local media

Must advertise, probably internally as well as externally

Selection by interview not very good – some sort of work simulation best – could create appropriate tests such as in-tray exercise

Must brief candidates fully on duties, terms and conditions

Training

Training - to satisfy clearly identified training needs

Probably based on immediate demands of marketing plan for hotel

Largely on the job – more experienced may guide more junior

Also provide element of career progression once satisfactory attitude established – encourage CIM studentship – subsidise if possible

Building and motivating the team

Six months to opening – time is limited.

Best team building activity is purposeful, co-ordinated and above all successful work.

Team will work together as much as possible.

If team can be created rapidly, organise social event early on to meet each other – should be easy as working in catering industry.

If launch goes well, suitable reward for hard work may appropriate - could be similar social occasion or day off. Reward/teambuilding activities/budget must conform to corporate policy.

Motivating the team

Motivating marketing people no different to motivating anybody else except to extent personalities differ – may be requirement to support volatile outgoing types.

In general, treat fairly both good and bad performance; manage in participative style without abdicating responsibility to lead; praise where appropriate; trust staff as far as possible; give clear directions when necessary; for new staff in new job, supervise constantly but non-intrusively – set clear objectives and plan times for reporting back.

Hard work likely for 6 months to launch – must set tone for longer hauls – job will settle down and motivation must be maintained. Be prepared to provide punctuating events if excess of routine work threatens tedium – perhaps with off-site team building.

(b)

> **Tutorial note**. Be very careful about the prohibition on lengthy environmental and situation analyses. You will be wasting your time if you ignore it. On the other hand, there are valid background points to be made. But they must be kept brief and to the point.

Situation analysis

City Sonata clearly a business oriented hotel ('every facility for the business traveller') – this trade very limited at weekends. Staffing can probably be adjusted, but premises and equipment will be under-utilised.

Need to market hotel services to different segment

Marketing strategy

Objective is to increase Friday to Sunday occupancy.

Target market is prosperous couples of any age

Product is weekend break at City Sonata – romantic weekend feasible ('romantic waterside') – cultural weekends – theatres, art galleries and so on. Opportunities for joint marketing with other city businesses – accommodation bundled with admission to theatre first nights/ art gallery travelling exhibitions and so on. Similar possibility of bundling with travel by air or train

Price must offer good value to be attractive. Must cover variable cost of accommodation but contribution to overhead and profit can be small – however, element of luxury important, so not too much of a bargain. Should be possible to provide eg theatre admission at attractive price as part of package.

Promotion will be largely via leisure and lifestyle publications, travel agent brochures and the website

Place is largely the hotel but co-operating businesses such as theatres must be carefully chosen for ability to support the overall style of the product.

People: the usual caveats for hotels apply. Customer care standards must be of the highest by all staff, especially for romantic breaks.

Process as above, plus co-operating businesses must be carefully chosen – probable need for high quality concierge staff to deal with problems

Physical evidence will be more important than for business bookings – perhaps a high quality brochure with confirmation of booking before the stay plus a souvenir of some kind to take away. Champagne and flowers for romantic weekends.

Numerical forecasts

Not possible at this stage in the absence of base data

Controls

Marketing organisation as eventually created – one assistant will have specific responsibility for promotion – marketing manager to organise co-operative ventures with other businesses

Question 2

(a)   Objective must be designed – along lines of: establish feasibility of weekend break product idea and appropriate parameters for product specification

Will include estimates of cost, number of rooms available, existence or otherwise of competing products and their prices, possibility and details of co-operative ventures, costs of promotion, travel costs

Much of this available in house and from desk research – competitors' brochures, promotional material from city centre attractions - Local Chamber of Trade or local authority may have promotional budget/facilities such as website – all to be established by secondary research

Potential size of market/existing market information probably available from national hotel trade association

Primary research may have to be undertaken – probably most appropriate after weekend break product launched – programme of interviews with hotel guests to establish profile, satisfaction, best and worst features, attitude to price and so on

Collation of results to be by assistant with primary responsibility for product

(b)   Define MkIS – framework for processing, structuring and managing information of marketing interest - internal transactional data – external data acquired *via* marketing research

Normally computerised, may be simple database or more complex groupware or knowledge management system

Inputs related to weekend business:

Transactional data – guest names, postcodes, billing details – permits analysis of distance travelled, popular and unpopular offerings for bundled weekends

Analysis of interview programme – will compare and contrast with above

Competitor information – activities, prices, promotional activities

Special information such as dates of civic festivals, opening nights and so on

Management use of system is to analyse degree of success of individual initiatives such as new products, new prices, special offers against background of changing influences

Question 3

Hotel catering largely to business customers – target public is individual business person plus corporate buyers of travel facilities

B2B market more rational than consumer, very price driven, will seek discounts especially for major business. Guest may not be purchaser – must provide evidence of benefits appealing to decision-makers as well as guests

Personal selling to large corporate clients may be appropriate

Repeat business very important – appropriate to use ideas of relationship marketing for customers of all sizes – should really be done at corporate level as many customers will use more than one Sonata hotel

National and international corporate promotion strategy will be guided at corporate level – at hotel level main task will be local promotion, maximising return on enquiries and building relationships – even these in modern corporate relationship marketing environment likely to be in accordance with corporate directions

Promotion strategy always to be in accordance with appropriate communications model such as AIDA

Attention probably generated by corporate promotion but also by guests' visits

Interest generated by our own web pages on corporate site, by our own brochures and by quality of service received by guests while here – emphasises importance of *people* element and internal marketing

Desire ditto but also specifically by sympathetic and efficient handling of corporate enquiries – possibly by personal visit

Action ditto – must make booking easy to do – proper use of on-line booking system, proper closing technique during telephone and personal interaction

Question 4

(a) Internal marketing in this context – promoting importance of customer service in all hands – people element of service marketing mix vital in hotel where so many largely unseen staff contribute to guest satisfaction eg cleaning staff

Must aim to convince all staff of importance of very high quality customer service

Frontline staff eg reception, bar, waiting, concierge/portering staff should be able to derive job satisfaction from immediate contact with guests – and possibly sour taste from grumpy or ill-mannered guests

Less visible staff must be convinced of equal importance of task – proper reward, proper supervision

Staff newsletter/notice board

Induction training – departmental training to be preceded by session with Marketing Manager

Employee of month? Presentation as matter of importance – General Manager input? Photo in prominent place in hotel public area

Proper feedback from guest comments essential

BPP
LEARNING MEDIA

(b)   *Zeithami, Parasuraman and Berry*

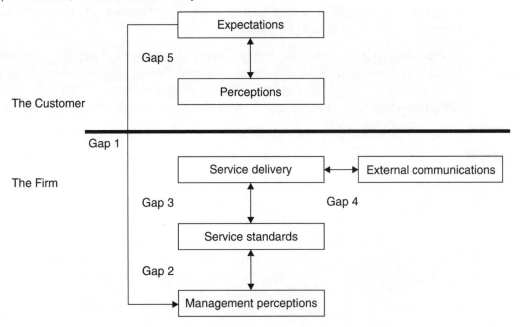

Gap 1:   Consumer expectations and management perceptions gap

Customers define high quality – manager must know levels of performance required by customers - feedback forms and interviews

Gap 2:   Management perceptions and service quality specification gap

Must ensure proper service standards defined - resource constraints and market conditions may result in this gap.

Gap 3:   Service quality specifications and service delivery gap

Ensure all staff including contract employees willing and able to perform to the specified standards.

Gap 4:   Service delivery and external communications gap

Exaggerated promises or lack of information will affect both expectations and perceptions

Gap 5:   Expected service and perceived service gap

The service quality gap - influenced by the preceding four gaps - design procedures for measuring service performance against expectations.

Question 5

Project – definition – beginning – end – meets goals – cost, time, quality objectives

Project life cycle – definition – planning – implementation – control - completion

Activities

Definition stage – outline planning of accommodation, staff and facilities – financial details agreed including credit check – quote and acceptance

Planning stage – detailed planning – consult customer on requirements, confirm booking of rooms, arrange audio visual facilities, confirm catering and overnight accommodation requirements – appoint subordinate staff – brief all staff concerned

Implementation stage – receive and facilitate conference organisers and speakers – receive delegates - monitor and control activities – troubleshoot – supervise catering – present bill and obtain payment

Completion stage – debrief senior staff for what went right and what went wrong – review arrangements – seek feedback from client

BPP
LEARNING MEDIA

Further reading

BPP
LEARNING MEDIA

Adair, J. (1983), *Effective Leadership: A Modern Guide to Developing Leadership Skills*. Macmillan. (Chapter 2)

Belbin, M. (1996), *Team Roles at Work*. Butterworth Heinemann. (Chapter 2)

Blake, R.R. & Mouton, J.S. (1994), *The Managerial Grid*. Gulf Publishing. (Chapter 2)

Drucker, P. (1993), *Management: Tasks, Responsibilities, Practices*. Harper Business. (Chapter 4)

Farmer, R.N. & Richman, B.M. (1990), *International Business*. Cedarwood Press. (Chapter 6)

Handy, C.B. (1992), *Understanding Organizations*. Penguin. (Chapter 2)

Haynes, M. (1990), *Project Management*. Kogan Page. (Chapter 7)

Herzberg, F. (1993), *Motivation to Work*. Transaction Publishers. (Chapter 4)

Hofstede, G. (1996) *Cultures and Organisations*. McGraw-Hill Education. (Chapter 6)

Kotler, P. (2002), *Social Marketing*. Sage Publications. (Chapter 1)

Maslow, A.H. (1987), *Motivation and Personality*. Longman. (Chapter 4)

Mintzberg, H. (1989), *Mintzberg on Management: Inside Our Strange World Of Organizations*. John Wiley & Sons Inc. (Chapter 1)

Ohmae, K. (1990), *The Borderless World: Power and Strategy in the Interlinked Economy*. Harper Collins. (Chapter 6)

Porter, M. (1996), *Competitive Advantage*. Simon & Schuster. (Chapter 6)

Trompenaars, F. (1987), *Riding the Waves of Culture: Understanding Cultural Diversity in Business*. Nicholas Brealey Publishing Ltd. (Chapter 1)

Vroom, V.H. (1964), *Work and Motivation*. John Wiley & Sons Inc. (Chapter 4)

Key Concepts & Index

BPP
LEARNING MEDIA

MEDIA

REVIEW FORM & FREE PRIZE DRAW

All original review forms from the entire BPP range, completed with genuine comments, will be entered into one of two draws on 31 January 2008 and 30 July 2008. The names on the first four forms picked out on each occasion will be sent a cheque for £50.

Name: _____   Address: _____

_____

_____

How have you used this Text?
(Tick one box only)

☐ Self study (book only)

☐ On a course: college_____

☐ With BPP Home Study package

☐ Other _____

Why did you decide to purchase this Text?
(Tick one box only)

☐ Have used companion Kit

☐ Have used BPP Texts in the past

☐ Recommendation by friend/colleague

☐ Recommendation by a lecturer at college

☐ Saw advertising in journals

☐ Saw website

☐ Other _____

During the past six months do you recall seeing/receiving any of the following?
(Tick as many boxes as are relevant)

☐ Our advertisement in *Marketing Success*

☐ Our advertisement in *Marketing Business*

☐ Our brochure with a letter through the post

☐ Our brochure with *Marketing Business*

☐ Saw website

Which (if any) aspects of our advertising do you find useful?
(Tick as many boxes as are relevant)

☐ Prices and publication dates of new editions

☐ Information on product content

☐ Facility to order books off-the-page

☐ None of the above

Have you used the companion Practice & Revision Kit for this subject?   ☐ Yes   ☐ No

Your ratings, comments and suggestions would be appreciated on the following areas.

	Very useful	Useful	Not useful
Introductory section (How to use this text, study checklist, etc)	☐	☐	☐
Chapter introduction	☐	☐	☐
Syllabus coverage	☐	☐	☐
Action Programmes and Marketing at Work examples	☐	☐	☐
Chapter roundups	☐	☐	☐
Quick quizzes	☐	☐	☐
Illustrative questions	☐	☐	☐
Content of suggested answers	☐	☐	☐
Index	☐	☐	☐
Structure and presentation	☐	☐	☐

	Excellent	Good	Adequate	Poor
Overall opinion of this Text	☐	☐	☐	☐

Do you intend to continue using BPP Study Texts/Kits/Passcards?   ☐ Yes   ☐ No

Please note any further comments and suggestions/errors on the reverse of this page.

Please return to: Kellee Vincent, BPP Professional Education, FREEPOST, London, W12 8BR

REVIEW FORM & FREE PRIZE DRAW (continued)

Please note any further comments and suggestions/errors below.

FREE PRIZE DRAW RULES

1 Closing date for 31 January 2008 draw is 31 December 2007. Closing date for 31 July 2008 draw is 30 June 2008.

2 Restricted to entries with UK and Eire addresses only. BPP employees, their families and business associates are excluded.

3 No purchase necessary. Entry forms are available upon request from BPP Professional Education. No more than one entry per title, per person. Draw restricted to persons aged sixteen and over.

4 Winners will be notified by post and receive their cheques not later than six weeks after the relevant draw date. List of winners will be supplied on request.

5 The decision of the promoter in all matters is final and binding. No correspondence will be entered into.